Passionate Soccer Love

A Memoir of 20 Years
Supporting US Soccer

Tanya H. Keith

authorHOUSE®

AuthorHouse™
1663 Liberty Drive
Bloomington, IN 47403
www.authorhouse.com
Phone: 1-800-839-8640

Published by AuthorHouse 5/7/2014

ISBN: 978-1-4969-1079-0 (sc)
ISBN: 978-1-4969-1080-6 (hc)
ISBN: 978-1-4969-1081-3 (e)

Library of Congress Control Number: 2014908375

Any people depicted in stock imagery provided by Thinkstock are models, and such images are being used for illustrative purposes only. Certain stock imagery © Thinkstock.

This book is printed on acid-free paper.

Because of the dynamic nature of the Internet, any web addresses or links contained in this book may have changed since publication and may no longer be valid. The views expressed in this work are solely those of the author and do not necessarily reflect the views of the publisher, and the publisher hereby disclaims any responsibility for them.

Contents

Acknowledgments   vii

Introduction   ix

Chapter 1 – Love and Soccer   1

Chapter 2 – If You Can't Beat Them, Referee   6

Chapter 3 – How You Know You're In Love   9

Chapter 4 – Referee World   15

Chapter 5 – Here We Go — France 1998 Coup du Monde   19

Chapter 6 – A Sea of Orange   23

Chapter 7 – Leibe Berlin   30

Chapter 8 – Blitzing France   33

Chapter 9 – 1999 Women's World Cup   46

Chapter 10 – The Road to Korea   52

Chapter 11 – That Pregnant Girl in Korea   58

Chapter 12 – Homeward Bound   94

Chapter 13 – Soccer Mama   98

Chapter 14 – Somebody Stole My Sombrero   102

Chapter 15 – Timbers Army Initiation   111

Chapter 16 – Weltmeisterschaft with Brucesliga   115

Chapter 17 – Reality Czeck for USMNT   124

Chapter 18 – You Mighta Won if We Only Had Seven   127

Chapter 19 – Wir fahren nach Berlin!   136

Chapter 20 – And Then There Were Two   145

Chapter 21 – South Africa 2010   149

Chapter 22 – Safari Adventure With My South Africa Husbands 176

Chapter 23 – Once More Into the Breach   184

Chapter 24 – Joburg Tourism   189

Chapter 25 – Soweto Inner Sanctum   191

Chapter 26 – A Whole Other Level   197
Chapter 27 – Ch-Ch-Ch-Ch-Changes   201
Chapter 28 – Eurotrip 2011   210
Chapter 29 – The Road to Brazil is Wet, Hot, and Snowy   226
Chapter 30 – Battle of the Hoth   243
Chapter 31 – USMNT vs. Germany, 20th Anniversary Edition   245
Chapter 32 – Summer of '13   252
Chapter 33 – The Next Twenty Years   257

Acknowledgments

This book wouldn't exist without my husband and partner in crime, Doug Jotzke. You promised me marriage could be anything we wanted it to be, and you delivered. Thank you for surprising me with the grand adventure that marriage to one person for decades can be.

Thank you to the Writers Group at the Des Moines Central Public Library for supporting me through the writing process. Especially I would like to thank Terry Crane, who never let me doubt I should go the distance. I'm so grateful for the hours you dedicated to helping me refine and edit this work. You've made me a stronger writer, and I will always cherish our friendship.

Thank you to every insane soccer fan I've ever gone to a match or sat at the bar with. I feel incredibly blessed for the depth and longevity of friendships soccer left at my doorstep. To my Kennedy/Kwiatkowsky family, I love you people. Whether it's the craziest win and the most visceral defeat, there's no better people to be with through it all.

I'm grateful to "Uncle" Jimmy LaRoue who cheered me on through the process of writing this book and made me feel like a legitimate writer every time he reposted my blog. Thank you for your encouragement, editorial help, for being my middle of the night sounding board, and last but not least, letting a tired pregnant almost-stranger put her feet up one long wonderful night in Korea.

To my new friend Renee Murphy, thank you so much for your help with editing and your support for this project. Even better than your help with the final polish were your margin notes of encouragement along the way.

American Outlaws Des Moines. Hey ... remember when I thought AO DSM would be the four members of my house? You all are like family to me, you make Des Moines feel more like home every year. You make me proud as hell to say I'm from this town.

To my parents and Doug's parents, thank you for watching the kids when four flights was just too expensive. Thank you for gifts, large and small, you ever gave us towards the travel fund, for the rides to the airport, for keeping me calm when I freaked out about leaving my store behind to chase another game or World Cup. We always knew the home front was covered thanks to you all.

Thanks to the places that fueled this book. Tacopocalypse's bulgogi tacos, Gateway Market's family night complete with Mario and the Mexican kitchen staff who always wave (usually smiling) from the back. And I would never have finished this without my friends at Mars Café. So much more than almond milk Sputnik lattes, I have made great friends in my months writing at Mars, and I've enjoyed our many chats on soccer almost as much as the coffee. Some people have soccer bars, I have a soccer coffee house.

Finally, to Aviva and Raphael, my amazing mini supporters. It has been my greatest joy to watch you grow up around soccer. I have loved virtually every moment of being your mother, both on and off the soccer field, and your patience with me writing my blog and this book has been wonderful. Thank you. It is an honor to pass my passionate soccer love to you.

Introduction

Sometimes when you think your life is completely falling apart, it's really just falling into place. I'd grown up in northern New Jersey, daughter of a pharmaceutical chemist and elementary school teacher. I had fought secondary glaucoma for the past six years and hadn't been allowed anywhere near sports for fear athletics would further complicate my eye pressure meds. Yet here I was at Carnegie Mellon University on the night of the last soccer game of 1992, meeting the senior defenseman and engineering student from Iowa who would one day become my husband. I was so detached from athletics I didn't even know I was at the soccer fraternity. I just knew by reputation it was really easy to get picked up there, at least according to one of the girls in my posse that night.

I wasn't paying much attention to anything that semester. Trying to hold some semblance of my old life together since two weeks before the semester started my life had turned irrevocably upside down. While I knew there was no going back to the way things were, I could not yet see where I was headed. Three short months prior, home on summer break was the last point everything was normal and sane.

My parents had left for their vacation house in New Hampshire where I was to join them in a week after picking up my little sister from camp. I was gearing up for my sophomore year as an industrial design major at Carnegie Mellon. I was enjoying being back with my friends and was happy to be in the same zip code as my high school sweetheart. Everything was copacetic.

That's when the bomb went off, a tiny little explosion inside my own head. My right eye, a troublemaker from day one, sightless and then diseased, had gone full traitor on me. I could tell my glaucoma was relapsing from that first night of pain … but this time was different than the previous six years of on and off relapses. One trip into Cornell Med in New York City confirmed my worst fears: I was losing my eye, sooner than later.

It seemed like the unraveling of my existence. I'd fought through six years of medication, arguments with my parents and specialists about the best way to manage my illness, the teasing, insecurity, and physical pain. I'd missed SATs, dates, family vacations, all due to this relapse or that appointment. I'd skipped all of middle and high school gym, which may seem like a privilege, but proved to be a lost part of being a teenager, denied such an important rite of passage. I had missed the chance to play any team sport, only to lose my eye as I was entering adulthood, leaving all those lost teenage moments behind me.

Three months dedicated to the end of life as I knew it, full of life lessons I didn't feel ready to learn. Three months of losing friends and the high school sweetheart who couldn't handle the stress of watching me go through the surgery or the gut-wrenching recovery. Three months (really 14 months) of Carnegie Mellon doing its deal-with-your-crisis-on-your-own-time thing, subsequently transforming from my first choice university to the very last place I wanted to be.

But this book isn't about artificial eyes or surgery. It's about my life as a passionate, devoted, traveling supporter of US Soccer. The thing is, without those three months, I never could have made the leap from nice suburban, non-athletic Jewish girl from New Jersey to Midwestern soccer fanatic. I had to strip everything recognizable out of my life before I could start rebuilding in the current paradigm. It looked like everything had gone completely off track when really it had all started to fall into place.

* * *

"You're a really good dancer. What's your name?"

Not the most creative pick up line in the book, but it certainly did the job. There's quite a bit of folklore around our "how we met" story. Tanya, "Commitment is Death," meets Doug, "the Scam King," on Halloween night. It was epic. Two commitment phobes brought down, or I suppose some would say brought together, by fate. Earlier that night, one of my girlfriends prophesized she wanted Mr. Right to walk up, plant her with a kiss, and off into the sunset they would go. That statement seemed ridiculous until Doug blindsided me with a kiss that first night and then asked if I wanted to go upstairs because "it's quieter up there and we can talk." I swear I was not at all drunk when I thought: "Oh my gosh, it's Mr. Right. I may not be the kind of girl that goes upstairs in frat houses, but I seriously can't blow this." When he asked again, thinking I hadn't heard him over the music, I decided in my naïve, Jersey Girl mind "he's from Iowa, he must be a nice guy." (Word to the wise, Iowa's just like everywhere else. You can't trust everyone, even in the heart of the polite Midwest.) Lucky for me, Doug was a nice guy for the most part. I mean … no 19 year old woman wants a perfect gentleman.

So off we went into the sunset. Doug stole my ID from me that night, pretending I had dropped it in his room so he could see me the next day (just enough trickery to be charming). We went along the path of our relationship never really acknowledging how entwined our lives were becoming. 20 years later, I still tease Doug I'm only promising the next six months or so.

Doug was a college soccer star and up-and-coming referee. My experience with soccer was a little less committed and a lot less diverse. At that time, it was based largely around Watchung Elementary School in Montclair New Jersey, where we would walk up to Mr. Dino's Pizza for lunch. They often always had Italian league soccer on the television and were usually passionately discussing whatever game was on the tiny little TV in the corner. Additionally, I'd traveled to Europe, mostly to Germany several times as a child, and remembered fondly watching my parents' European friends gather around the TV to watch a sport I rarely saw in the US with more passion than I'd ever seen from any American sports fans. I had also played a little soccer on the playground at lunch, even co-captaining my lunchtime soccer team, the Strikers, to first place in fifth grade.

My less than promising athletic career was cut short at age 13 by glaucoma made meeting Doug like a revelation into the new-to-me world of athletics. I had been a hockey fan thanks to the left wing hockey player who was my high school sweetheart and our high school's state championship team, but I had never immersed myself into a sport to learn all the ins and outs of it. I had been to a few professional sporting events but had never become a passionate fan of any one particular team.

Our relationship progressed and I slowly learned the depth of Doug's obsession. He had played his entire childhood, certified as a United State Soccer Federation (USSF) referee in 1989, and had aspirations of becoming a National Referee. He refereed youth, high school, and college soccer, both locally and by traveling to tournaments. He talked about soccer almost constantly. It was clear if I wanted to be a part of his life soccer was part of the package.

What I needed to figure out now was how I was going to fit into this new world. It took years of experimenting with different aspects of soccer, from refereeing to coaching to following the team as a supporter and blogger. I think will always be adopting and adapting to new segments of the American and International soccer landscape. One thing is certain though: I have fallen in love with the US Men's National Team (USMNT) and that team is a permanent part of our household.

You can read plenty of books on the history of soccer, or why soccer explains everything from politics to economies, but that is not this book. This book is my story of how I fell in love with American soccer and the resulting adventures that have come my way via my love affair. It is my own personal history in the swelling tide of American supporter culture. It is our how-to manual on soccer travel, and a guide to the changing landscape of what we, in the United States, have done with the world's game of football. It is my book of lessons learned from living my life on the quadrennial cycle of the rise and fall of international soccer's ebb and flow of the World Cup and tournaments built around it. I hope reading it will give you a sense of American soccer history from a fan's perspective and inspire you to find something to love passionately, and pursue it without reservation.

1

Love and Soccer

"I am myself sifting my memories, the way men pan the dirt under a barroom floor for the bits of gold dust that fell between the cracks. It's small mining– small mining. You're too young a man to be panning memories, Adam. You should be getting yourself some new ones, so that the mining will be richer when you come to age."
    –East of Eden, by John Steinbeck

I love the idea of a life lived gathering stories and adventures. After reading this passage, I decided my guiding principal would be to live my life without holding back from any opportunity for adventure. If there was a choice between a wild adventure and taking a break and catching up, we would be off to adventure. I'm often behind on paperwork, laundry, housecleaning, seeing friends, and sleep, but I never regret the adventures we've shared along the road.

My first adventure with Doug's soccer world came seven months after we met. He lived in Iowa while I spent the summer in New Jersey, and the Region II (Midwest) Youth Regional Soccer Tournament was in Canton, Ohio, or about halfway between us. I didn't have much interest in the tournament but the opportunity to see Doug was too good to pass up. So off I went in my parent's Chrysler E-Class, headed further west than I'd ever driven before.

I was about one and a half hours from home when I stopped at a rest area and locked my keys in my car. I was super annoyed with myself, having left for my journey later than planned. I sat by my car and stewed, thinking about each moment I could be spending with my boyfriend as I waited for AAA to arrive. I stared at the keys sitting tantalizingly close but locked behind the glass windows of my secured car. Forty-five tortured minutes later, AAA rescued my keys and I was back on the road.

A little further into Pennsylvania, my car started making a horrible noise and slowly lost speed. I got off I-80 in Lewisburg, Pennsylvania and found a service station. The mechanic said it was the catalytic converter and he wouldn't be able to get a spare one until the next afternoon. I was furious. My parents had just had the car checked by their mechanic and had asked *specifically* about the catalytic converter. Now I was not only going to lose a day with my boyfriend, but I needed to find a place to stay and pay for two hotel rooms (the one in Lewisburg and the one in Canton). I sat down on the grimy chairs at the side of the auto shop and put my head in my hands and started silently crying. I was absolutely devastated. I was not going to see Doug or the tournament. I had no idea how to reach him to tell him where I was (the days before cell phones!) I proceeded to lose it.

The mechanic, so undone by my undoing, came up with an ingenious plan. He told me he could take apart the catalytic converter, take all the junk out of it (my technical term) and weld it back on. It wouldn't be legal, but I'd be on my way in about 4 hours. Four hours sounded a whole lot better than overnight, so I signed off on the plan. A few hours later, I was on my way.

Of course, things like these always come in threes, don't they? But I was too young to pay any attention to superstition. I was speeding along trying to make up some time before nightfall when I came up over a bend on I-80 and too late to slow down, saw the state trooper hiding out behind a boulder with his radar gun. I couldn't even get upset. I was so disastrously late already, and more importantly, if you've ever driven across Pennsylvania, you know it is a VERY expensive place to get a speeding ticket. In a full-out panic I was about to triple the cost of my trip with this ticket. I began to think of ways to beg for mercy. I rolled down the window for the Trooper.

"Miss, do you know why I pulled you over?"

"Um, no officer, I don't."

"I clocked you doing 83 miles per hour in a 55 zone."

"Really? Well, I kept getting boxed in by all these semis, and I was trying to pass one when you clocked me." If you're going to lie, at least start with the nearest thing to the truth. It was a bit terrifying doing my first major road trip on I-80.

"But ma'am, (long pause) 83 miles per hour?" Touché, officer.

I chuckled. "Well, I'm not going to tell you that I drive 55, but I don't do more than 10 over. I live in New Jersey and I go to school at Carnegie Mellon in Pittsburgh. I drive back and forth across Pennsylvania all the time, but I usually take the Turnpike, and there's a lot less trucker traffic. I just got freaked out by all these trucks. You can check my record, I've been driving for over three years and I've never had a ticket." The three years part was a bit of a stretch to include my year with a permit, but it was close to the truth.

The Trooper looked skeptical, but continued, "Well, I'll check your record, and if you're telling the truth, I'll let you go with a warning."

In a day of frustration, I'd finally caught a break, and I couldn't believe my luck. I was hoping to get my ticket reduced to under 10 over, which still would have cost $100 in 1992 money and who knows how much on my insurance bill, but the Trooper kept his word and I had told the truth. I had just talked my way out of my first speeding ticket.

The rest of the way to Canton was uneventful and around 11 pm, I found the referee hotel. I had no idea how to find Doug, but I didn't have to wonder too long. Most of the referees had their doors open as they joked around with each other and it didn't take long for someone to crack a joke about the Iowa referees. I followed the ruckus and soon was reunited with my beau.

My first glimpse at "Soccer Referee World" certainly had its highs and lows. Midwest Regionals was a huge production of the best of the Midwest soccer teams. State Champions from all over the Midwest from age Under-14 through Under-19 travel to Regionals to try to advance to the National Championships. It's played in a different state every year in huge soccer complexes. There are soccer games as far as the eye can see, interspersed with medical, referee, and merchandise tents. It is serious business for youth soccer.

The tournament was very strict and had rigid rules of conduct and modes of behavior. Young, ambitious referees were out all day in the sun, striving to referee top flight youth games to the very best of their ability, knowing they were always under the watchful eye of assessors that could and would control their careers. Not just for the weekend but for as long as they wished to advance. After their grueling day, the refs would gather to go out every night and talk over dinner, always anticipating their assignments for the next day, which wouldn't be handed out until they were slipped under the door at four or five in the morning. Referees struck me as obsessive compulsives. Some needing to recite rules by their number in the rule book, others that would religiously prep for a game in the same order of pocketing cards, score sheet, whistle, and almost everyone shining their shoes before every game (making Canton, Ohio, temporary shoe-polish capital of the world). Games went from dawn until dark every day, but the referees did all this not for pay but for the honor of working these games. It all seemed cult-like to me, but I had to admit it was a fun atmosphere with really great people.

My second night at the tournament, we went out to the Olive Garden and sat around a huge table. The referees at the table talked about their games of the day. The banter over dinner was entertaining stories about what some crazy coach had done or a point of interest in a game. The dinner devolved into a noisy, out-of-control affair complete with a wild game of Frisbee played with restaurant coasters.

I met some of the Iowa referees such as Janet Larson, future Godmother to our daughter, and Doug's roommate, future Federation International de Football (FIFA) referee Terry Vaughn. These referees were funny, raucous, and entertaining, like a supportive sibling-esque group of people who were at the very least passionate about soccer refereeing, if not soccer itself. It was entertaining to spend tournament down time with this engaging group and nice to feel a part, however far on the fringe, of the referee family.

During the tournament, I made several new friends and became conversant with the Laws of the Game, as the soccer rule book is called. It opened my mind to just how big soccer had become in the US and how important it was to the man I loved. I wasn't a part of it yet, but watching some of the best referees and youth players of the Midwest,

I wanted to find the path from novice soccer girl to in-crowd. Casual spectator was not enough.

This was how Doug, however inadvertently, seduced me into soccer. During the long-distance phase of our relationship, we kept scheduling our visits around soccer games. First, it was Regionals. Then, in the fall of 1992, it was the Carnegie Mellon vs. Chicago college game. Doug was living and working in Des Moines, and I was chipping away at earning my degree from Carnegie Mellon in Pittsburgh. Chicago was as close to halfway as we got.

Being a broke college student, flying was out of the question. Driving made sense, but I had no car and 450+ miles to go. Most of my connections were East Coast based, so I posted a ride request on CMU's electronic bulletin board (think Craigslist, before Craig). Then I packed a bag, conveniently neglected to notify my parents of my whereabouts for the weekend, and made my way to Chi-town, sharing a ride with another woman going to visit her boyfriend.

I had never been to Chicago and ached to see Doug again, even for just a weekend. We walked around downtown, went out for dinner, went to museums, but most importantly, we watched Carnegie Mellon play University of Chicago. I don't even remember who won; it didn't really matter. We had a blissful weekend, and once again, soccer was involved. It was a strange pattern developing: love and soccer, always together.

2

If You Can't Beat Them, Referee

By June of 1993, I'd had enough of sitting in the bleachers, watching Doug referee high school soccer. I think most people get involved with refereeing after watching their children's games and thinking, "I may not know much, but I could do a better job than these guys." That thought occurred to me about three times a week and I figured I could make money while spending time with my boyfriend (who had recently been promoted to fiancé) instead of watching him from the stands.

Doug promised me it would be a piece of cake to pass the entry-level referee exam. I had watched so many games and could discuss the game and its rules with ease. He was so confident, I signed up for a course the weekend he would be out of town for Regionals; thus marking the beginning of several years of stressful Regional tournaments for us.

I got to the referee clinic and immediately felt out of place. There were several people there I am still friends with today, but at the time, I didn't know a soul in the room filled with smart, well-versed youth players who knew the rule book inside and out. There were a few parents who also seemed to understand everything the instructor said. Not only was I the only kid-free adult in the room, I seemed to be the only one who had no clue what the instructor was talking about. How was it possible I'd watched soccer endlessly for months but now was completely lost in the entry-level referee clinic? Was it possible refereeing was not as easy as it looked from the bleacher seats?

I got home after that first night and was freaking out. I am not good with failure. In fact, I'm not really great with mediocrity. I'm used to being in the top of my class; the best at my work. I was totally unprepared for how to deal with the possibility I might fail this test and embarrass myself and my newly minted fiancé. It would be a disgrace for me to not achieve a passing score on the entry level referee exam. Did I sit down and pour myself into the Laws of the Game? Nope. I called my already-stressed Regionals referee man and cried my eyes out. "How could you tell me I would be fine in this clinic? I don't know anything compared to these kids. What am I going to do if I fail this test?" Not a bright point in our relationship.

Beware, if you have ever thought refereeing is a breeze, try it first. I nearly choked before I ever set foot on a U8 field. Lucky for us, I pulled it together and passed the exam. I went through the typical fits and starts of a new referee. I got thrown into a contested U19 game for my first line (yes, my referee career pre-dates the term "Assistant Referee"). Doug was in the middle, and the assignor had a last minute cancellation and believed I was better than nothing.

For those of you who have never refereed, it is not for the faint of heart. There are only about a trillion things you're trying to watch and if you're conscientious you really don't care who wins but you do really care about getting it right. An experienced referee can just automatically manage about half of the trillion things going on around her, but in the beginning, it's intense and over-stimulating enough to force catastrophic brain shutdown. The first time I refereed with a flag in my hand, I was so focused that I forgot the teams switch sides at half-time. Suddenly, I wasn't paying attention to blue as the last defender but the white team. Alas, in the time it took me to put that together, the ball was in the back of the net and both teams were ready to eat me alive as I stood frozen to the ground trying to sort out why the guy I thought was the last defender was celebrating the goal he had scored from an offside position. I got the call right in the long run and learned the hard lesson that getting it right slowly is significantly worse than getting it right in real time. I lived to referee thousands of more games, but I'll never forget that first one.

My referee career took me all over the United States, refereeing various youth and amateur tournaments. I loved hanging out in nerdy referee tents discussing the finer points of soccer we'd seen that day and the latest pro soccer developments. Through refereeing I made the leap to soccer supporter. Major League Soccer (MLS) was starting as my travel referee career took off, allowing me to tour the professional games of the mid 90s. I saw DC United during the WAGS Tournament, Columbus Crew while at Warrior Classic, and Dallas Burn during Dallas Cup. Refereeing not only made me a soccer nerd, but sent me on a guided tour of early supporter culture in America.

In a perfect world, refereeing could have been all I ever loved and needed in soccer. It's a geeky bunch of people … so many of them are funny, charming, and entertaining, and alas, living far, far away from me. Iowa in the mid 90s offered plenty of nice people, plenty of talented people, but a serious shortage of truly passionate for soccer fans. Only one other family, Lee Tesdell and his two sons Omar and Ramsey really seemed to get soccer on the level Doug and I did. More about them later.

Worse than the shortage of passionate fans was the dark side to my referee experience, brought on by some mean-spirited people in the Iowa referee community, many of them were in positions of power (isn't that always the way?) It seemed they were convinced they had been put on this earth to: 1. ruin my referee career, 2. ruin my marriage, and 3. all of the above. They blocked my assignments, blocked my assessments, and tried to tell me I would never be good enough for them. In general, they tried to make me miserable, and it's a little sad how often I let them succeed.

But have no fear! I had to be shoved out of the referee nest before I could fully embrace the supporter community and find my true home amongst the most amazing people in American soccer, the supporters. I'm grateful for many of the lessons I learned refereeing (I'm pretty sure I could write a book titled "Everything I Needed to Know About Parenting, I Learned Refereeing Soccer") but I'm most grateful for the introduction to the love of the game. Refereeing gave me the opportunity to travel and become deeply ingrained in soccer culture … worth any heartache that came with it.

3

How You Know You're In Love

It all started on June 10, 1993. USMNT vs. Germany in a "friendly", a game that is not in qualifying for anything but played for fun, show, or practice. Since I had lived in Germany for a summer and the game was to be played in nearby Chicago, Doug suggested it would be a great game to go check out as my first international game. Chicago was less than six hours from our apartment in Ames. As an Easterner, I considered five-and-a-half hours was a bit of a schlep, but in the virtually traffic-free Midwest it was nothing.

US Soccer sells tickets months in advance of the game which can lead to some sticky situations early in a relationship. We had purchased tickets together with my future in-laws and Doug's sister. In the time between tickets going on sale and the game Doug and I had a falling out with his family. We had just gotten engaged and initially my husband-to-be's parents were happy for us. To be honest I'm not sure what happened. Sometime over the holidays the engagement honeymoon glow wore off and their Midwestern Lutheran-ish son marrying a nice Jewish girl from New Jersey lost its luster. I became the enemy. It caused enough of a rift they did not speak to us for several months. Fast train to mega-tension central.

I'm part Greek and all Jewish, my people don't stop speaking (or yelling). Ever. It's an expression of love: I care about you enough to fight this out. My ancestors would argue until some resolution could be reached. Doors may be slammed, voices may be screamed hoarse, and to people of quieter persuasions it may appear we're about to fight to the death or at least to never speak again. But we would reach a resolution or agree to disagree, and life would resume as normal. Not talking, silent treatment, and passive aggressiveness were things I had only read about in books. Not so much for the family to whom I had committed myself.

They are Midwestern Protestants, a misnomer considering how little they protest in the modern era. In the Midwest, it's not polite to argue. Everyone is supposed to get along and if you don't you certainly do not bring it up. You sweep that stuff under the carpet or give coded, innuendo-filled messages no Easterner is ever going to interpret. It's taken me 20 years of Iowa residency to achieve Iowan decoder level "Occasionally Understands Coded Messages," making me feel like the smartest cryptologist in the whole world. To make matters worse, I had just moved to Iowa, and hadn't yet figured out that there was a code, let alone how to begin deciphering it. Enter the US vs. Germany game with assigned seats right next to my future in-laws.

We arrived at the stadium and met up with Doug's parents and sister outside the gate. It was June and we had hardly spoken to them since December. Doug and I had hoped somehow over the past 6 months things would magically improve between us. Alas, nothing could be further from the truth. My future mother-in-law's pursed lips and chilly silence interspersed with curt, sharp sentences loaded with bitterness and sneer created more tension and suspense than anything on the field. A guaranteed tense situation became an all out stand-off of epic proportion. Future mother and daughter-in-law, squaring off at the soccer stadium as if it were still World War II and we were US vs. Germany. At the beginning of the game I wasn't sure I could endure the 90-minute onslaught of weaponized silence, often lethal to East Coast Jews. It should have been grueling sitting a couple seats down the row from my future mother-in-law as she tried to kill me with passive aggressiveness. But as a testament to the power of soccer, I loved the game and became enthralled by the match. Every moment I spent in the stadium I fell deeper in love with soccer, even more shocking, American soccer.

The game, a short-lived tournament called the US Cup, was an invitational with the US, England, Brazil, and Germany. There were American soccer fans out there, crazed soccer supporters, ancestors of mine and 21st century American Outlaws creating a great party atmosphere around the stadium. The game was a score-fest by soccer standards; Germany won 4-3. My hero, Jürgen Klinsmann, a star in Germany and future coach of USMNT, scored the first goal in the 14th minute allowing me to sit smug in my Adidas hat with black, red, and yellow stripes. Not for long though as the score was tied 11 minutes later by a goal from Tom Dooley. I knew enough about soccer to know the Americans should not be tied with the German Fussball machine. I sat up and took notice of these American characters who'd dared to tie my Germans. The shock and awe swung from one team to the other as Germany scored three more goals, then answered twice by the US substitute Ernie Stewart and again by Dooley. Alas, not the charmed third time. Germany beating the Americans was not a surprise at all, but the sensation that the Americans might have tied it given another few minutes earned the USMNT the respect of many Americans who'd been biding their time watching European soccer, waiting for America to wake up to soccer culture. I walked into the stadium a fan of German soccer and walked out ready to follow American soccer.

It's not as though one particular day I woke up and thought "I'm going to be a US Soccer ultra fan." It snuck up on me like a thief in the night, creeping around all the soccer in my head in the early and mid-90s, infiltrating my decidedly neutral soccer referee world. Somewhere, in between scoring against my previous home soccer nation, Germany, and our ground-breaking performance in the 1994 World Cup, I became seduced by US Soccer. I can't really explain why we were among the earliest adopters of the US Soccer phenomenon, I can only tell you along the way my passion for soccer in general became my obsession with the American game, and now I can't imagine it any other way.

1993 had created a perfect storm for me to fall in love with soccer. As a brand new twenty-something soccer referee, I was getting assigned to as many games as my schedule would hold. I'd attended my first real international game, and people were beginning to talk about a tournament coming to the United States for the first time ever, the 1994 World Cup. The previous World Cup had taken place in Italy in June of 1990, the summer I graduated from high school. Germany won the World Cup that year, and despite spending the summer traveling with my German friend, I have zero recollection of the '90 tournament being played. Flash forward four short years and I crash landed into the middle of American soccer culture, at least the referee corner of it, and the World Cup coming made for big news. I remember my husband standing in the doorway of the kitchen at his parent's house, discussing what tickets we should purchase with our US Soccer referees early ticketing privileges. The United States only played in Michigan and California. If we wanted to stay close to home we would be in Chicago, five hours away. Was it worth a five hour drive to go see four countries I didn't care about? Luckily, still in search of adventurous memories to sift in my old age, I agreed to go, launching my love affair with World Cup soccer.

If we hadn't traveled to any games at all the 1994 World Cup still would have had an impact. The United States had a better showing than anyone ever anticipated. We were living in a tiny apartment in Ames, Iowa, while I finished my bachelor's degree at Iowa State University. My first cap convinced me I liked soccer, though not yet a supporter, but my betrothed, was passionately glued to the action. The games in Chicago had me pumped, but I paid only passing attention to the US games on TV at the time. Doug's unforgettable reaction the US vs. Colombia game in the first round of World Cup 1994 could not be ignored. The US had tied its opening game against Switzerland, but Colombia was a contender for the World Cup title. They had just beaten Argentina at home and were supposed to be a tough opponent for the US, a team trying to avoid being the first host nation to get eliminated in the opening round of the World Cup Final. I was studying for summer school courses while Doug screamed at the TV throughout the game. Not too uncommon for a man to be screaming at a sporting event on TV, but my quiet Midwestern mechanical engineer rarely has emotional outbursts. So when he shows emotion, I am often startled to attention.

Colombia, considered one of the potential dark horses to win the World Cup, lost their first game against Romania. Two losses meant almost certain elimination. In the 34th minute, the US passed into the penalty area towards American Ernie Stewart tearing down the right side of the field. Before the pass reached him, it slid in front of Andrés Escobar, who in desperation to break up the play, miss hit the ball and scored an own goal for the USMNT. No one could believe it! The US was winning against Colombia, my husband uncharacteristically going berserk, captured my attention and for the next 55 minutes the game had both of us riveted. Ernie Stewart scored for the US in the 52nd minute and Colombia got a mercy goal in the 90th minute to lose the game 2-1. The United States continued the line of every host nation before it that advanced to the second round of their host cup.

For Colombia, the shame and humiliation of losing to the USMNT was intense and serious. Escobar was murdered days later when he returned home; a dark reminder of just how passionate so many nations are about soccer. It cast a pall over the our second round game, a patriotic July 4th match up against perennial powerhouse Brazil. No team in any World Cup wants to go up against Brazil. They had exceptional players and were known for beautiful soccer. I thought after so many close calls and near misses maybe, just maybe, we could take down the giant. Everyone would love that story, right? The host nation takes down Goliath on Independence Day! (Can you hear the patriotic music in your mind right now?) Alas, we held Brazil to 1-0 but fell to the soccer juggernaut who went on to win the entire tournament. It softened the blow to go out to the eventual champion but not by much.

Adding more phenomenal experiences on top of the pure joy of watching the USMNT exceed expectation in 1994 were the games we watched live in Chicago. Still in transition from Germany fan to US supporter, I was grateful to see the two games Germany played in Chicago, Germany vs. Bolivia on June 17th and Germany vs. Belgium on July 2nd, the latter a lucky draw to see Germany a second time in their second round berth. The two games were ridiculously exciting with Klinsmann, my favorite German player, scoring the game-winning goal in the first game. The second game resulted in one of the biggest controversies of the tournament. FIFA had just introduced a law against taking a player down on a goal-scoring opportunity, making it a red card offense. Taking a player down in the penalty area would mean not only a penalty kick (with a high probability to score), but also the fouling player would be ejected from the game and his team would play short for the rest of the match.

A German player took down a Belgian clearly in a goal scoring opportunity position. Despite the obvious call for the new rule, the referee did nothing. Havoc ensued. The referee was chased by three Belgian players pleading for the call that would give them a penalty kick and a chance to make the score 3-2, forcing Germany to play short for the rest of the game. Insult to injury, Belgium scored again making the "should-have-been" score tied at 3, but the actual final score line 3-2 for Germany.

Showing me some of the best soccer I had ever seen, the World Cup, unlike any event I could even imagine, locked down my love of soccer. There were people from all over the world coming together to celebrate their common love of the game. People were in all sorts of international traditional dress, speaking so many different languages, like the United Nations of Sports, but with everyone happy and celebratory. My favorite quote regarding World Cup soccer came from then USMNT player and now soccer commentator, Alexi Lalas. He was talking about Americans needing to have tolerance for World Cup culture when he said: "We need the culture police in the stands saying 'Hey, it's culture, leave it alone.' So what if they're sacrificing a goat, let it go. It's the World Cup."

Once I'd experienced the world's biggest party, I never wanted to miss it again in my life. On our five and a half hour drive home from Chicago I was high on the drug of World Cup soccer. I had a beautiful hallucination of our future together and Icurled up my legs in fidgety excitement in my seat. Doug so deeply passionate about soccer, and I had started my love affair with the sport. Even more, I loved to travel, and I loved to see and learn from cultures around the world. We absolutely needed to do this. I told Doug we should take my love of travel and his love of soccer and go to every World Cup, wherever it was in the world. For three out of four years, we would travel to different tournaments to referee along our individual career paths. Then once every four years, we would have an epic, life-altering journey together to see the World Cup. Little did I know I was proposing what would become a defining principle of our relationship. It seemed brilliant and attainable in our young and naïve kid-free world.

That one crazy proposal has gotten us through so many of our challenges. No matter what happens, we have to find a way to get to the World Cup. Focus on that quadrennial goal that has carried us through more struggles than we could count. It all started with one crazy idea on the way back from Chicago. My commitment to my husband-to-be that my new love of soccer would be emblematic of us for the rest of our lives.

4

Referee World

Our passion for soccer smoldered for a few years before bursting into flames. We were early in our professional careers and both deeply involved in refereeing soccer. Our vacation time spent traveling to tournaments to referee. Iowa experienced dramatically rising participation in youth soccer, and faced the growing pains of not having enough experienced referees to keep up with demand. An adult referee with even a couple years experience would find plenty of work. We were young and broke and virtually every weekend from April through October filled with soccer games: high school games in the spring, and college games in the Fall, and club youth soccer almost year round. On summer tournament weekends we would do five or six games each on both Saturday and Sunday. Plenty of Mondays I'd have a knee or an ankle wrapped and would be on massive doses of ibuprofen, just trying to get well enough for the next weekend's slate of work. We flew back to New Jersey for our wedding during this period with me still on crutches from some soccer-inflicted injury. You can file that under "How to Make Your Mother Very, Very Angry." For the record, I required no assistance getting down the aisle.

Everything in our lives started to revolve around soccer. However, with Doug in pursuit of his National Referee badge, and me in pursuit of my State Referee badge, we were often in different states at different level tournaments "The best of times, the worst of times." We were always on the run from one game to the next, tournament after tournament, exhilarating and exhausting all at the same time. Some tournaments paid, Some volunteer. All driven by desire to advance a referee career or knowledge of the game. Engaging and thrilling, like a new club I'd never experienced before. I never went to camp or joined a sports team, and there were very few prior opportunities to get together with such specifically like-minded friends and geek out for the weekend.

As an advancing referee, I spent my summers traveling around the Midwest to various tournaments, meeting up with other referees from around the US. We would work from early in the morning until dark, watching each other, trying to become better and help our fellow referees improve. We would sit in the referee tent and put on sunscreen, polish shoes, or try to catch up on a few calories and rehydrate. The ref tent served various purposes throughout the day as a place to gossip, sleep, refuel, and get away from the harassment and/or glory we faced in front of the fans and players. It's the clubhouse where we get to tease each other and compare notes.

"Do you need to put some adhesive on your flag to keep from dropping it?"

"Was that a new record for yellow cards?"

"Did someone commit a murder over there, because you blew the whistle and people on our field stopped."

"I heard so many whistles on your field, I thought you were directing traffic."

The days, entertaining, but long, were full of adventure and enjoyment. After the games of the day, we'd go back to the hotel to shower and drain some of the lactic acid from our legs by chatting with our roommates with our feet up on the headboard while we had confessional on whatever game situations demanded feedback. We'd wait for everyone to get showered, dressed, and anti-inflammatories on board, and then back out we went to go eat and drink over stories of the day's games. Those referees were among the best storytellers I'd ever met. We would talk for hours about the crazy things we'd seen on the soccer pitch. We shared great comebacks we'd heard someone use on an obnoxious fan and the hilarious things coaches said as they came unglued over one of our calls:

"There was this fan complaining about every little thing I did, so I went up into the stands and said 'By gosh, you can see it better from up here … play gentlemen! Play!'"

"I was running at full speed after a break away, and a player cut across my wake and clipped my back heel. I fell head over heels and popped right back into stride without stopping."

"Blow the whistle! It's not a pacifier!"

"And then I just told him "Coach, you better warm up your assistant!""

The referees I worked with were smart and funny, sharp and outgoing. I loved going around the country and refereeing with people as passionate about soccer as I. To referee at the State, Regional, and National level is to be a part of a huge family of the biggest characters I've met in the game. There became a time keeping to our year based on the tournaments we refereed. Memorial Day weekend was synonymous with Warrior Classic in Canton, Ohio. We didn't end the Summer with Labor Day but with the WAGS (Washington Area Girls Soccer) Tournament in Washington, D.C. on Columbus Day in October, preceded by the September weekend in South Dakota at the Sioux Falls Fall Classic, and followed by the college playoff championships that raced the early winter frost and snow annually. There were some fun Iowa tournaments back in the day, like the Just for Girls Tournament and Iowa Games, but when you live locally, you miss the referee culture that develops after the games in the hotel and when you're out for dinner. I loved traveling and meeting new people while learning better referee techniques from other referees and assessors.

Through refereeing, I learned how to anticipate a play building. I learned to think about coaching styles and tactics. Refereeing gets into the technicalities in the Laws of the Game and forces you to think about player formations and how play flows throughout the game. Referee World is a great place to really delve into soccer and get to know it, though I felt most soccer referees missed the experience of soccer. Referees like to know the game very well, but they don't seem to experience soccer with the same passion as supporters. How can they? They have to view each game with clinical detachment. Refereeing was the antithesis of being a supporter as the referee must be completely impartial while the supporter could not be more committed to one particular team.

While I still love refereeing, it was never going to be enough for my personality. I love to dive all the way into something and become completely immersed in it. When I'm passionate about something, I want to feel it coming out my pores. I want to be gushing with excitement. Referee World was a nice stop, but I was headed for Ultra Fandom.

5

Here We Go – France 1998 Coup du Monde

The time came to put our money where our mouth is. In the car ride back from Chicago in 1994, we promised to go to every World Cup. As the calendar turned the last corner on 1997, our plans started to take shape. I changed jobs; leaving my job as a sales rep and taking a job doing inside sales and interior design for a local flooring company. In my interview, I explained my passion for soccer would require two and a half weeks off in summer 1998 for our already planned trip to France. I was told this was no problem. They must not have taken me seriously. When the schedule came out for June with my traded days allowing for my vacation, the store owner called me into his office. The conversation was tense and baffling, considering my position as one of the store's consistent top sellers.

"I see you've arranged to have more than two consecutive weeks off." Pat scowled.

"Yes." I said. "This is when we're doing the World Cup trip I told you about in my interview."

"Well," he said in an "Office Space" manager tone "that's just against our company policy to let people take so many days off in a row."

"Um, well, that's why I clarified in my interview I would need an exception to that rule for this trip."

"Yeah, well … we're not going to be able to do that."

By now, I let out a nervous chuckle, in awe of what was going down. "Um, heh heh, I already have airline tickets purchased. I'm going on this trip."

19

That's when Pat lowered the boom. "Well, if that's how you feel, we're going to have to let you go."

In my head, my voice shouted "You're what?!" However, only a meek "Well, I guess if that's how you feel, that's the way it is" escaped my lips. In retrospect, I should have been jumping up and down thanking him. Getting fired meant I didn't have to work ten days straight on either end of the World Cup in order to make up for time off. I had time to get last-minute errands done and pack, and it meant I got to pull unemployment insurance all summer long while working on our photo album when I returned. It also meant I'd earned massive respect from virtually every soccer fan around the world.

We were on a train in the middle of France, chatting with a group of Scottish supporters. They were curious about an American woman at the World Cup.

"Ay, so you came with your husband to see the Cup?" One of them said.

"Oh no, I follow soccer just the same as he does. I'd come by myself if he hadn't wanted to go." I said

"C'mon now. Really? You watch football?"

"Watch it? I got fired to come here!"

"Fired? What'cha you mean now?" slipping into an adorable Scottish accent to match his kilt and traditional attire.

"My job, they wouldn't give me the time off to come here, and I told them I was going, so I lost my job." I said, with no small amount of pride.

"SACKED! You were sacked to come to the World Cup?!"

I nodded.

"Ay, we're buying you a beer, right now!" as he stood up to wave down the beer cart.

I drank so much free beer at that World Cup, it dramatically offset my loss of income.

Controversy ruled the 1998 World Cup and its ticketing scandal which sold many seats two and three times over. People who thought they had tickets, actually did not. After failing to win tickets through several rounds of FIFA lotteries, we were getting a little desperate when a solution presented itself. My house father, Wolfgang Trommer, from the summer I spent living in Germany as a teen was a Super Elite Double Golden Awesome Frequent Flier with Lufthansa. As a sponsor, they had tickets to sell to their double secret most favorite fliers, and Wolfgang had purchased tickets to the three US games on our behalf. But when the ticket scandal broke, we learned we would only have tickets to the last game the US played of the three-game opening round. We were heartbroken. We had all our travel booked at this point and decided to see what we could find on the black market for the other games. Wolfgang and his family, wife Jutta, and daughter Tanya (my namesake, even with the Russian spelling, much to the chagrin of German authorities that thought they should use Tanja) would be integral in our black market adventures, but first, we had to get to Paris and meet with them. Our first international World Cup trip was definitely not for the faint hearted.

We got to Charles De Gaulle Airport after a flight that seemed to take forever for us, a young married couple eager to get off on our first big escapade. When we finally landed, we searched for our bags but could not find them. We were jet lagged, dispirited, anxious to get out of the airport, and neither of us spoke French. We thought we must be misunderstanding where we were supposed to go for our luggage, but we could not sort out where we were going wrong. Finally, we gave up and went to the luggage office to beg for help. The woman at the counter looked a little surprised, and seemed to recognize our names. We soon understood why. She disappeared into the back and came out with our mangled, open suitcase with our belongings spilling out of it. She explained they would replace the bag and compensate us for the trouble and what had possibly been lost. Luckily, there didn't seem to be anything missing, and we were free to explore the streets of Paris with a brand new, lighter weight suitcase.

We ditched our bags at our hotel and set out for the Champs Elysees for some sightseeing and shopping, since the dress boutiques were one of the few things I remembered from my previous trip to Paris as a teenager. The Champs Elysees during the Coupe de Monde is unlike any other time in Paris. People from all over the world are sightseeing in their country's soccer kit or traditional dress. There's a party atmosphere, and instead of Parisians glaring at you, you get the sense the really obnoxious Parisians have all fled the city in anticipation of this world-scale party ruining their proper world.

As we walked, we discussed particularly entertaining groups of people to each other. I wanted a photo with a group of Scottish guys with kilts on, but I was a little wary of one group walking ahead of us. They were young and clearly drunk, and they seemed to be perpetually on the verge of causing trouble. We did not have to watch for long before the antics began. They were calling out to a few American girls up the street, and the girls called back "Is it true what you don't wear under your kilts?"

If they had rehearsed, the coordination of the move that followed could not have been more precise. In unison, all five guys turned around and lifted their kilts exposing what I can only describe as what I imagine shorn sheep rumps to look like, complete with balls hanging out in the breeze. It is now 14 years later and that image is burned in my brain clear as the day I saw it. Surrounded by all the architecture and old world class of one of Paris' most famous streets were five white Scottish asses glowing in the sun. Let the World Cup party begin!

6

A Sea of Orange

When planning our trip, we wanted to arrive in Europe with plenty of time prior to the first USMNT match. Therefore, when our arrival went relatively smoothly, we had time for a side trip to Amsterdam. I had never been there before and proximity allowed us the experience of visiting a second European country. We collected our gear and headed to the train station to get our rail passes for the rest of the trip.

You would think you'd be safe counting on English speakers at the main rail station in Paris but not so much. We communicated how many days we needed and where we were going, but somehow ended up buying First Class rail passes. My newly unemployed budget wasn't first class qualified, but everything happens for a reason. Our First Class purchase actually ended up being the steal of the trip. Not only do First Class passes come with better sleeping accommodations but press, players, and the rest of the so-called "elite" all travel First Class. I met and chatted with the Editor of San Francisco Bay Soccer, and by the end of our journey, he had signed me as his Midwest photography stringer which later scored me press credentials for the 1999 Women's World Cup and several USMNT games. Well worth the price of the First Class pass upgrade!

We arrived in Amsterdam in the morning and found our hotel after wandering the streets for a while in those confounding pre-GPS days and began our discovery of just how sketchy cheap hotels in Europe could be. Our room was on the sixth floor of the walk up hotel, and it had a double bed, one chair, and a sink. There wasn't room to walk by the chair to get to the window beyond it without climbing on the bed. There was barely enough room to stand at the sink without stumbling backwards onto the bed. There was a shared toilet on every floor and showers on every other floor. However, the clerk warned us we should mind the floor in the fifth floor shower because it was a little soft. When my husband, the engineer, went to check it out, he informed me we would be going down three floors to the "safe" shower. He wasn't confident the fifth floor shower would last through our stay. Despite its sketchiness, we were young and broke; so we stayed in the ridiculously cheap hotel laughing about it for the rest of our lives. It's about the adventure, after all, whether going to great soccer matches or practicing extreme showering!

While the Netherlands was not a host country, all of Europe is caught up in World Cup fever, and the orange-outfitted Dutch were not to be outdone. There were posters of a huge orange face proclaiming "Friday the 13th ... unlucky for some ... like Belgians," promoting the match between rivals Netherlands and Belgium. We were excited to be in Amsterdam for the game, to see how a non-host European city functioned during the World Cup. We were thrilled to learn the fervor in Paris spread throughout Europe. People might work in the morning, but when the matches played, people would gather in bars and in the streets to watch every match on any screen they could find. Two or three times a day, productivity would suspend as we all hung on every last touch and volley. Phenomenal to experience as an American, having lived all our lives in a place where the majority of people could care less about World Cup soccer. We expected France, as the host, to have a great atmosphere, but here we were in an average European city, finally in a place where our obsessive passion for soccer was appreciated and understood. For the first time, we got to witness what soccer means to the rest of the world, to get a sense of the intensity and focus people had for games completely unrelated to their home nation. It was incredibly gratifying and made us dream of the day when we might find that atmosphere in the US.

We went out that night, sat in a bar drinking beer and chatted with two women from Long Island and two men from Italy. We talked about soccer and accents as the Italians were struggling to understand the New York spin on the English language. The girls were a little ditzy, and once they realized the Italians weren't imminently taking them to bed, they wandered off. After a few rounds of drinks and soccer talk with the Italian guys, the four of us left to go dancing. A couple bars later, we lost one of the Italians a woman who wanted to leave with him; thus leaving myself, Doug, and the remaining Italian to drunkenly dance our way through Amsterdam, flirty and lighthearted. It was only when we stumbled out of the bar at dawn and our Italian friend said an especially wistful goodbye that I realized this had been a three-(or four?) some waiting to happen. I was completely disoriented as I looked around the square with its fountain pleasantly splashing, trying to sort out where the night had gone. As we hit the reckoning hour of daylight, we dragged ourselves back to our sketchy hotel laughing about my naiveté and cluelessness to when I'm being hit on. Everyone should be able to say they've danced until dawn in Amsterdam and then laugh about the ménage-a-trois that might have been.

Friday the 13th arrived with the city of Amsterdam bathed in orange. Everywhere we looked the Dutch were in head-to-toe orange eagerly anticipating the game. Everywhere we went there was an electric excitement in the air. We wandered through galleries and cafes until the evening matches. Many of the bars that looked like they had the best atmosphere were jam-packed with no room to stand. We gave up on comfort and smashed in with the other fans from around the world.

A bit disappointing as the game ended in a 0-0 tie with the Dutch losing one of their stars, Patrick Kluivert, to a red card towards the end of the game. It felt as though all of Amsterdam would have erupted into total bedlam had the Dutch scored, but alas not meant to be. They would eventually advance out of the group along with Mexico, so at least the tie caused no permanent damage. It's funny to look back on the statistics from this game and realize how far I've come as a supporter. Today, I would never have been so laid back about the result of a game in the group containing our soon-to-be arch-rival Mexico. I liken it to becoming a parent. When you look back on your life without kids and wonder what you did with all that time, money, etc.

I got the chance to do that as the night went on as people began to drink and party as if they'd won because it's the World Cup, and Amsterdam is always a party. We went to one bar where they were playing loud house music and everyone had bright orange whistles on lanyards. There was no souvenir I wanted more than that orange whistle. I asked around and finally worked my way around to the deejay and asked about the whistles. He reached under his counter and pulled out a t-shirt with huge fat guy jumping around with a whistle and the text "Wilt u een fluitje?" Now that I had my coveted whistle, I had to solve the next puzzle before donning a shirt of questionable message. We finally managed to shout back and forth over the music loud enough to get the translation: "Would you like a whistle?" Well, yes I would!

The following day, we headed back to Paris for the USMNT's first game of the tournament. We went out sightseeing and after walking the sights all day were getting tired as we schlepped ourselves up the hill to Sacre Coure. By luck, we were startled out of our late afternoon lull by the growing sound of drums and music coming up the hill. We looked down and saw a huge parade of musicians and women dressed in white with flowers in their hair. As they approached, we realized these were not Parisians but a huge mob of hundreds of Brazilian soccer fans coming to make an offering for their team at the cathedral. There were women with huge feathered headdresses and white gowns, men with big drums strapped to them and people as far as you could see with Brazilian hats, shirts, and banners (and several nervous-looking French police officers). With all the joy and exuberance of a wedding procession, they climbed the hill singing and dancing in front of the cathedral before finally entering to pray for their players. The most passionate outpouring of soccer love we'd ever seen; it was contagious. Brazilians are good role models for young American soccer fans and we drank as much of it in as we could. I may be Jewish, but I don't think a supporter can go wrong joining Brazilians in a prayer vigil the night before a USMNT match.

We got settled back into Paris and all its World Cup entertainment as we prepared for the United States' first round-robin match: US vs. Germany. Wolfgang, Jutta, Tanya and Tanya's fiancé, Georg, had all traveled to Paris to meet us for the game. None of us had tickets to the match, but the two Tanyas and our men were going in search of tickets, and if nothing else, we'd all watch together at the bar. We met my host family several hours before the match and after some good-natured trash talking, we left my host parents and went with German Tanya and Georg down to find a bar near the stadium and check out the black market for tickets.

We checked the market. Still so long before the game, the prices were still way too high. Georg was confident prices would drop as kickoff time approached. He suggested we chill out in a bar and get something to eat and drink. We found a bar nearby and sat in the glassed in-patio area and ordered a round of beers. My high school German only required a couple beers to start flowing again, and soon Tanya and I were chatting in German while Doug and Georg got to know each other in English. We were deep in our respective conversations when we noticed a table of German soccer fans staring at us perplexed, trying to figure us out. An American couple supporting the US and a German couple, but the women were speaking German to each other and the men were speaking English? What is THAT about? They were four German men in their mid-thirties and once we explained the situation to them, they were thrilled to spend the afternoon exchanging stories and drinking songs with us in English and German. Soon we were laughing and joking like old friends. It took the edge off our nervousness about getting tickets via the black market.

About 45 minutes before kickoff, we decided to resume our ticket quest. We asked around and discovered that the prices had dropped substantially since our previous check. We split up and wandered through the available scalpers, searching for the best deal. We struck up a conversation with one of the ticket sellers who had two tickets in a section we could afford. We were chatting and joking around with the guy and finally agreed on a price. We wanted Georg to come and check out the ticket since he'd seen the authentic tickets and would be able to tell us if these were fake.

"Is it all right if we have our friend check the tickets to make sure they're authentic before we exchange money?" Doug asked.

"Yeah, sure. No problem" the scalper answered.

We called Georg over, and the expression on the scalper's face turned from jovial to nervous distress. Georg is over 6 feet tall and a pretty strong looking guy. The scalper weighed in around 5'4" and scrawny. The look on the scalper's face could not have been more panicked if a battalion of police had just pulled into the square. Fortunately for all of us, the tickets passed inspection and the scalper was able to leave peacefully with our money, and we were soon inside the stadium just in time for kickoff.

In his career as a US Soccer National Referee, my husband has had the opportunity to talk to many of the professionals associated with the US Men's National Team including the sports psychologist that works with USMNT. Doug shared many times the story he heard from the team psychologist about what happened immediately prior to the start of this match. In the tunnel just before walkout, the USMNT lined up ready to take the field. They watched as the highly-ranked German National Team walked in perfect linear precision to their place, turned with domineering synchronized superiority to look down at the US team, then in coordination snapped their heads back to look forward again. The psychologist said you could feel all the energy and determination evaporate from the US side, and when they took the field, they played like a team that had been completely psyched out. By the time the US had regained their composure, Germany had beaten them 2-0.

The beauty of being a USMNT supporter in 1998 was we didn't have any expectation of performance. We just wanted to have a good time and not get completely embarrassed in a blow out. The game was respectable enough to return to the Trommer's hotel and allow Wolfgang to buy us a bottle of consolation champagne. We had a great time catching up with them, reminiscing, and letting my husband get to know my German "family." Wolfgang even gave us a little bear dressed in a German soccer kit to comfort us to sleep that night.

We said goodbye to the Trommers, and with them bid farewell to our French translation services. On the train back to our hotel, we were immediately confronted with communication issues not addressed in the dictionary and phrase book I carried everywhere. A French gentleman was trying urgently to communicate his concern about our stop at the line terminus. In his search for a common language, he had no trouble communicating his disgust that I had bothered to learn

German before I learned French; yet he could not clarify his warning about our stop. It took almost the entire 45 minute train ride before he finally expressed his concern: our hotel was in an Arab neighborhood. Imagine our disappointment learning all that effort was just to learn our travel mate was racist.

The communication fun didn't end there. I caught a cold, requiring pantomime of my symptoms at the pharmacy to procure the proper cold medicine. Later we tried to order dinner from a lovely woman who actually spoke English and was translating the menu for us. We got stuck on a salad that she kept calling "ohndeev salad," insisting that these were English words and we should know them. Doug and I looked at each other trying to figure out how we'd become so uncultured we couldn't figure out what "ohndeev salad" was; desperately wanting to put our translator out of her misery. Finally, I asked her to write the word down, and when she did, I shouted, "OH! Endive!" frustrating the poor French woman even more. To this day, I can't see the word "endive" without smirking inside.

We spent the next day walking around Paris, young American soccer fans in love, in a city known for romance and transformed by the world's biggest soccer event. I told my husband I never wanted to come back to Paris again after seeing such a beautiful city at the height of soccer fever. To us, there was no better way to see Paris than with soccer fans from all over the world. There were fans everywhere you went, from Louvre and Notre Dame and all the way to the Eiffel Tower, wearing colors of every nation in the tournament and then some. A blissful walk around Paris. A gorgeous experience only heightened by ubiquitous world soccer fans.

7

Leibe Berlin

One of the great things about World Cup travel is the several days between each country's opening round games, leaving us with plenty of time to see surrounding areas. I had traveled to France twice as a teen and wasn't in love with it, but I had been completely in love with Germany. It was time to introduce my husband to my second homeland and that tour had to start with my favorite city, Berlin.

My previous trip to Berlin had been as a 17-year-old in 1989, the last summer before Germany unified from East and West Germany, and I remembered Berlin to be an incredible place before reunification. It was located in the middle of East Germany but was divided into East and West Berlin. Therefore, tourists traveled through East Germany to visit West Berlin. Brave foreigners could go through a checkpoint and spend a day (and the government required 50 East Marks) in East Berlin. To me, the trek didn't require specific bravery, but when my brief 5 Mark phone call to my parents ran out as I said "Tomorrow we're going to East Berlin," it sent my mom into a minor panic that she'd never see me again. While on the East side in 1989, I saw a handful of people protesting; a demonstration that eventually led to the fall of the Berlin Wall. Seeing a communist country and getting to know the people of East and West Berlin was a defining moment for me, and I was excited to see the city post-unification and to introduce my husband to my favorite city in the world.

Berlin once again blew my mind. There were construction cranes everywhere you looked and so much had changed in nine years. I would often walk by familiar places and not recognize where I was until some landmark would jog my memory. The TV tower with the round ball, which would be turned into a soccer ball eight years later when Germany hosted, was ever present. Remnant World War II bombed-out buildings were everywhere in 1989, but the 1998 development quickly swallowed them up to make way for new construction. In 1989, there was stark contrast between East and West. Cars, food, culture, and people were all easy location identifiers. The West was bright, creative, punk, and riotous with color. The East side was grey and black without much variety. On both sides of the wall, the people of Berlin were thoughtful and kind, intelligent and engaged. Before, the Brandenburg Tor was essentially a demilitarized no-man's land between East and West, but in 1998, people were driving THROUGH it. I stood frozen when I saw it, tears in my eyes, unable to reconcile the radical cultural shift that had taken place in my absence.

In 1989, Berlin was the first German city I toured and I was still upgrading my American high-school German to native-speaker speed. I was traveling with Tanya Trommer then so when I got desperate, she would help me. However, at East Berlin checkpoints, Germans and Americans were split into two lines, and suddenly, I was 17 and on my own trying to cross into a communist country. Once I was in checkpoint interrogation, my mother's worry made more sense. The border guard was a huge German woman who spoke high-speed German with no tolerance for English. She demanded to know why I had chocolate bars, a book, a jacket. Terrifying. At the end of our 1989 day with Trommer relatives, we wanted to cross through the infamous Checkpoint Charlie. I was bitterly disappointed we were required to exit as we had entered, and I missed the chance to cross at a landmark. I think it was anticlimatic for Doug, but I was very excited to finally get to see Checkpoint Charlie in 1998, even though it had been largely dismantled into a historic marker.

1998 Berlin also offered the chance to see another cultural embrace of the Weltmeisterschaft, as Germans call the World Cup. We would stop along our sightseeing for a bier (or four) and watch the game of the day at outdoor cafes or restaurants. There was a Mexican place called

Las Cucarachas (I know, it sounded sketchy to me too, a restaurant named "The Cockroach," but it seemed clean and the food was good). They'd set up benches on the streets in view of TVs with World Cup matches playing constantly. We often stopped there to watch games before heading out for the night.

Berlin was a perfect blend of the best of East and West: fantastic art and music with street painting and galleries around every corner, incredible museums and architecture, and the people ... I will never get enough of talking to the people of Berlin about the history of their city. Lucky for me, they were equally enthralled with an American woman who spoke German and had seen the city before reunification. I talked to gallery owners, shop keepers, and people on the street ... it was wonderful, and an even better experience having my husband with me. It was like sharing a piece of my soul with him, eating in cafés where I had been as a teenager, and walking streets that are now forever part of my journey.

We left Berlin and headed back to France for the USMNT's next game. It's a long trip from Berlin so we stopped along the way in Köln, or as Americans call it, Cologne. One of my great regrets of my 1989 trip was that I made it to see friends in Bremen but missed out on seeing Cologne. We just had to include it as part of our side trip. We were only there for a day, but Kölner Dom (Cathedral), Gross St. Martin, the mikva from 1170, and the walks along the Rheine River were totally worth it. This taste of Köln was one of the reasons we decided to return to the city in 2006 when it would be Germany's turn to host. One more brief stopover in Geneva and we were finally in France for our next round of games.

8

Blitzing France

When I look back at what we did for the rest of our trip, I think either Wikipedia must be wrong or we were very young and very crazy about soccer. We were in a different city every day for the next four days. I have photos of us at the games, and the internet makes game places and details delightfully easy to verify. It still seems impossible this is what we did. I'm starting to understand why my parents thought we were nuts, but we thought, it's once every four years, we can certainly sprint the finish!

We took the train to Lyon, the site of the US vs. Iran game. Our tickets to this match were lost in the ticketing scandal, but we thought we would travel and at least absorb the atmosphere of the city and have the opportunity to meet another old friend from my 1989 trip to Europe. In 1989, my house father, Wolfgang, had a conference in Morzine, France which I attended along with the family. My first stop that summer resulted in an abrupt and thorough initiation into the difference between European and American culture. Tanya and I met Elnou Roby, a French girl our age whose mother was running the conference. Because Elnou's mother was American and from the town next to my hometown in New Jersey, we became friends and spent the week going out to bars and clubs, drinking and smoking, chatting it up in any number of languages with the young chemists from the conference. The three of us had such a great time. We were friends and pen pals for many years to follow. Elnou and I met up in the US once or twice, but she was kind enough to meet us to watch the US game at a bar in Lyon, about 60km from her home.

The pre-game chatter was full of tension, hypothesizing that the political strife between the US and Iran would come to a head during the game. Security was on high alert around the city of Lyon. There were police everywhere, but we were able to find a pleasant café to watch the game. We figured our chances were very good against a smaller nation like Iran, better than against the powerhouse of Germany, so we were in high spirits having met up with Elnou and excited for the game. We didn't even get to carry these dreams into halftime, however, as Iran went up 1-0 in the 40th minute. During the entire second half, we were desperate to will our team to score, but it wasn't meant to be. Iran went up 2-0 in the 84th minute, and McBride scored a mercy goal in the 87th. The game ended 2-1 for Iran. No political excitement but no US Soccer excitement either. We left thinking it was impossible we would have come all the way to France to lose all our games, but it certainly wasn't looking good for the US.

The next day of the sprint was bound to be more fun, since we were watching a game just for fun. Through the insanity of ticketing, we had ended up with tickets to England vs. Romania in Toulouse. We were excited to see a contested match played by teams we respected but did not support. We knew England had fantastic football supporters and at the very least it would be a great learning experience for us as a new soccer supporters. Although the game was just for fun, the photos we have of this match are (sadly) the happiest we looked at the 1998 Coupe du Monde.

We arrived in Toulouse and after a few hours of walking around the city center, we headed to the stadium to check out the fan zone. Doug was wearing a US flag shirt, and I had a flag as a modified toga with my Dutch orange whistle around my neck to complete the look. We stopped to get flags painted on our faces; English on one side, Romanian on the other. There were street performers and musicians all around the stadium, and while the Romanians were having fun, the English were there to party and they could not get enough of the American woman there to party with them. I saw very few women from any country at the World Cup and my presence was far from unnoticed amongst the European fans. I had many great conversations with Europeans about what I was doing there. It became very clear that Europeans did not expect to find American football fans, let alone a female US supporter.

Dance parties would break out everywhere we went. One shirtless English guy saw me standing on the edge of their dance circle and grabbed my hand and pulled me in to spotlight dance with him in the middle of a circle of soccer fans from around the world. With maybe one or two other women among the spectators, it was a rousing display of awkwardness, yet a very entertaining drunken pre-celebration that I happily joined in with for a few minutes.

We left the impromptu dance party and continued walking around, charmed by all the English accents talking trash outside the stadium. We found one group of men who were particularly proud of their banner, and they were all too happy to explain it to us in English accents so thick you could almost not understand a word. It was an England flag with Bristol City FC in the cross, and Bedminster and Hen & Chicken in two corners. They explained.

"Well, we're from Bedminsta [you have to read it in full-on English accent], and this [pointing to BFC] is our cloob, and this [pointing to Hen & Chicken] in our Poob."

It took me until 2011, when I watched "Rise and Shine: The Jay DeMerit Story" to figure out exactly what Pub Leagues in England are all about and started to understand why these guys were so mad proud about that banner. Of course, I understood it a little when I first got the American Outlaws Des Moines banner and started carrying it around the world, but that's three World Cups away. Suffice it to say that English fans had much to teach about supporter culture.

We went inside the stadium and took our seats next to a guy wearing an FC Bayern München shirt and scarf who schooled us in all things club vs. country. I asked him why he wasn't following the German team.

"Ugh, I can't watch those games. I am a supporter for Bayern München, and when I watch the national team, it's all the Bundesliga players I hate from other teams. I can't watch Germany play. It makes me too angry." he answered.

"But it's your country." I said, perplexed one would be German and NOT cheer for their national team, especially since I wasn't German and had a thing for them.

"It's not that I don't want them to win, I just don't get any pleasure from watching it. So I come here and watch really great football and enjoy myself." Club vs. Country, a totally new concept for me.

Major League Soccer was just getting off the ground and was comprised mainly of very young or almost retired players, and there wasn't any one team I was passionate about. I could start to understand that I would not want to watch a club that had a player on it that I loathed from the National Team side. This was something I got to know all too well when the Mexican (inappropriate language censored) player Blanco started playing for Chicago Fire, the team I was following at the time. Fire and I went on a break … real fast.

Back to the game … which did not disappoint in the slightest. Romania racked up their first of 4 yellow cards in the 4th minute. We were in view of the score board which lit up "BUT!" (French for goal) with every score, much to the entertainment of our second-grade humor level. Despite eventually losing 2-1, the English fans sang all night long. The only song I remember is "There's only one Michael Owen!" which they sang for their super sub, the teenager Owen. I remember being completely impressed they would even have a song for their substitute, although strangely not for the other sub of the game, 23-year-old pre-stardom David Beckham.

After the game, we said goodbye to our German seat mate and headed back to visit Elnou in Grenoble. It was lovely to stay with her family and catch up as well as spend a little time resting the cold I had picked up while running around the country. Her mother made me an herbal infused steam that cleared my head so fast I wondered why we ever messed around with American cold remedies. It was glorious to have a couple quiet days before taking off to our next adventure, especially when I could catch up with my friend. While she was at work, Doug and I explored the town, trying not to upset people with our lack of French-speaking skills and our desire to eat food while walking … very anti-French culture, but baguettes were perfect grab-and-go food!

The day after the England match we got introduced to just how small and riddled with danger the world of soccer can be. The referee from the US, Esse Baharmest, was scheduled to referee Brazil vs. Norway. There was no television in Elnou's house. Her family knew it was important to us, as referees, to watch our hero referee. Not every country gets to send a referee to the World Cup, so to have one of our own selected was a big deal, and we were very excited to watch him work. Elnou's neighbor had a television and kindly offered to let us watch there, even knowing that we could not speak French and they could not speak English. We figured we would communicate through the language of soccer, and we weren't concerned. We enjoyed watching the game with them but realized early on they cared about Brazil winning. Brazil's win would put Morocco through, and Morocco was coached by Frenchman Henri Michel. This is when we learned national teams are more than just about one nation; it's about who is coaching them and where the players predominantly play club soccer. There can be fans from several countries all cheering for one country, much like in 2012, when the Americans supported Egypt because their coach, Bob Bradley, was the former US coach. Brazil was the favorite, and even a tie meant Morocco would go through. We were having a great time … and then came the 88th minute.

That's when the biggest referee controversy I had ever witnessed happened. Baharmest called a penalty kick for Norway while the score was tied 1-1. It was awful … he motioned a shirt pull but every camera angle replay showed no infraction. This was Esse Baharmast, a man who could do no wrong in our eyes. We were baffled, but worse, we began to think we were in some trouble with our hosts. The French hosts' speech became intense and heated. What little we could understand was about the American referee, and let's just say the words were not kind. Norway scored their penalty, the game went on for a few more tortured moments, and then ended with Norway winning 2-1, sending Morocco home. We wanted to see the replays and figure out what Baharmest had seen. It was impossible for us to believe. He couldn't have made a mistake. We respected him so highly. After half a dozen camera angles showed nothing, and the tone of the French was getting faster and hotter, we said the most awkward thank you and goodbye in the history of farewells and walked back to Elnou's house. Days later, one unique camera angle vindicated the call, showing the penalty kick was warranted, but it was an awkward couple of days to be an American in small-town France until our referee was cleared.

Elnou's house was like heaven on Earth. She had beautiful gardens and her family was lovely. We were relaxed, dining on French food and surrounded by beautiful lush gardens. We weren't really focused on leaving, but as the next day rolled along, we had to face packing for the last game of our trip: the USMNT vs. Yugoslavia in Nantes. We wanted to spend a little extra time packing since the day after the game we were taking the train to Paris to fly home. We needed to organize and do the serious trip packing but leave the things we needed for the last couple days in one bag. We were so relaxed in the garden after breakfast, lazily procrastinating the big pack when I got a bad feeling that we were forgetting something. I went to our room and got out our train reservations. I was horrified to realize I had looked at the departure time for our connection; not the first train. Our local train was leaving almost immediately! There was no time for careful packing at all, it was time to throw it in a bag and run for the door. It was a terrifying race against time, but in retrospect, it was a hilarious French caper of shoving huge American bags, packed haphazardly, into Elnou's tiny car, and racing breakneck to the station. Elnou parked her car completely illegally in front of the station and ran with us at full speed into the station and down to our track where our train was just barely starting to pull out of the station. We threw our bags on and jumped onto the train already in motion, throwing kisses and thanks back to Elnou before collapsing in a sweaty, exhausted heap of spent adrenaline.

We then had the unenviable task of opening all our luggage in a baggage room of the train and spreading out over the grimy floor everything in our immediate possession. It took almost the entire trip to sort out what we would need in our final city so we could leave the rest of our bags in the train station lockers. Every conductor on the train stopped in to see our chaos, but no one kicked us out. We repacked, although not as calmly as we might have at Elnou's, in a constant juggle of keeping clean things off disgusting floors, while still packing fast enough to complete the task before our next connection. It was complete chaos and horrifying to be rough-traveling Americans rudely rearranging everything mid journey, but we finished the job and caught the night train to Nantes without further incident.

We arrived early in the morning not-so-fresh from the night train. Our final game was versus Yugoslavia in Nantes, we had decided to take another night train back to Paris to save time and money since our flight was the next day. Our brilliant plan involved leaving our bags in the luggage lockers that were available all over French train stations allowing us to see the city and attend the game luggage free, then pick up our bags, and catch the last train back to Paris. It was a great plan, if only the train station lockers had not been closed due to a bomb threat. Doug and I spent a few minutes just staring at each other at the train station trying to reformulate a plan B. Our next idea was to get a hotel room for the night and get a shower, leave our bags, and then figure out which train to take when we got out of the game. How tough could that be?

This is when we learned our next lesson in French: "*hôtel est complet ce soir*" (the hotel is full tonight). We schlepped our luggage, rattling up and down cobblestone streets like beggars, hotel after hotel, an endless chain of obnoxious front desk clerks saying "*hôtel est complet ce soir*", "*hôtel est complet ce soir*", "*hôtel est complet ce soir*". It droned on without variation or apology, and we started to get anxious. Our next idea was to convince a hotel to let us rent a room for an hour and get a shower and then leave our bags for the day. We didn't care how much it cost. We just had to ditch our bags somewhere before the game or risk losing them at the stadium. We were feeling desperate and pathetic after almost three hours of searching for a hotel when we finally came upon the small Hotel Le Richebourg … not that we cared what it was called at this moment.

I almost didn't hear her when she answered "Oui." I was so accustomed to the no answer, "yes" sounded especially foreign. I did a double-take and nearly fell to my knees in relief. My hopes were dashed again when she explained that it was their most expensive room, sort of the honeymoon suite. Doug and I exchanged anxious glances; we had finally found the last hotel room in the entire city, only to be priced out of it. As we approached the end of our trip, the reality of my joblessness was setting in and neither one of us was too excited to spend huge piles of money on anything, even on our most coveted hotel room. We asked her how much for the night. She told us in francs, and it took us a moment to convert the sum to dollars.

Fifty dollars!! Our most expensive hotel room by far but so far superior to dragging bags around the city and to the game that night. We followed her to our not too fancy but spacious room and private bath (another first for the trip!) It had a tiny balcony that overlooked the alley, which was now swarming with American soccer fans. We were so incredibly excited to have escaped our plans gone awry. We thanked our host and began to prepare for the game.

We decided to paint our faces. We'd brought paint with us but hadn't had a good opportunity to use it. We were inspired by our good luck and by the neighboring American fans. Doug painted USA on both sides of his face. I painted a flag across my face with the blue and stars over one eye and red and white stripes across my face. It was quite impressive. We left our hard won hotel room and headed for the fan zone, walking quickly, excited to watch the earlier games on the big screen. Doug and I talked about the day's adventures and about our plans for getting to the game as we walked. The streets were mostly empty as people slowly gathered for the afternoon games.

As we turned up the hill toward the fan zone, I felt something blunt slam into the back of my head and felt someone push by me. I looked up through the stars now floating before my eyes and watched Doug rocket up the street in front of me chasing after the kid who had just stolen my red baseball cap. What was terrifying in that instant became comical in the passing seconds as my husband, looking like a superhero in face paint and cape-like flag sailing out behind him, chased the teenager who had just stolen my hat. My fear turned to pride as my late-20s husband had almost caught him within a block. The thief gave up and tossed the hat back to Doug who returned the hat to me triumphant. My hero!

We continued on to the fan zone and stayed there for the end of the afternoon game. All of the hype before this World Cup involved hypothesizing how Americans would interact with Iranian fans. We saw no trouble between Americans and Iranians, but we were quickly becoming uncomfortable with the Yugoslavian fans. We had already experienced one crime, and it seemed like there were lots of Yugoslavians, not too many Americans or police, and the tension was mounting. There was far more negative energy from the Yugoslavian fans than any of the Iranians. Apprehension mounting, we determined it was time to leave. The stadiums all had a "safe-zone" around them where only ticketed fans without weapons were allowed past security, but there was entertainment before finally entering the stadium. We decided it was in our best interest to head there quickly and directly.

We walked together towards the shuttle in full city-alert mode. My hometown is just outside New York City so I had plenty of experience navigating New York before Mayor Ruddy Guiliani cleaned it up and made NYC tourist-friendly. We made it to the stadium shuttle, and while I was relieved to be there, a huge crowd had formed at the stop. We were almost home free, but there was a group of four Yugoslavians at the bus stop that wanted to take pictures with us. Their request was pretty aggressive, and we told them we would, once we were at the stadium. They kept asking, with increasing intensity as the bus pulled up in front of us. My anxiety was through the roof. This group was bad news, but the bus was pulling up and there was nowhere to run.

I stepped on first, but as I did the photo-request guys grabbed ahold of Doug and tried to pull him off the bus steps. I hooked my arm through Doug's and lifted, screaming for help. I had my right arm locked around the bus handle, and my left arm around Doug's upper arm trying with all my might to pull him aboard the bus as the four guys were punching him and trying to drag him away from the bus. There was no way I was letting them get my husband. I've jumped in front of angry players coming after my husband as a referee, but this threat was far more real, and it was all happening in a blur. Somehow, I pulled Doug out of the chaos and onto the bus as the crowd pulled his attackers away. The doors finally shut and we were on our way to the stadium, with a moment to assess the damage.

We were so grateful to be on the bus with only bruises to show for our trouble when Doug checked the security waist pouch with all our documents. It all came crashing down ... we had been mugged. We were in a city where we didn't speak the language or know anyone who did. My panic turned to a hollow, empty terror. They'd gotten our game tickets and train reservations. I tried to be grateful that they had missed our passports and cash, but this occured just a couple hours before the game and the tickets we had worked so hard to get were gone, and we had no record of our ownership of them. Post attack, there was no satisfaction that we had been justified in our suspicion that there was no safe place in the city for an American couple on their own.

We took the shuttle round trip past the stadium and back to our hotel. I was sobbing, quickly ruining my first attempt at face paint. The American fans were still congregating in the alley outside our hotel, drinking and gearing up for the game. They asked what had happened, and I told them, sobbing, that our tickets had been stolen. The stunned looks on their faces did nothing to make me feel better. We went to our room and washed off our face paint. We got the address for the local police station from our hotel front desk and headed to the station.

The police station was the darkest, most dismal place on Planet Earth. We were supposed to be partying in the fan zone with our fellow soccer lovers, ablaze in all the colors of their respective countries, but instead, we were sitting on a hard, lumpy couch in the middle of a gray French police station. I would start sobbing every time I thought about our trip ending on such a low note. The fact that we were broke and could barely afford our first train reservation, let alone a replacement, was hitting me hard, and there was no comfort to be found in a blue-gray monochrome police station with cops who only spoke French. Officer drones were buzzing around us speaking their fast, accented French that we couldn't follow at all. We were told that a translator was on the way, but as it ticked closer to game time, I grew more and more apprehensive and depressed, bottoming out in a pit of hopelessness.

Finally, our translator and his partner arrived. I can only describe them as the Laurel and Hardy of French policing. Both officers were from another town, brought in to help with the influx of foreigners. They had developed a very funny communication style that needed no translation. The tall skinny one, who we'll call Laurel, didn't speak English and was all business. The heavyset one, Hardy, was joking around, all charm, and within minutes he had us relaxed and smiling and explaining our story. We thanked them for coming to help us, as after our trip, our vocabulary was limited predominantly to food and soccer terms. They were thoroughly entertained that we clearly knew almost no French but could say yellow card, red card, and goal flawlessly, a finely-honed vocabulary that would only be useful for the stadium portion of our travel.

If you have seen any cop show on TV, you know they like to ask you the same questions about 47 times. Only here, each time it had to be translated into French. Luckily, Hardy's patience ran out before ours. We could understand enough French to get that after going over our story about 10 times, he turned to Laurel and said something in French that would loosely translate to:

"Look, the game's about to start. They were on their way to the stadium, four guys asked them for photos, they assaulted them and took their tickets and rail passes. They know the tickets were in the orange zone but not the row and seat. Let's get them over to the stadium so they don't miss the entire game."

Well, alright … you go, Hardy! The lesson here is if you're ever going to a major sporting event take a photo of your tickets, passports and other documents, and then email them to yourself. It will make life so much easier if you have to recreate your identity or game passes with nothing in your pockets.

We piled into a tiny French police car, Doug and I in the back with a third officer who was catching a ride to the stadium, Laurel driving, Hardy in the front passenger seat. Hardy started to talk about how French officers were superior to American officers.

"In America, they are so serious. They have hands like this (on the wheel at 10 and 2) and they have the windows up and they look like this." He said, scowling intensely. "But in France, we drive like this (one hand on the wheel, one hand waving out the open window), and we say 'Oh Cherie, hello! How are you?'"

We didn't know quite what to say to that, but we had to laugh at his antics flirting with French girls as we drove through city streets on our way to the stadium. His cell phone rang and he took a moment to answer it.

"*Oh! Brigitte! Cherie! Bon jour!*" He spoke in French for a moment before he handed me the phone full of glee and said "Brigitte wants to talk to you."

I took the phone and said "Hello?"

"*Allo?*" came back from Brigitte.

"Does Brigitte speak English?" I asked Hardy.

"No!!" he answered, now hysterical with laughter, the other officers chuckling at his prank.

I sat there for a moment trying to think of something I could do to get out of this gracefully when my husband leaned over and said conspiratorially, "Why don't you tell Brigitte the only French you know from high school?"

There wasn't even a moment for the mischief to register on my face before I exclaimed "Oh Brigitte! Hardy has been teaching me French! *Voulez-vous coucher avec moi ce soir?* (translation for those of you who didn't have friends taking high school French: Will you sleep with me tonight?)

At this point, Hardy dove into the back seat for his phone while everyone else in the car burst out laughing. Hardy put the phone to his ear and said "Allo? Allo? ... Ach, Brigitte! She's gone. I take my black book and I cross her out!" We all laughed the rest of the way to the stadium with the remaining apprehension about the mugging gone.

We were surprised that a flash of a badge waved us right through the security blockades and we drove right up to the stadium with our police escort. We entered through the security entrance and made our way up a series of corridors deep into the stadium. We came out into a room that housed more technology than I thought existed in 1998. Hardy's always joking demeanor became hushed and awe-struck as he explained that we were about to meet the head of all of the French police. He said he'd never had the honor of meeting him before and started thanking us profusely for bringing him into this situation. We met the Chief of Chiefs, and he asked us to look through the section we were supposed to sit in and see if we could recognize the guys that had robbed us. We walked into a room of screens that were trained on fans all over the stadium. The operators were trained to scan the stands for trouble in order to mobilize police to problems as fast as possible. We watched as they zeroed in on a shoving match, and before it could become a full-blown fight, there were officers sent to break it up. We used this technology to scan where our seats had been, but we couldn't spot the guys that had stolen our tickets. After searching for the first half, the police thanked us, explaining that the tickets had probably been sold on the black market, and offered us seats with the American supporters. We said goodbye to Laurel and Hardy, thanked them again for everything, and went to join the game in progress.

The seats they moved us to turned out to be a critical formative experience. They sat us behind Sam's Army, the newly-formed supporter's group for US Soccer. Sam's Army had started in 1995, after the '94 World Cup, but in those pre-social media days, we had heard very little about it before this match. They sang and cheered and looked like they were having a great time. It was our first introduction to US Soccer supporter culture, and we were only there because we'd been robbed. It was our first lesson in "whatever happens, just go with it." Much like Alexi Lalas asking people to not be culture police in the stands in his 1994 quote, my theory of the World Cup is that it's like life ... sometimes it's going to be awesome and sometimes it's going to suck. You just have to roll with it and trust that at the end, you'll wind up with a great story.

As if our introduction to Sam's Army wasn't enough, we did score one final great tale on our train back to Paris for our flight. We still had our first class rail passes and bought a new reservation for the morning train leaving for Paris. We got on and became aware of a buzz a few seating compartments up from us. Eavesdropping heavily, we figured out that it was Tom Dooley, USMNT captain, sitting with his wife, fielding questions from other fans on the train. We were over-hearing happily all the way to Paris when we made our move. We said hello and told him that we were American fans who had this great adventure all through France following the National team. He apologized that the play wasn't better, and we laughed telling him about how we'd missed half the game in our madcap mugging misadventure. Now Tom Dooley looked impressed that we might have had a better time than he had but looked a little skeptical, and his wife was looking a little impatient. I quickly produced the crime report we'd been given at the police station as proof of our story and asked him to sign it, which he happily did. Don't get me wrong. Getting mugged was rotten. It was a very stressful night for us, but coming home from France '98 with a police report signed by Tom Dooley ... Priceless.

9

1999 Women's World Cup

By 1999, my obsession with soccer was in full swing, and it was a good time to be a soccer-obsessed American. The United States hosted the FIFA Women's World Cup, and the US Women's National Team (USWNT) was the team to beat, at least in my opinion. Kristine Lilly, Michelle Akers, Mia Hamm ... so many superstars of the women's game ... who had been playing together for so long. I was sure we'd make it out of group stage, and I was pretty confident they had a shot at the final. I decided a little low-budget traveling to see the women play around the country was a good way to spend the summer, since my career remained freelance after my 1998 World Cup firing. With my parents still living in New Jersey, the opening ceremonies at Giants Stadium were an obvious choice, and I decided to take my mom with me to show her what my soccer obsession was all about. I also bought tickets to the games in Chicago (driving distance!) allowing me to see the USWNT play twice in the opening round.

I love my mom very much, but we do have one of those relationships that never really gelled up nicely. I love her and she loves me, but as much as I try to understand her, I am not sure I get what she's about and I know she doesn't get what I am about. I love adventure and risk taking; she hates it. I love to travel; she is a home-body. I'm sure many mother/daughter pairs get past this sort of thing but having weathered my many eye surgeries and medications with our wildly differing world views, we weren't really all that good of friends. Despite our history, I have a daughterly desire to be understood by my mother. I used to dream of the day when my mom would look at me and say, "OK, I get it." Whether it was an education, romantic, or geographic decision (yeah, that moving to Iowa thing didn't go over so big with my folks), I just wanted her to get where I was coming from and love that I was loving my life, even if she didn't. I have not felt that satisfaction for many days of my life but June 19, 1999, was probably the best day of my relationship with my mom.

Taking my mom to the Opening Ceremonies of the Women's World Cup, and watching the US Women take their first step in the final tournament into their destined role of champions, was an impressive bonding experience for both of us. The ceremonies were very cool: a flood of confetti, bright colors, and music. The opening ceremony was stunning and beautiful, entertainment enough on its own. Then the US team took the field against Denmark, and the fun really began. It was so nice, after being the underdogs in 1998. We could kick back as fans and not be in constant panic about every game we played. And my mom, while not really happy in a crowd, enjoyed being surrounded by chill women's soccer fans. It was manageable for her, and my excitement about the double header was contagious. US vs. Denmark with a Canadian referee I was familiar with followed by Brazil vs. Mexico. Great lineup for the day.

It did not disappoint. Mia Hamm scored in the 17th minute of the US game and Foudy scored in the 73rd. All the while, I explained refereeing to my mom and the various rules that came into play. I taught my mom about the Women's team, and why I liked Lilly better than Hamm, even though Hamm got all the press. I always liked that Lilly was the unsung heroine of the team, not so marketed, quieter, nicer, and getting more caps. She reminded me of the type of person I was in high school: hardworking, dedicated, but outside the limelight. She was the most capped player, male or female, in the history of the sport, retiring at 352. My husband and I summed up our feelings for players of this era as, "We named our cat Mia, but our daughter's middle name is Lilly." So you can imagine, in the waning moments of the game, when Kristine Lilly scored in the 89th minute, I pretty much went ballistic. Brazil trouncing Mexico in a 7-1 goal-fest was just icing on the cake for me.

The thing I most clearly remember about that day is my mom looking at me, and saying, "I can really see how much you love this. It's great to be here with you. I get why you love it so much."

I can't see a single goal or really bring back any details of anything else that day, but I can tell you exactly where we were sitting and exactly how my mom looked, telling me that she got it. It's funny. Most sports books are about a Dad taking a son to a game and imparting wisdom, but for me, the opener of the '99 Women's World Cup was an opportunity for my mom to have a fleeting unforgettable moment of understanding who I am.

The Opening Ceremonies would be a tough experience to beat, if not for that San Francisco Bay Soccer connection I had from the 1998 World Cup. My editor came through with press credentials for the Women's World Cup in Chicago for me to take photos and interview players at the double header there. I got to report on Brazil vs. Italy and then US vs. Nigeria. I was excited to see Brazil vs. Italy but that game just seemed like the local comic sent out to warm up the crowd for the main event. It was a fine game and all; however, as the kickoff for the US match approached, the energy in the stadium crept higher and higher to pandemonium.

It was a moment I will remember for the rest of my life. I was on the field level, between games, waiting for the USWNT to take the field. They were to play in front of 65,080 fans at Soldier Field, and there was a hush between games throughout the stadium as people got their drinks and made their bathroom runs. Then, it happened. You could hear the noise travel like a tidal wave across the stadium as 65,000 little girls and their families realized their heroines were coming out of the tunnel. I had never heard anything like it before and never so clearly since. The wave of communal joy that spread through the stadium as the team took the field was deafening and powerful, and its might was only multiplied from my vantage point at field level. It was an awe-inspiring moment in history.

Then the impossible happened: Nigeria scored in the 2nd minute to go up 1-0. All those little girls devastated their team wasn't living up to the hype ... their tiny hearts breaking all over the stadium for what amounted to nanoseconds in sports time. Nigeria had rattled the hornets' nest, and they were going to pay. USWNT pressure caused Nigeria to give up an own goal while still in the 2nd minute, and then it took a short 18 minutes for the gloves to come off. In the 20th, it was Hamm, Milbrett in the 23rd, Lilly at 32nd, Akers at 39th, Parlow at 42nd, and before they could get to the halftime lockers, Nigeria was down 6-1. The match continued to slide into ugly, with frustration fouls that bordered on violence. We later joked that the Swiss referee was ill equipped to deal with the level of fighting that was taking place on the pitch. Milbrett scored once more for the US in the 83rd minute to make it 7-1 USA at the final whistle.

Soccer fever had taken over the United States, and people were talking about the USWNT in the final with greater and greater certainty. While I was home in New Jersey, I had coffee with a few friends from high school including Jon Czar, a guy from the class ahead of mine, who had been dating one of my friends, Nicole Scheller. Nicole was not entirely impressed with soccer but was entertained with my obsession and got me talking with Jon, who had also shown interest in the game. As the summer and the tournament rolled on, Jon and I talked more than we'd ever talked in three years of high school together, and the conversations became more serious about traveling to see the final match if the USWNT made it that far. In "I dare you to go/I'll go if you go" terms, we discussed going to the final game in Pasadena if the USWNT advanced to that game. After every round, we would touch base by phone and have the "I'm still in, are you in?" talk, until finally, the semis were over and the final match lined up the US vs. China to win it all. We bought tickets and planned to meet in California.

Truth is, there was no way I was going to be in Des Moines for the Women's World Cup Final of 1999. My husband had ascended to National Referee Candidate for US Soccer, which is the year that you have to get everything right and get very lucky. In 1999, candidates needed five games including three center referee and two assistant referee assessments from a National Referee Assessor. Trouble is, there were no National Referee Assessors in Iowa so Iowa National Candidates had to do all this out of state or pay to have someone come in to assess them. Doug had gotten all of his assessments passed at out-of-town tournaments, except the last one, which was going to be an assessor brought in to watch him referee a Des Moines Menace PDL game on … July 10, 1999, the day of the Final. There was no way I was going to take responsibility for distracting, jinxing, or otherwise screwing up his mojo. He'd passed four without me, and I was crazed with superstition, so off to Pasadena I went.

I really don't remember the flight or how I got to the stadium or any of the details at all until I got to the game. It's not even a blur … I just remember being at the Rose Bowl Stadium with Jon. Our seats were so high up, I thought my nose would literally bleed, or I'd fall off the mountain and die somewhere on the steep trek up to our seats. But we were in the stadium, and that was all I cared about. The atmosphere was great … lesbians and soccer moms and daughters everywhere soaking up all the girl power. There wasn't a defined supporter's section, at this point, I'm not sure I would have recognized one if there had been; however the whole stadium was electrified with the hopes and dreams of over 90,000 fans eagerly anticipating the history about to unfold.

Game day was blisteringly hot, and we were so high up in the Rose Bowl, I had the sensation that we were an important distance closer to the sun, and in danger of frying in the atmosphere. The game went on and on, scoreless for the full 90 minutes and 30 minutes of overtime as we sweltered in the sun. There was excitement with scoring chances, some blisteringly close. After just two shots on goal during all of regulation, China had three shots in sudden-death overtime; one a header directed off a corner kick that would have surely won the game for China but was saved off the line by a jumping header by Kristine Lilly. I love watching a match and getting a growing sensation that my team's net is protected by a force field so strong there is nothing their opponent will be able to do … they will not score. I had that sense, and after Lilly's save, I wholeheartedly believed we would win the Women's World Cup.

The game went to penalties and the stadium was thick with energetic tension; kick after kick, until all ten shots of the opening round of PKs had been fired. It only took one Brianna Scurry save because all five USWNT shots were perfect goals. The stadium went crazy; the players went crazy. The players were tiny ants from our seats, but I was there when Brandi Chastain whipped her shirt off in celebration of their victory causing a national controversy for flashing less skin than most beachwear allows. It was an incredible victory and a great game to witness firsthand. I was so grateful to be a part of it and was flooded with an even deeper gratitude for the post-game swim in the hotel pool.

After the game, we met up with Janet and Carly. Janet was from Iowa who had grown up refereeing and playing with Doug, and Carly was her girlfriend. The four of us went back to the hotel, learned that my husband had passed his final assessment to become a National Referee (making 2000 the first of his 10 years as a USSF National Referee), and took a much deserved celebratory swim. A doubly memorable day in the history of my soccer life.

10

The Road to Korea

It had been almost three full years since my last USMNT cap when qualifying got started in 2001. Seems impossible to me today, over a decade later, when I could never go a year without a game. We joke that with every World Cup cycle we get a little more serious, so the low cap count I could accept a decade ago seems ridiculous today. A decade from now, I won't be able to believe how comparatively little I traveled in 2013. I imagine the fire of my passion for soccer will continue to rage for decades to come, hindered only by budget. Back in 2001, that fire was a smoldering ember, growing from a spark struck in the early 90s that somehow didn't extinguish at the 1998 World Cup, and was fed just enough in 1999 to begin its slow burn.

I was still reporting for San Francisco Bay Soccer, and when I heard that USMNT would be playing a qualifier in Kansas City, I immediately requested press passes and received field-level passes for Doug and I. I may not be the greatest cook or keep an awesome clean house, but I think scoring your husband field passes for a USMNT qualifier is wifely bonus points for a solid 20 years. Half the fun of that game was watching Doug as we walked around field level as his referee buddies from all over got their first-row seats one-upped by his field-level access. Doug is a quiet guy and he doesn't ask for much. He's not even the type to boast about his accomplishments, which makes it even more fun to pull out all the stops for him at times.

The crowd of 37,319 was less than halfway to filling Arrowhead so the atmosphere could have been a little more charged up, but the game was exciting and intense. Tied until the 70th minute when Clint Mathis received a pass from Jeff Agoos and headed the ball down in the penalty area for Josh Wolff to tap in for the winning goal. Supporter's groups were still nothing like what we have today. There was a small group of Sam's Army together for this match, but those were the days when we could not fill one whole section. We would maybe get enough people to go a third or halfway up one section with people singing and cheering. The upside of this was that it was very easy to have very creative chants for almost any situation and player because you didn't have to teach it to two or three sections. You only had to lead maybe 100 people. We had songs like "Show us your Clint" for when Mathis was warming up or had scored. It makes me a little sad that we don't sing it for Dempsey but time rolls on.

The article Doug wrote for that game was about how the USMNT had essentially qualified for the 2002 World Cup at Arrowhead. We were nine points up in three games, and it was almost mathematically impossible to imagine we would not end up qualifying. Officially, however, it took us until October 7, 2001, a day we would not never forget. The USMNT defeated Jamaica 2-1 at Foxboro, but Doug and I couldn't watch the entire game live because we were refereeing the Washington Area Girls Soccer (WAGS) Tournament in metro Washington, D.C. There's something really special about being at a top-flight tournament with expert referees and assessors while a US Soccer game is going on. In between my game assignments, I went into the sports complex building and huddled with the other USMNT fans who watched the match. Referees are very interesting to watch games with, because they tend to over analyze everything. They refuse to scream at the referee for not rewarding a particular foul or card, because they're aggravatingly objective about the game. I can be objective about some games, but not when the US is playing. Still, we won and we were through to the World Cup. Doug and I were going to going to Asia for the first time, and there was great rejoicing and celebration. That is, until we got back to our hotel room.

A soccer tournament is like a hive of information ... but only about what's happening at the tournament. Teams and referees to watch.

Exciting game situations. All buzz around the referee tent, but very little from the outside world gets in. We got back to our hotel and turned on the TV looking for game highlights but instead learned we had declared war in Afghanistan with the opening of Operation Enduring Freedom … the US response to the attacks of 9/11. We had only been officially dreaming of Korea for a couple hours, and now, we were at war, back when being at war was not commonplace. We sat on the edge of our bed watching the attacks unfold wondering what it would be like to travel through Asia in eight short months. We talked late into the night about "what if" things escalated and Americans weren't allowed to travel. That couldn't happen, could it? It seemed unlikely, but we were freshly into post 9/11 world and nothing seemed guaranteed. Do not mistake me if I sound calloused, as if the World Trade Center and Pentagon bombings meant nothing to me because 9/11/01 was a pivotal day in my life.

I grew up looking across the river at those towers, and I was devastated that morning when I pulled into work and realized the Iowa high school deejays on the alternative station I listened to back then were not kidding … someone had flown a plane into the World Trade Center. I arrived at work just in time to see the second plane hit on our conference room TV. With phone lines jammed, I couldn't reach any of my friends in New York nor could I immediately reach my Dad, who was supposed to be flying from Boston to California that morning but thankfully not scheduled until late morning. It took me until 4 PM to reach my mom at her elementary school in Montclair, NJ, where she sat with her kids trying not to cry as it took until 7 PM for the last parent to walk out of the City and pick up their child. Although I lost no one, the suffering of so many was not at all clouded for me. But even a month later, you knew life had to go on somehow, and for the first time, I had a sense of how important it was to me that we continue our streak of World Cups. That day and several times since, I have wholeheartedly believed that if I could just get to the next World Cup everything would be okay.

In our conversations that night, we decided that we would go to the Cup if it was at all possible. It became a rallying cry around the house for a while: "If we don't get to the World Cup, the terrorists win!" No war would keep us from going. However, there were other storms brewing on our horizon. For me, 9/11 was a wakeup call on two fronts: Work and Home. At work, I was a sales rep for an office furniture company and realized that day no one cared about all the office furniture destroyed in the attacks. There had to be thousands of miles of totally irrelevant panel systems furniture lost on 9/11, and thinking about it made my work seem unimportant. No one wants "She put people in cubicles" written on their tombstone. I needed to find more meaningful work, and it needed to happen soon.

On the homefront, my pre-9/11 position on kids and parenting was not very positive. I had talked to my Rabbi, Steve Mills, about my complete lack of desire to have children and my feeling of obligation to have them for my husband's sake. I was as sure he would be a great father as I was unsure I would thrive as a mother. I presented him with my pros and cons list of parenting as I saw it and asked why people would do such a thing when children seemed to drain all your resources and offer very little in return. Rabbi Mills laughed.

"You're absolutely right. If becoming a parent suddenly became a rational decision, the human race would grind to a halt instantly. One day, you may wake up and decide, despite it not making any sense, you want children and you'll have them. Or you won't and that's fine too. But it will never be rational."

I found this concept totally unbelievable, but testing it as a theory was pretty simple: just keep on keeping on until a thunderbolt from above changes you from a rational person into someone who wants kids. Yeah, right.

But on 9/11, we went home after the futile and obligatory blood donation and made dinner in front of CNN, drowning ourselves in the horrific images of the day. At one point that night, I turned to Doug.

"I think we should have children, like soon."

Doug turned to me, stunned at my abrupt change of heart, "Uh … OK. Why now?"

"Here's how I see it. In order for this to have happened, there had to be, like, at least a dozen really truly evil people in the world. I'm not saying I think our kids will cure cancer or anything, but I think they'd be good people. Good citizens. Maybe we owe the world a few good people." I said, stunned the shift from rationality had taken place.

"Let's see how you feel in a couple weeks." said my ever-practical husband. However the shift had been made, my pre-kid days were numbered from that day forward.

Those two life-focus shifts joined forces, and I left my job at the end of December 2001. I started doing community-based work, first for the Des Moines Marathon as the Assistant Race Director, and then as the Events Coordinator for the Stadium Foundation, working in partnership with the Des Moines Menace PDL soccer team in an attempt (which died in an Urbandale City Council meeting) to build a soccer specific stadium in Des Moines (shakes fist at short-sighted Urbandale City Council). It was work I loved; and perfect for where I was in my personal life.

My idea to start our family didn't fade in the months that followed 9/11, and while my husband was away at National Referee Camp that January, I did some calculating. I announced at our post-camp celebratory dinner that if I got pregnant, my due date would be after the Des Moines Marathon race day, but that "prime time" for the month had passed while he was at camp. Another cautionary tale for all fertile people reading this: when calculating 40 weeks of pregnancy, you start from the first day of your last period, not conception; and when they told you in seventh grade family life class that you can get pregnant any time, but you're more "likely" to get knocked up on day 15, they are not kidding around.

Two weeks later, I was sitting at my annual torture session, aka Iowa High School soccer rules meeting. I lamented I just wanted to get assigned to the high school State Championship so there would be nothing left to achieve in high school refereeing and I could retire and quit going to those idiotic meetings. Lou Agocs, a 60-something referee from Italy, looked at me and started to create a scene.

"You're retiring? You're pregnant! I knew it! Look at you! You're pregnant!"

As if it was not hard enough being one of 3 women in a room of 300 men, now I had a guy practically shouting I was pregnant when we'd barely thought about trying to conceive. I squelched it, saying, "I am not pregnant, I'm just sick of these meetings! I want to retire from the meetings … sheesh. Keep it down."

I swear, at the time, I had not one single clue that I was, in fact, already pregnant with our daughter. Those old Italian referees, they're pretty tuned in to the universe or something, because he knew a week before I did. I walked out of the meeting thinking, "Huh … when was my last period?"

11

That Pregnant Girl in Korea

When I finally confirmed my pregnancy in the third week of February 2002, it never once crossed my mind to cancel our trip. We'd won the FIFA lottery and had Team Specific Tickets (TST) for the United States' first round. Literally a lottery drawing, in which one can request tickets that are Team or Stadium specific, a choice between following a team or basing in one city and watching whoever plays in that stadium. We always select TST for the US, but the only time we've been selected by FIFA (the earliest round of ticketing) was in Korea. The soccer gods smiled upon us as if to say, "We will not let them make any excuses about not going to the World Cup." In my mind, it was just a pregnancy, and I would "only" be there for weeks 20, 21, and 22; just past halfway. It seemed perfectly reasonable to Doug and I, but I'd have a funded college account if I had five bucks for every wide-eyed stare reaction we got after mentioning our travel plans. I found a red sleeveless maternity shirt and a backpack I could wear low on my hips. Ready to rock out pregnant Korea style.

The 2002 World Cup predated American Outlaws, Facebook, Twitter, and a thousand ways soccer fans connect with each other today. Sam's Army existed, but there was no way for Sam's Army members to connect directly with each other back then. They had a website with information they wanted you to have but no way to connect with other soccer fans in your town or fans traveling to Korea. BigSoccer.com was at the height of its relevancy and served as the main communication point for fans. In 2002, on BigSoccer's travel thread, someone posted a link to a Yahoo group "Yanks In Korea," a private group for people traveling to Korea to watch the USMNT. People discussed hotels, bars for pre-game drinking, transportation, and more. We had locals that were helping us sort through Korean culture, cutting edge crowd sourced information. We used it to meet up with other Americans in Korea and to help us sort out housing.

The hotels in Korea were of two general classes: business and "love hotels." The business class hotels were way out of our price range and pretty far out of the crowd we were hanging with. Let's face it, how much fun can you have worrying about your $150-$300 a night hotel room? So, love hotels for us! What's a love hotel? Well, in Korea, they have several generations of families living together in one house. So, if you, as husband and wife, wanted a little private time, to say … balance the checkbook, you could rent a love hotel room and work out your … checkbook calculations. This doesn't really explain why you would drive into parking lots hidden behind strips of plastic to have others immediately cover your license plate. I guess it's a big secret in Korea when a happily married couple just needs a little quiet time for checkbook balancing. Strangely, married couples looking for a little private time also needed an extensive porn collection, fluorescent undersea murals under black light, and round beds with mirrors on the ceiling. And they say Americans are repressed!

Most love hotels had "Western" floors which looked like your basic average motel, assuming you could pretend the porn collection in the lobby didn't exist and disregard the strange parking situation. Otherwise, it seemed legit. As we traveled and changed hotels, we'd check in every once in a while before a Western room was ready and be put in a bowchickawowwow room, or I'd be looking for a quiet place to order pizza and I would wander onto a floor straight out of a porno. You could peek behind the curtain of what must be a very interesting world of Korean sexuality. Only one night were we put in a Korean style room from which I requested to be moved. It felt like it had not been thoroughly cleaned in months and so over the top with forced sensuality I told my husband our unborn child could not sleep there. I would imagine those sort of situations only got more awkward with the groups of single guys traveling together, but the rest of the time the 24/7 staff, kind and efficient, with translation services, made the love hotels a great place to stay.

A third option for accommodations was referred to as "Home Stay." We home stayed when we were in a city for three days or more. A Home Stay Korea website, part of the Korean Federations' coping mechanism to deal with their very limited number of hotel rooms, listed Korean citizens willing to host travelers. They posted their parameters (nationality, number of guests, etc) and their rates for a room plus breakfast. The fees typically converted to about $8-15 per night for both of us, which was less expensive than the love hotels at $30 per night. Homestaying allowed us to meet locals we thought would add to the experience of traveling on the other side of the world. Our homestays ended up being the highlights of our trip. In fact, we have incorporated them into every World Cup since.

Once again, we were leaving for the World Cup in a state of transition. We had the "Engaged World Cup" in 1994, the "Married, No Kids World Cup" in 1998, and as we boarded the plane for the 14-hour flight to Japan followed by the hour jump to Korea, we were quite clearly embarking on the "Pregnant World Cup." At four months along, I definitely showed and had outgrown even my stretchiest regular clothes but was not yet comfortable in my maternity wear. Our baby's kicks weren't strong enough for Doug to feel yet but I had felt the baby move for the first time while assistant refereeing an April amateur game in Des Moines. Pretty fit, having refereed Dallas Cup, high school, and amateur soccer games right up until we left; however, nothing could have prepared me for a 14-hour flight at 20 weeks pregnant. Walking and fluids were the key to not blowing up like a balloon during the flight, and fortunately I got the bulkhead seat and could easily stretch and walk almost whenever I wanted. I was exhausted when we landed but no more than non-pregnant travelers. Even through the extreme fatigue, I felt exhilarated to be in South Korea for the first time in my life. Seeing Korean written everywhere induced momentary panic we wouldn't be able to read anything that wasn't ours for the next three weeks. What were we doing here, thinking we could navigate this country … pregnant no less? I remember thinking I didn't have to get through the next three weeks in my weary state; I just had to collect my luggage and find my way to Homestay #1. We called our host and found our way to meet Phillip Cho in the middle of Seoul by way of the city bus; a feat I can't believe we pulled off so jetlagged and disoriented. Somehow we made it without GPS or a cell phone. We survived on handwritten notes taken from a payphone conversation in the middle of the night in Korea.

The next morning things looked brighter. Our host, a Chinese Christian Reverend living in Seoul with his mother, in custom of caring for parents by living with them in their old age, spoke English relatively well. His mother spoke none but clearly expressed her excitement over my pregnancy. She would smile at me and nod with an ancient, all knowing smile. Only looking back I understood that she looked at me as the next in a neverending line of mothers and children, seeing me as a prospective member of a sorority I hadn't known existed yet. She seemed to be trying to telepathically communicate her "Wisdom of Mothers" to me and I only got the message in retrospect. She did one really cool thing one day towards the end of our stay. She took me over to the couch and sat me down with a calendar, pantomiming that she wanted to know my due date. I pointed to October 21. She frowned and shook her head a vehement no. She placed her hands on my belly and then waved them over the calendar and then my belly. She went back and forth until she landed on October 16th, looking very pleased with the number. Later, when Western medicine decided I should be induced several days before the 16th and intruded on our sacred little moment of prediction, it upset me for years. There are very few decisions I would do over, but I do think I would tell them to stick their Pitocin elsewhere until October 17th.

Day One in Korea was a gorgeous sunny day. Phillip made us a decent American breakfast, but it paled in comparison to the traditional Korean food he prepared, at our request, for the rest of our stay. Koreans eat fish and vegetables at every meal and very little grains or rice. My three weeks there were quite possibly the healthiest of my life. After breakfast, we decided to explore the city on our own for the day. Getting out in the sun is supposed to help your body adjust to the new time zone, though it would be some time before the realization we were finally in Korea settled into our existence.

We took the opportunity to check out one of the famous sites in Korea, the Demilitarized Zone, or DMZ. It's the no-man's land zone between North and South Korea and visiting it was serious business. We had packed business-casual clothing specifically for this tour as we'd read in the guide books that women had to be dressed in skirts and men had to wear long pants that were not jeans. These were two countries still at war with each other, and the closer we got to the DMZ, the more real that seemed to us. As we went through the tour, our guide told us about attacks that had taken place in the DMZ as people had occasionally tried to defect from one side to the other. We finally arrived at the border and were inspected on the bus by our border tour guide. She stopped at our row and then went to have a discussion with one of the other guides. When she returned, she told me that my knee-length khaki skirt was not appropriate, and I was going to have to change into something else from their collection of clothes. I pointed out that their own directions stated skirts needed to be worn but did not state a requirement for calf or floor length. She said they needed to present a professional appearance for the people on the north side that may be taking photographs. At this point, I almost lost it … wearing a skirt I'd regularly worn to work. There was no way I expected Koreans to have a skirt that would fit a 5'8" tall, pregnant American woman. When I told the tour guide this, she finally backed off and let me continue the tour dressed as I had come.

The DMZ tour was thrilling, especially to see the seriousness both sides had about maintaining the sanctity of the boundary. There was a concrete valley that marked the North/South border with row buildings built spanning the border in order to have meetings between the two countries where neither country would have to cross the border to meet. There were armed guards all around, but once in the building, we were allowed to cross to the North side of the conference table to take a photo of what was technically North Korea, just so long as we did not try to exit the guarded door to the north side. We found the culture of both sides riveting and recommended to everyone we met that they tour the DMZ while visiting Korea.

Seoul is both modern and ancient at the same time, with gleaming skyscrapers interspersed with ancient buildings. There were city gates, built in the late 1300s, that stood in stark contrast to the tech-entrenched modernity that surrounded them. The people were friendly and we found plenty to explore, sightsee, and shop until the evening when we were to meet up with Americans for the night-before-party at Nashville Bar. After shopping for World Cup official souvenirs, we had a meal of delicious Korean street food and headed to the bar.

It was a huge relief to get to the bar and see so many American soccer fans and hear fluent English spoken for the first time all day. My pleasure was short lived as people had drink after drink and I was the one sober pregnant girl. My jet lag was still catching up with me, and the more people drank, the more alienated I felt amongst my own people. We called it a night earlier than we ever had before and found our way back to Phillip's apartment. As we walked under streetlights, I thought about the trip and the pregnancy, a once in a lifetime experience multiplied by another once in a lifetime experience. In Asia for the first time ever at the first Asian World Cup and carrying my first child, I made the decision as we rounded the corner into the courtyard facing the apartment, that I would not allow myself to let the trip ruin my pregnancy or the pregnancy ruin our trip. I would figure out a way to be the best pregnant girl at the World Cup there would ever be, and no matter how the games played out, I would appreciate my good fortune.

The next day we got up and had breakfast with Phillip; this time a traditional Korean meal with fish, noodles, and vegetables. It was tasty and filling and prepared us for the task at hand: supporting our team through what was supposed to be our toughest opponent, Portugal. They were number four in FIFA rankings and had the current FIFA player of the year, Luis Figo. Doug, Phillip and I talked about the game and discussed possible outcomes that would have both Korea and the USMNT escape the group. It was nearly impossible to imagine an outcome which would allow us to advance while not having a hand in sending the host out in the first round for the first time ever. We tried not to think about how our trip would look as we got closer to the likely faceoff between us and our host in group play since first things first, we had to take it to Portugal.

The "Yanks in Korea" group had planned to meet around noon in a bar district near the stadium shuttle bus stop. We took the subway to the district in Suwon, a suburb of Seoul, and when we surfaced, we were looking out over a busy roundabout lined in businesses shouting things to us in Korean. I had to stop for a moment and take it all in: here we were, in Korea, going to the USMNT's opening game. It was breathtaking and overwhelming in emotion and unfamiliarity. I had been in foreign countries before; but in European languages, you can figure out what most places are by reading the foreign words and extrapolating. There was no faking your way through Korea. Even after three weeks, the only sign I could find on the street was for the PC Bangh, or internet café, and that was only because the PC was written in Roman characters. Determined not to panic, we headed across the street in search of our fellow Yanks.

We found a group of about 15-20 people at the designated bar, but the bar wasn't supposed to open for at least an hour which meant we'd be cutting it close getting to the shuttle buses. Our nicely-formed plan fell apart, and people were hanging around in the pedestrian area trying to sort out plan B. I didn't really care to stay at a bar and was much more in favor of getting to the stadium. We knew from France that the fan zones around the stadium were places where you could easily spend a couple hours hanging out. Not wanting to go alone, I walked up to a tall guy in a tie-dye goalkeeper jersey and his friend and suggested heading to the shuttle buses. Goalkeeper jersey and his friend were Jimmy LaRoue and Andy Gustafson from the Washington, D.C. metro. They agreed and we headed to the stadium together and look for fan-zone activities. If you've read Andy's book, "23 Days in Korea," then you already know the fan-zones were non-existent. Andy spent the rest of the afternoon reminding me that we had just walked away from all the food and drink outside the stadium, as if my pregnancy didn't remind me of hunger and thirst enough. We came across some fans who'd been drinking a while and they tossed us a few extra beers. Even I took a few swigs believing dehydration was worse than a few gulps of second trimester beer.

Along the shuttle ride and walk to the stadium, we got to meet Andy Mead, a journalist documenting the World Cup. It was cool to meet so many people that were spreading the joy of soccer to the masses, and so nice for my tired, pregnant brain for them all to be named Andy. As we walked up the hill to the stadium, we met a few more American fans. One who stuck with us was Kaela Porter, a woman traveling solo from New York. A little further into it, we met Monty Rodriguez who became affectionately known as "Korean Citizen" as we teased him mercilessly for getting his passport stolen. There was Sean Kennedy and Brock Kwiatkowski, whose last names now make up the official name of our band of soccer travelers. Now we had a little family of supporters to enjoy the atmosphere with us. Little did we know, a dozen years later we'd still all be traveling together.

When we got to the stadium, Jimmy and Andy wanted to find Chuck, an American who'd been living in Korea as an English teacher. This venture ended up a pivotal decision. Chuck, who was helpful with local information in the beginning, was also loud, overbearing, and socially awkward to the point of being mildly aggravating to annoying depending on the day and our relative fatigue with him and/or the trip. For the first few times I interacted with him, I tried to see past his more irritating qualities, but soon it became clear, he wasn't going to settle down and get used to us. He was just going to be annoying. He would brag about being a millionaire in South Korean Wan, which was exceptional only until you realize that was less than $1000. He would complain about his experiences in Korean culture, but we soon realized his frustration was self-inflicted. It only took about a week for us to learn more Korean than he had in a year. As we racked up fabulous experiences in Korea, we began to develop that the hypothesis that Chuck's frustration with Korea and Koreans had more to do with him than his surroundings.

Chuck was hard to miss that day, standing at well over six feet tall in a bright red Ohio State shirt. He had his usual stream of complaints. However, now that we were outside the entrance to the stadium, nothing could bring me down. There were women dressed up in traditional Korean hanboks, acrobats entertaining the soccer fans, and then the soccer fans themselves, entertainment in their own right. A computer error had left hundreds, if not a few thousand tickets, left unsold for most games in Korea. In an effort to fill the stadium, many tickets were given away to Korean school children. They came to the stadium excited and full of wonder and were not shy about walking up to us and practicing their English, a hand extended with charming and adorable greetings. "Hello, my name is _____, what's your name?" Sprinkle in some international media, and the party was definitely warming up. We spent some time walking around the outside of the stadium, chatting it up with the foreign press and making outrageous projections of a 3-1 or greater score.

"To Portugal?" The journalist said in disbelief.

"No, to the USA! We're going to get 3 points today." We replied. The result was memorable, and our wild-eyed boastful projections were not far off. Even BEFORE the game, 3-1 to the USMNT was an outlandish prediction that bordered on insane delusion. The American team, a bunch of kids, against one of the powerhouses of Europe. An impossible dream we might escape with a tie, but when we were off camera, the discussion was more focused on hoping our goal differential wouldn't be wrecked by this game. Looking back, I'm amused by the split personalities we were all developing: our private hand-wringing distress at our impending doom and the on-camera bravado of singing songs and gleefully making projections of the college kids from America pummeling the Portuguese Goliath.

We left the reporters shaking their heads at us crazy Americans and continued our trek to the stadium. We came upon what has to be one of the most fascinating things I have ever seen at all my World Cup matches: a few hundred people dressed in identical baseball caps and vests, half in blue and the other half in red. As we approached, we saw that the blue people all had American flags and their uniform read "Suwon Supporters for USA." I'd assume the other half of the people were for Portugal, but I'll never know for sure. We were so excited about the Suwon Supporters for USA group that we mobbed them and sang them our supporters' songs, thrilling the media people and Suwon Supporters alike. They had paid supporters to make the World Cup a success, both amusing and awesome. We had stayed with them in the courtyard until we were ready to go into the stadium. When we left, they gave us vests and caps. I still have the patches, which remain one of my favorite souvenirs of all time. We went into the stadium and found our seats. We were split from Kaela, Jimmy, and Andy, but we agreed to all meet after the game.

What I'm about to describe to is the greatest game I've ever been to of any sport and of any team. It was so great because there was nothing expected of us. We went from being a bunch of young players maybe going to make it out or maybe not, to the story of the World Cup in 90 minutes. Everything changed, and in an hour and a half, our group had been turned upside down.

If you're a sports fan, maybe you've gone to a big championship game and you can relate. Upon entering the stadium it takes a few minutes of pinching yourself that you're even there, in that stadium, and in this case halfway around the world. Pure nirvana, I was so happy to be there with my husband, expecting our daughter, and having met such cool people right off the bat (can we change that phrase to "right off the boot" once soccer overtakes baseball?) It was euphoric to be in the stadium, maybe 20 rows up behind the right goal post; it was surreal just to be in the stadium after waiting four years for the World Cup cycle to reset. Here we were, finally kicking off against the giant, Portugal. And then it happened.

Three minutes into the match Ernie Stewart takes a corner kick right in front of our section it arcs into the box, pings off a few players, and John O'Brien buries it in the back of the net. The stadium erupts in a way I'd never experienced before or ever since, as if the electricity of 37,000 people simultaneously shocked lights up the air so it crackles with a collective "now we got ourselves a ball game." This is what I assume the unaffiliated fan thought. I think the feelings of our section were summed up by my husband who grabbed me by both shoulders and screamed. "Oh my G-d! This is going to be the longest 87 minutes of my life!"

I will tell you of the moments that I can remember how my husband looked at me: when he first saw me on our wedding day, when he first held our children, and when we closed on our dream house. But nothing is as clear to me as that moment in the stadium when we went up 1-0 against one of the best teams in the world. No amount of pinching ourselves made it seem real. We just kept jumping around trying to believe the scoreboard.

Things were just starting to settle into believability: Could we hold a 1-0 lead until the end? That's when things really started to get crazy. In the 29th minute, Landon Donovan made a cross that deflected off the

Portuguese player, Costa, and then off their keeper's glove and into the net! Impossible! Now we were up 2-0 on Portugal? It defied all logic, and yet just seven minutes later, Tony Sanneh launched a cross onto the diving header of Brian McBride and we were up 3-0. By now the American section was completely ridiculous as we hugged, high fived, and joyfully mauled each other in pure glee. We were all pretty sure we had died and gone to heaven or would sometime in the remaining 54 minutes of the game. We were insanely and blissfully happy, and we probably would have hurt ourselves in the celebration had we not been summarily returned to Earth moments later.

In the 39th minute, Portugal had a clinically good corner kick delivered to the net with such authority; a sobering reminder we were far from victorious in this game. No one would remember us for having lost to Portugal 4-3 if we didn't walk away with the win, and the three point lead would be totally meaningless. I remember going into the halftime break thinking now we would see who had the better coach. It was all too possible that António Oliveira would take his busted up team into the locker room and inspire them or humiliate them into thinking that getting beaten by US Soccer was unacceptable. In refereeing, we say every game is really two games: the first half and the second half. What was Portugal really capable of? Were we really talented enough to beat them on this day? Was that dream really possible?

We were just starting to believe it to be true when Jeff Agoos makes what has to be the worst attempt at clearing a ball in the history of clearances. I'm not even sure what he tried to do, but it looked like a shot into the Portuguese net. This game we, the routinely disappointed Americans, could believe. Yes, the story line of a three-goal American lead with three points for a win against Portugal in our hand, or even one point for a tie, but they crumbled under the pressure. Twenty minutes, plus added time … plenty of time for another mistake to end our short-lived dreams of triumph. It was agony, imagining how many ways there were for us to be knocked back to a tie or the total humiliation of a loss. But the minutes clicked off as time crept at a barely perceptible rate towards the final whistle, brutally dragging us closer and closer to what we thought was a certain failure of a mission that had only seemed possible for the past 84…….85…………86………………..87 minutes.

Then the final whistle did come, and we had done it! We had gotten three goals, and held it for three points against Portugal, the team we thought was our toughest opponent. The rollercoaster game had been exhausting, but you couldn't help but be swept up in the celebration first in the stadium and then spilling out into the grounds outside the stadium. No one wanted to leave. We reunited with Andy, Jimmy, and Kaela, and Andy, who continually shouted at me that I had to name my baby "Suwon" in honor of the victory. We had already chosen her name, but I did spend several nights awake trying to think of how to rearrange our plans to include Suwon in her full name.

USMNT winning the perfect game was incredible, but the emotional fatigue of the game started to catch up with all of us. We looked for the shuttle buses while talking to the foreign media along the way. There was no way to really express how I felt about the game at my level of pregnancy exhaustion for the night, but we had fun getting mobbed by the occasional camera crew. Following Chuck, who swore he knew where the buses were lined up, we walked around the stadium for what seemed like an hour only to find out the bus lines were still so long I thought I would sink to the ground and start crying right there. That whole "creating life" thing is draining enough without the emotional blowback of turning the soccer world upside down. Determined to not show the weakness of my "delicate state" nor let it ruin my night, I asked Doug to hold my place in line so I could go sit on a bench near the bus line. Jimmy came with me to keep me company which was very sweet but a little problematic. Sitting with company was nice, but what I really needed was to put my feet up to get the swelling to go down. I turned to Jimmy and delivered the quote that I think cemented our friendship forever. "I know we just met and all, but I HAVE to put my feet up, so if that's going to freak you out, you need to get up now."

Jimmy just laughed and told me to go ahead. From that moment forever, he was to be known as "Uncle Jimmy" in our house. As if the game itself hadn't been enough of a bonding experience, here was someone willing to bypass all social construct and let me get 45 minutes of relief while the rest of the crew waited for the buses on our behalf.

When we got back to downtown Suwon, on the way to the train station, we found a Pizza Hut. It looked like it might be the best option for food that would still be open late. Generally, I try to avoid American chains while overseas. What's the point of flying for hours just to eat at a McDonald's just like the one down the street back home (no, calling it a "Royale" does not make it different). But late at night, a hungry pregnant girl's got to eat at what's still open. We went in and sat down and looked at the menu. Instead of the American toppings we're familiar with, there were all sorts of Korean toppings including Bulgogi Pizza. Bulgogi is a type of Korean barbeque I have come to love, and it is not bad at all on a late night pizza. It seemed a fitting end to a fantastic day.

The next day, Korean Memorial Day, our host Phillip Cho had the day off from work. As a war veteran, he said it would be an honor to show us around Seoul for the day. After another delicious Korean breakfast at the apartment, he took us to the Changdeokgung Palace, a stunningly beautiful ancient royal village built in 1405. Incredible. Built 600 years ago and still standing. Phillip told us little tidbits about the architecture and Korean history as we did the English-language walking tour.

After we'd gotten our fill of ancient architecture and culture, we walked out the gates and back into the modern city. We went out for lunch to a Korean café for barbeque. They grilled the beef at our table, and Phillip showed us how to properly eat it: take a lettuce leaf, place some grilled beef in the leaf, smear in some tangy red pepper sauce, wrap and eat. The combination of the cool lettuce with the spicy beef tasted amazing. We enjoyed getting to know our host a bit better on our last full day staying with him in Seoul. We spent the rest of the day walking around Seoul, seeing the sights, and chatting with Phillip. In the evening, he took us to one of his favorite places for another incredible Korean meal. It was one of our best soccer-free days of the trip.

On June 7th, we left on our way to Daegu for the June 10th USMNT vs. South Korea game. The trains required a stop in Jeonju; a perfect excuse to see another city and catch another World Cup match of Spain vs. Paraguay. We arrived in the morning and found a hotel through the tourist information booth. Tourist information was extremely helpful for last-minute travel planners like ourselves, but we did have the occasional awkward exchange with the young Korean women working the booth. At this stop, we asked for something to drink and they thought we meant alcohol. I told them no, just water or tea, since I was pregnant and pointed to my belly. The guide looked surprised and said "Oh! I just thought you were fat!" Ah yes, that lovely reputation that Americans abroad have for being a nation of beer-guzzling fat people. Sigh.

Finding a hotel room was far from the end of our adventures. We were about to discover the secret world of Korean addresses. Armed with our hotel information, we found a cab and gave him the address scrawled in Korean, but here's the thing you need to know about Korean addresses (explained to us later in our trip). Koreans do not write addresses like we do: in this city, go to this street, this house number. We were later told the Korean address system is more like: you know that neighborhood over by Bob's place? It's that street with the big trees at the house next to Mark's. Our poor cab driver stopped at least four or five times to ask for directions and finally found the hotel after about 20 minutes of driving around. He felt awful for not being able to find it and refused to take payment. It hardly seemed fair as an address just isn't as clear in Korea.

After all that, the hotel we'd been sent to was a dive without air conditioning (critical for pregnancy comfort). We walked around the corner to a nicer hotel that was the splurge of the trip at about 70,000 won, or about $60. The guy running it had the translation service on speed dial speaker phone which was a huge plus, and using it, delivered one of the best food stories of the trip.

We wanted to eat bulgogi, the Korean barbeque rumored to be at its best in Jeonju. We asked the hotel front desk clerk, via the speed-dialed translator, to direct us to a good place to get bulgogi. He replied back, also via translator, confirming we wanted a place for dinner. No, we said to the translation person on the phone, we want specifically bulgogi. The translation girl then quizzes us to make sure we know what that is, and once we confirm, she says to hand the phone back to the clerk. A long, disconcerting conversation in Korean of which we understood nothing ensued, but once he hung up the phone he came out from behind the desk and led us outside and down the alley way to the street. He then proceeded to hail a cab and had a long conversation with the cab driver that offered very little reassurance other than we did hear the word bulgogi a couple times back and forth. With a growing sense this game of telephone had decreasing chances of getting us to lunch at every turn, we got into the cab and went with it. The cabbie turned and looked at us and said "Bulgogi?" and we nodded … this could work out after all. He drove us to a very nice looking restaurant which would have been enough, but then the cab driver got out of his cab and brought us into the restaurant and told the owner what we wanted. The owner spoke English and confirmed we wanted to order bulgogi for two, and miraculously, we had pulled off an international accomplishment.

The meal was nothing short of amazing. The beef, marinated and then cooked table side, by far the best meal we'd had all trip, but the best part of this traditional meal were the side dishes. We were seated at one end of a table big enough for four to six people. In small saucer-like dishes, they set out about 40 little side dishes of various vegetables, kimchi, fish, and other delectable treats. Some were so good, we couldn't help but eat it all, which we soon learned one should never do in Korea. As soon as we emptied one of the little plates, the staff would fill it and bring it back. Thus, the phrase it inspired "You can't beat the kitchen, do not try."

After the meal, the owner of the place came over and offered us coffee, special coffee. I explained I couldn't drink coffee because of my pregnancy. Then he said it was like an after dinner drink which I thought would be liquor but he said no. We could not understand, so he brought us the drinks on the house as an explanation. It was the most delicious drink I've ever had. We later discovered it to be spiced persimmon juice drink. It was heavenly after our huge meal and we were thoroughly satisfied with our hard won find of a restaurant. We got up to leave and the owner walked over with car keys. He said it was so nice that we came to eat at his place and offered to drive us himself back to our hotel. We'd seen some neat little shops and a festival on our way, so we thanked him but said we'd walk. He practically insisted on driving us until we told him we'd taken an interest in the festival and wanted to stop on the way home. We gave him one of our Iowa Soccer Association pins and headed out to shop and sightsee our way back to the hotel.

On the way, we stopped in a bedding store to see if they had cool things for our new nursery-to-be. They didn't have anything that worked, but we found little baby pillows. One that was yellow with little sheep … just like our nursery plan. As we talked, the owner came over to talk to us, or I should say pantomime, that this little pillow was not for grownups. He pointed to the pillow and said "Child," so I pointed to my belly and said "Yes, *agee!*" (The Korean word for baby). This made him very excited … he asked where we lived, and when the baby would come (most of this with hand signals). Then we asked how much for the pillow. He suddenly looked very frustrated shaking his head no, then said "I gift to you!" He absolutely refused to give us a price so we left him with another Iowa Soccer pin and our thanks for the little pillow that ended up the basis of our first baby room.

As we sat next to German fans from Hannover at the Spain vs. Paraguay game later that day, they talked about how they were taking notes and planning how they could possibly match this when they host in 2006. We shared the story of our afternoon, and they just shook their heads. We agreed that while Germany would certainly be great hosts, you can't out-nice the Koreans.

While we enjoyed our chat with the Germans, Jimmy was stuck sitting with Chuck who reportedly talked his ear off the whole game. Jimmy's part Spanish and was really excited about the game, but by the end of it, he looked like he might lose his mind if he didn't get a break from Chuck's verbal onslaught soon. We all headed back to the hotel together looking along the way for a place where we could eat and watch the England vs. Argentina game. We had endured the long search for buses and a longer fruitless search for a restaurant before finally giving up and enlisting the help of a translator from the nearby train station in the ordering of pizza. The pizza ordering, yet another adventure in culinary Korea. In my search for a quiet place to order pizza, the translator and I went up a level to the hallway of the next floor's rooms. When we stepped out into the hall, there was a dazzling, glowing, black-lit underwater scene in garish neon colors on both the walls and the ceiling. When I stepped into the hall, black and glowing walls enveloped me, and a day-glow fish with ocean scenery was trippy and overwhelming. So completely over the top, I had to call the others up to come look as well. I could only imagine, if the hallway was this ornate, what must the individual rooms look like on this floor. I never did get to find that one out, but the hallway was unforgettable.

On the morning of June 8th, we got up and walked around Jeonju for a while, taking in the exhibits at the Dynamic Korea exhibit. There were cultural displays and a place where you could buy World Cup themed (knock-off) Monopoly, a required purchase for our game room. We then started the long trek to Daegu which involved not only a train change but a station change in Daejeon. While there, we stopped at the tourist information and asked for a place for a fast meal. The translator not only found us a place, but helped us place our order, then entertained us with stories about his kids and family, and shared our excitement about our pending parenthood.

We made our train and continued on to Daegu, the home of the next USMNT match against Korea. This would be the most intense game of the US schedule, because it is the chance for both teams to get six points, a guaranteed advancement. As if that wasn't enough intensity, there was a huge rivalry developing from the Koreans toward the US. The Americans, outnumbered, were trying to lay low, but there was really no hiding foreign in Korea, particularly as a 5'8" pregnant, white woman. It seemed the US would be satisfied with a tie or a win, but the Koreans would only accept a win against the United States, a country they held responsible for their speed skaters' elimination from the Olympics. The "Apollo Ohno incident" where the South Korean was DQ'd after an altercation with Ohno. To make matters worse, Ohno subsequently got the gold medal. As the game approached, we heard more and more intense Korean spoken, and while we may have only been able to specifically understand a few words of the story, we knew this World Cup match represented vengeance for the speed skating incident.

Fortunately, the group we'd met at the first game kept in touch via the Yanks in Korea Yahoo group, so we knew we'd be able to meet before the game and have a good-sized group for strength in numbers. However, first we needed to find and get settled in our homestay house. We were met at the train station by the father of our scheduled host and the family chauffeur. The father quickly informed us his son had been called to the US on business, and he would honor his son's commitment to us, with displeasure. He told us directly he thought Americans were stupid and annoying and complained we probably did not even understand Celsius. I'm not accustomed to such a stream of negativity, but I swear I only attempted a little self-deprecating humor. "Well, I don't know much about Celsius, but I know 34 degrees is REALLY hot!"

My attempt at lightening the mood only backfired. I only knew the Fahrenheit conversion of 34 degrees, but what I didn't know is in the front seat on the dashboard, the AC was set on the nose at 34 degrees. At least when I'm an obnoxious American, it's inadvertent.

We met our host's family, who were all lovely, and began to understand the root of the father's attitude. There were three generations living in the beautiful suburban home, and the son, our absentee host, had two little boys who were very modern in contrast to their grandfather's more traditional ways and ideals. The boys' room was an "English Only" room, aggravating their grandfather to no end. We were the embodiment of our host's desire for his sons to learn English in preparation for some day working in America, much to the chagrin of the eldest generation of the house. As he got to know us, he became more and more kind and friendly, and our stay that started out quite rocky eventually ended beautifully.

We had a day to explore Daegu before game day and, by coincidence, met the guys who sat in front of us on the plane to Korea. They remembered us and inquired about the pregnancy and if I was feeling better now that I had more than a tiny bulkhead to move around within. We joined them for their trek up a mountain-like hill to the Korean War Memorial. One of the guys, a history buff, could explain most of the exhibits to us, a handy skill to have in a country with very few English translations. We usually have a general sense of things such as what place serves food and what hotels look like but beyond that, we are at the mercy of the World Cup tourist maps and the translators provided by FIFA and the Korean Tourism Board.

Even armed with maps and a phrase book, we would still get lost, because our cab driver wouldn't understand the English map and our pronunciation was often not enough to communicate our destination. One night in Daegu, our cab driver, who was half blind and of questionable intelligence, couldn't find our homestay house from the address we had given him. We circled closer and closer until finally Doug figured out where we were and then had to convince the driver to follow our directions. The cab driver got so flustered these *waygooks* (foreigners) knew where they wanted to go, he actually stopped at a police station (to report us for the suspicious behavior of knowing where we were). Doug had to go in with him so the officer and Doug could convince the driver to go where we wanted. It was comical to watch the cab driver, the Korean police officer, and Doug hash out an understanding of what would happen. The gift of Korean addresses and the madcap adventures they inspire were a continuing theme throughout the trip.

We decided to try our hand at exploring the Daegu street market on foot. We headed into the heart of the city, thrilled to find an authentic Korean shopping experience that seemed like a place that very few tourists see. There were animals slaughtered and hanging in windows or waiting in wheelbarrows to be purchased, cooked, and consumed. Market stalls were everywhere we looked with spices, carvings, dresses, blankets, and so much more. We found a blanket to match the pillow given to us for the baby, and the seller was able to pantomime an explanation that the character on the blanket was a popular cartoon character. It was a puppy dog, not a lamb, as we had originally thought, although it remains a sheep to us. We also achieved the goal of finding a hangbok for our daughter-to-be. It was a beautiful red, gold and cream outfit complete with skirt, jacket, and crown. We were told it was for a baby, but ended up being huge on her at her naming ceremony, overrunning her tiny toes by several inches and requiring a more fitted top. It was perfect for her baby naming and still worked as a Halloween costume when she was two years old.

That night, we went out for a traditional Korean meal with our homestay host complete with floor seating, tableside barbeque, and the amazing little plates of food as far as we could see. We must have had 40 little dishes on the table that night; almost all of them a delicious, flavorful, and healthy treat. Once again, we could not beat the kitchen as every time we finished a plate they would bring five more out. My pregnant belly was happy and full of healthy food, and the after-dinner drink of cherry blossom fruit wine would have been the perfect finish to the meal, if I'd been willing to drink more than a sip of it.

After dinner, we attended the night-before party of Sam's Army soccer fans now gathering in Daegu. We went to a Blues bar to meet with the American fans for drinks, camaraderie, and singing. Having spent the past several days as isolated Americans amongst frenzied Koreans, who broadcast their cheers on every morning, midday and evening news program, we were really looking forward to spending time with fellow US supporters. Our group took the bar over singing and chanting through the night. Koreans would walk in, take a look, and walk out somewhat baffled at the passion of our group. Americans from the coast were surprised when our Iowa friends, Lee Tesdell, and his sons Ramsey and Omar, showed up at the bar. Suddenly, there were five people representing the state of Iowa … impressing Sammers from New York, D.C., and New England. Americans from all over the US were finally figuring out how to be soccer fans, and we'd never again have to go seek out the Brazilians to party at a World Cup.

Game day arrived and somehow we managed to be calm enough in the morning to visit an orphanage director who our next door neighbor in Des Moines was friends with in the early 90s. Our connection with our host had become strong enough he let us take his car and driver to the facility. The children were beautiful and sad, and it broke my heart to leave them there despite already having a baby on the way. We talked to the director and had a lovely time walking around the gardens before heading to meet with the Americans. It was probably more emotionally draining than we needed on a game day, but it was the only time we had been able to work out to meet with her and deliver regards from our US neighbor.

We made our way to lunch at TGI Fridays, not our first choice for dining, but the rallying point for the Americans' trek to the stadium. I was a little tired from the morning so it was nice to grab a table and some food. I started to perk up about the time we were heading to the stadium and I was determined not to end up in a cab with downer Chuck after having worked so hard to get my spirits up for the game. Big Dog, a huge guy from New York who was fast becoming one of my favorite supporters, got into a cab with us successfully averting Chuck. Just as we were about to leave, I saw poor Jimmy LaRoue getting stuck with Chuck again, and I couldn't abandon my hero from the Portugal game. I called out to Jimmy to join us which unfortunately left Chuck to fend for himself, but when it comes down to the guy who misled for me hours of looking for shuttle buses vs. the guy that let me put my tired feet up, there's absolutely no question what's going down. All's fair in pregnancy and World Cup soccer.

Incredibly, we found the Tesdell family from Iowa upon arrival at the stadium. They walked around the outside of the stadium with us until we came upon the photo op of day: former US Soccer coach, Steve Sampson. We'd been joking about Steve Sampson being the anti-hero of the US team and how he'd ruined the 1998 World Cup team. Then, as we were laughing, he materialized out of the crowd. We greeted him and talked about the current and previous team. After taking a few photos with him, we said goodbye and headed for our seats laughing in disbelief at meeting him.

Along the way, I decided it was best to find a rest room before the stadium got too packed and the lines were even longer. I got in line behind a group of women all wearing USMNT jerseys with player names on them, a rare sight at the time. As we waited, I realized each woman looked like the player named on her jersey. I worked up my nerve and asked what the story was and found out they were a group of national team mothers and sisters. There I was, in line with the moms and families of Reyna, Hejduk, Beasley, and more. I started to gush about what a pleasure it was to meet them, the mothers of my heroes, particularly while pregnant with my firstborn. Beasley's mom said "Well, if you're pregnant, you should definitely cut in front of us." Now I was really losing it … I was cutting in front of women who'd raised the coolest men in the world. I asked Hejduk's mom for the secret of raising a soccer star (especially one with the fantastic personality of her son). In a manner of awesomeness you'd expect from a Hejduk, she said you just give your kids the space to find their own way and they turn out as they should. It felt like a rite of passage into motherhood, receiving the wisdom of USMNT moms and bonding in the ladies room line.

We continued the walk up into the stadium through thick concrete tunnels that insulated us from the stadium noise. As we walked out onto the terrace between the two stadium decks, the Koreans let out one of their "Tae Ha Mingo" cheers with an intensity and coordination I had not witnessed before. It was as if their voices were so perfectly in sync it created one sound wave compounded by 60,000 voices. The sound hit me with such physical force it seemed to push me back into the walkway. As it did, I felt the baby in my belly do a startled full roll, registering her own shock at the intensity of the moment. It was a bonding moment for me, one I relive every time my daughter sees something amazing at a soccer game and looks up at me in wide-eyed amazement. It was the beginning of our supporter relationship, still four months before her birth.

We got settled into the section, sitting at the bottom of the stadium flag. The flag on this trip was the 20' x 30' US flag, nicknamed the "Baby Ass Flag," as the smaller counterpart of the 30' x 60' "Big Ass Flag." Somewhere along the way, I became obsessed with needing to sit under or within reach of whatever stadium flag was with us at each game. We seemed to play better when I had a good time and the best time in the supporters section is under the flag with the craziest of crazy fans. The stadium flag was like my security blanket and I needed to have it with me at all times during games.

A hostile environment, the stadium was filled with the strongest opponent's showing I'd seen. The sportsmanlike Korean hospitality began to deteriorate a couple hours before the game as things became increasingly uncomfortable for American fans. Not with violence so much, but with rudeness, behavior so un-Korean we wondered what life in Korea would be like if we beat them. We had to work to cheer above the Korean crowd as they booed Coach Arena and were loud and clinically coordinated the whole game. They had a beautiful tifo display at the start of the match, an enormous Korean flag that covered the entire end zone. However, even a flag hundreds of feet wide was more impressive than the intense sound the Koreans were able to generate throughout the match.

The game was chock full of action on both ends, full of aggressive fouls and many, many scoring opportunities. Our keeper, Brad Friedel made saves that even the most passionate supporter wouldn't expect of him. He was absolutely on fire saving virtually everything that came his way including a penalty kick and a shot that he seemed to save from within his own net as if he had some sort of force field set up. His heroics were legendary and earned him "Man of the Match" honors.

It was Clint Mathis of "Show Us Your Clint" chant fame who would be the offensive hero of the game for the Americans. In the 24th minute, he scored a beautiful goal my husband describes in play by plays form as "Right foot, left foot … clinical." Mathis received a pass from midfield which he dropped to the ground with his right then smashes into the corner of the net left-footed. It was a beautiful shot. We went nuts, enjoying being up a goal, while experiencing the sinking feeling of winning on the road: "How are we going to get out of this stadium safely after this game?" We didn't have to worry about escape plans for our win as Korea came back to tie it up in the 78th minute. They celebrated by running to the corner flag and pretended to speed skate, in reference to the speed skating incident in the 2002 Winter Olympics. American Apollo Ohno, South Korean Ahn Hyun-Soo, and a Chinese skater got tangled up in a speed skating race. Ahn was disqualified and most South Koreans (and some others) disagreed with the ruling. What the skating incident had to do with soccer was less clear, but it's hard to think nice things about the team that just dropped you from three points to one, despite concerns for your own safety. In the end, the defensive battle ended in a one-all tie. We were lucky to escape with a tie as it would make our lives much more pleasant during the rest of our stay.

Things were difficult enough with the tie. There was a strong US Military presence in Daegu, and Americans were not well received before the game. The tension only rose after the game. We saw a video later on of shoving matches between American and Korean fans, and we personally had a very difficult time getting out of the stadium zone. Our experiences after the game, and that of our fellow supporters, made any US racial bias event I have witnessed pale by comparison, and I do need to set the record straight. In Andy Gustafson's "23 Days in Korea," he writes about this game, he accuses me of being a cab stealer which is completely untrue and as incorrect as his spelling of my name. Here is the real story.

We had been turned down by at least a dozen cabs who did not want to take American fares. I was frustrated, exhausted, and feeling very pregnant. I went and talked to a nearby police officer. I told him we'd been waiting forever for a cab and no one wanted to stop for a bunch of Americans. Indicating my pregnancy and fatigue, I begged him to help. I slipped him some money and asked if he'd be able to help us score a cab. He accepted my bribe and hailed the next taxi for us, a cab Andy somehow deluded himself into thinking was his. Not my fault I was better at manipulating public officials, Gustafson! (Despite our difference of opinion, Andy and I are friends to this day, although we will probably debate the proper ownership of that cab for the rest of our lives). Even with the bribe, we weren't out of the woods. The taxi driver was very upset that he'd been tricked into picking up Americans, and while we were shielded from the precise list of complaints he had about us by the language barrier, I think it's safe to say he was not a fan. He tried to drive off when he realized what the police officer was doing, but the cop wouldn't let him. We sat quietly for the ride with the two other Americans with us and endured the diatribe en route to the American-friendly bar for the post-game meet-up of US fans.

Really more of a US-tolerant bar … we had to pay for dinner when we ordered because they didn't trust Americans. We ate but never really felt welcome as we talked with other American fans and compared experiences from around the stadium. On our way home, we decided to stop in a shop looking for some small souvenir from the day. From the moment we stepped in until we left, we were followed and watched with intensity. They leaned in every time we reached to touch something, making it clear we were untrustworthy Americans and not welcome. The experience lasted only a few minutes, but it was so unnerving and awful that it renewed my sympathy for what American minorities must go through. It was horrifying to think we experienced something that happens to Americans, by Americans, every day based on the color of their skin or their perceived ethnicity. I felt enormous relief to make it back to our homestay, baby kicking in my belly, calmed after the shock of stadium noise, and home safe and sound from the adventures of the day.

Americans didn't fare much better in the Korean press in the days that followed. Korean and international press coverage of the game was definitely slanted towards Korea and away from the Americans. It seemed the world is a little annoyed with us for beating Portugal and not leaving space for the host to advance as if it were just the nerve of these upstart Americans coming in and wrecking everyone's plan

81

for a nice orderly World Cup. Strangely, no one was complaining that Portugal played so disappointingly that the Americans got not only one but three points from them nor that Portugal must beat Korea to keep them out. No, it was all our fault, and by now, we were prepared to take on the role of upset. We refused to care what the world or our hosts thought. We wanted to advance by any means necessary and anyone who wanted to escape the group would have to go through us as well as Korea, Portugal, and I suppose the sleeper Poland, although little was said about them before our fateful match against them.

I realized one of the things people with unhealthy obsessions will do is point out they are not the only ones with said unhealthy obsession. Those cohorts were supposed to make the "crazy" decisions we make seem less crazy. In Korea, we were not the only young family traveling. The Flannigans were a family from Chicago traveling with their one-month old baby girl. It was great to have another family on the road with us and to catch a glimpse of where we'd be living in a few short months. At the time, I thought it was crazy and daring to take a one-month old to Korea (who knew you could even get a passport that fast!) Now that we're experienced parents, I get it, and I'm grateful for the lessons in parenting they taught us. The babies just become part of the organism of the family, and why wouldn't they come with you to soccer matches? We joked with the Flannigans that someday our girls would be sitting together in the supporters' section, cheering on the Nats together. The Flannigans don't go to as many games as they used to but our prediction played out when the girls got to play together at a USMNT game in Chicago several years later. The girls had a very limited grasp of their connection, but it was fun for us as parents to see the Korea babies finally reunited.

The following day we said goodbye to our hosts and left for Suwon, home of our memorable first game against Portugal, for a homestay with Mrs. Young and her nieces, Rosa and Louise. They met us at the train station and were very excited to meet us. Mrs. Young was active in the hosting committee for foreigners and was very proud to be our host. She had us sign our names on the board at the tourism station and presented us with gifts from City Hall. We returned to her house for a lunch she had prepared for us and tried not to upset her too much with the news that we intended to go to the Senegal vs. Uruguay game at 3:30 PM. She was a little frustrated that we wanted to go watch soccer so soon after our arrival, but let us go.

We walked up and bought tickets from the ticket booth … something we have not been able to do at any World Cup since! We traded some US Soccer swag for a Senegal handkerchief and then went to our seats in the middle of a sea of Irishmen in the scorching sun. Senegal went up 1-0 on a terrible penalty kick call in the 20th minute and then made it 2-0 in the 26th minute. The Irish surrounding us were fun with their songs and jeers, but the sun was exhausting, and at halftime we moved next to a Korean family in the shade. They shared their Korean vegetable rolls called Kimbap with us. The rolls were delicious and got us through the second half which ended 3-3 with an equally bad penalty call to even the score. There were no fewer than a dozen yellow cards in the match so the game wasn't dull for a moment, and we thoroughly enjoyed it. We dashed out of the stadium in time to catch the first bus back to the house and enjoyed a traditional Korean dinner with our host. The girls were seated at the table with us, and the two Aunties were traditionally seated on the floor.

We spent the 12th sightseeing and visiting the Insadong art market in Seoul. After weeks of perfect weather in Korea, we stepped out of the subway into pouring rain. Our first stop was a news stand to grab umbrellas which I thought might be something interesting. Perhaps Koreans had some new cool way of collapsing umbrellas into impossibly small spaces. The joke was on me when I discovered that the umbrellas in Korea were exactly the same as in the US. In fact, precisely the same as umbrellas at UCLA: we had traveled halfway around the world to find a logo umbrella for UCLA. With that purchased, we were able to continue on to lunch at a street café that served *mandu gui* (fried chicken dumplings) and *bulgogi*. It was delicious and fortified us for the day of shopping.

We went through the art market shopping for gifts and mementos. There were wood carvings, jade, celadon green ceramics, and more. We found gifts for our families and our housesitter as we ducked in and out of souvenir shops and art stalls in the market as the rain poured down. We wanted to find something for our family, and when we found a small inlaid bentwood tray, we decided to try to build our own havdalah set. Havdalah is the Jewish service for ending Shabbat, or the Sabbath. We had a great time going from booth to booth searching for the perfect ceramics for a wine cup, candle holder, and spice box that all coordinated with each other. We found all of those pieces and continued our tradition of buying a World Cup necklace. This time the necklace was a silver ellipsoid with pointed ends encasing a blue crystal (it only later occurred to me I'd bought an American football-shaped necklace on a World Cup trip).

The subway back to Suwon took too long to leave much time for pre-dinner sightseeing in Suwon. and our lack of commitment to Suwon sights was starting to aggravate Mrs. Young, but she did have the most amazing dinner reserved for us. Her niece, Louise, told us we were going to have "dog" for dinner which set off a bit of panic until we realized we had just misheard "duck." We breathed a sigh of relief and set out for the restaurant for a dinner that needed to be ordered at least a day in advance. When we arrived, we were seated on the floor around a low table in a beautifully austere, sunlit room. Without a doubt, one of the best meals of my entire life. The duck was slow cooked all day, stuffed with a rich, purple rice and seasoned with a blend of 12 different spices. It was so flavorful and layered with so many tastes in every bite, I could have eaten it forever. A decade later, I still treasure the matchbook from the restaurant in desperate hope we will one day return to Korea and I can repeat the duck with purple rice meal.

After dinner, we walked around old Suwon and the Hwaseong fortress gates. We walked along the city walls and enjoyed the ancient Korean architecture as Mrs. Young finally seemed pleased that we were getting to enjoy her beautiful city. It really was one of those perfect days from the art market to that incredible dinner to walking along ancient walls as the sun set. I really could not imagine a more perfect day at the World Cup, of course ending with us watching the evening games back at the house.

The 13th was another game day in Suwon, but we dedicated ourselves to being good guests for the morning, now that we understood how much time Mrs. Young wanted to dedicate to our visit, and joined her and the girls for further touring of the old city gates and fortress. We also trekked out to the most wonderful art museum set among gardens and ponds just outside the city. The Ho Am Art Museum galleries were beautiful, peaceful galleries of Korean and Buddhist art. There were exhibits of celadon and white porcelain, rooms of ancient Korean paintings and calligraphy, and Buddhist relics from past centuries, combining into a total experience of Korean culture and serenity.

The surrounding Hee Won Korean Gardens were stunning, each section of the garden an exquisite outdoor collection of plant life and sculpture combined to create spaces that were simultaneously elevating and enveloping. The gardens were designed in 1997 to commemorate the 15th anniversary of the Ho-Am Art and were designed following the natural contours of each garden site, incorporating naturally-occurring elements into the final design. Their website described this as "borrowed landscape," but the effect was more a garden perfectly at peace in its own corner of the world. The boundary between developed and natural blurred to create an atmosphere that was the perfect respite from the color and sound riot of the World Cup.

We couldn't stay in Korean Zen for the whole day, however, as we had plans to watch the afternoon game, Brazil vs. Costa Rica at Suwon Stadium. We were dropped off at the stadium, close to game time, and were looking forward to watching the matchup between a CONCACAF team and one of the best teams in the world. Costa Rica could advance on a loss if they didn't let the goal differential get out of control. Better than needing a win, but still a tough job against Brazil. The atmosphere at the stadium was electric, and we were happy to be back among Brazilian fans, reminiscing about celebrating with them four years prior at Sacre Coeur. They were out in force, the under-dressed and over-the-top Brazilian women and other assorted passionate Brazilian fans, as well as a smaller contingent from Costa Rica. The reserved Korean crowd did not know what to do with Brazilian women in bikinis. The stadium was crazy with passionate soccer fans.

Once the game started, it did not take long for Costa Rica to get into goal differential trouble. Ronaldo put Brazil up 2-0 by the 13th minute, meaning if Turkey beat their opponent by more than a goal, they would be tied with Costa Rica for points at four points apiece (three for a win, one for a tie) pushing them to a tie-breaker situation. In the

World Cup that tie would be broken by goal differential (the difference between a team's "goals for" and "goals against" numbers). It's enough to make your head swim late in a tournament and the reason final games in the round robin stage are often played simultaneously so teams can't throw a game and keep another team out on minute by minute goal differential changes. Not having web-enabled phones at this World Cup meant we were waiting for stadium updates on the other match score

Brazil scored once more in the 38th minute before Costa Rica finally sprang to life and answered in the 39th minute and then again in the 56th minute. It looked like they might actually stage a comeback and hold out for at least advancement, if not victory. But then, even though they looked like they had fallen asleep for a while and might allow our CONCACAF friends through, Brazil lowered the boom and dropped goals in the 62nd and 64th minutes by Rivaldo and Junior and nailed the coffin shut on Costa Rica's advancement. Dreams of Costa Rica advancing were nice for the six minutes it looked possible. But that's how Brazil plays. You can't ever count them out. As I wrote in my journal, "Brazil can turn on goals like they are turning on the faucet."

We met our hosts in Suwon for a final dinner of *Kalbi*, a local specialty of grilled beef that they cook at your table. It was a delicious meal, although bittersweet for us as we prepared to leave Mrs. Young and her nieces. We thoroughly enjoyed our time with the Young family, but we were excited for US vs. Poland the next day in Daejeon, I remember her fondly every time I try to iron. Once when I borrowed her iron to smooth out my shirt, she looked at my work, shook her head and took it to correct my lackluster efforts. I also think of her as I strive to have as much pride showing people around Des Moines as she had showing us Suwon. The tournament marched on, so we packed our bags one last time and headed out for the final adventure of our trip.

There were very few times I questioned the wisdom of going to a World Cup at five months pregnant. As the anticipation climbed as we approached our final game, the image of a peaceful pregnant serenity faded in my rearview. I wrote in my journal, "It's 2:22 PM on game day (8:30 PM kickoff) and my heart is already racing! This is the BIG DAY! We are all waiting to see if the dream can happen, the US and Korea, like high school seniors waiting for a fat envelope, telling them they get to move on to the next round. It feels like an entire country is holding its breath!"

I'm sure all that breath holding and heart racing wasn't the best thing I could have been doing for the baby, but I suppose at least in Korea I was eating a better diet than I would have back in the states watching games in the middle of the night. Overall health wise, it was probably a wash.

The Korean press had done almost a perfect 180 flip from focusing on the US as the spoilers to turning the focus (finally!) to Portugal. Emphasis turned to how beatable they were and that Korea's chances were good for a tie sending them through. The conventional wisdom among US fans was to win and let the Koreans worry about themselves. Back in the US even my mom was learning about soccer as the tournament progressed and announced she wanted to name her new Jeep after US Goalkeeper Brad Friedel. It may not seem like much, but I took it as a hat tip from my mom that she was at least getting caught up in World Cup fever the only way she knew how.

We were pretty confident the worst of our World Cup was over and Poland should be beatable enough to push us through. We walked around humming the tunes to the Sam's Army chants of the trip, such as the following.

To the tune "She'll Be Coming 'Round the Mountain When She Comes"

> Agoos has more goals than Figo,
> Agoos has more goals than Figo
> Agoos has more goals
> Agoos has more goals
> Agoos has more goals than Figo!

Agoos, of course was the own-goal scorer from the Portugal match. Figo was Portugal's star player.

And to the tune of Old McDonald:

> Bruce Arena had a team, e i e i o
> and on that team he had a Wolf, e i e i o
> with a goal goal here and a goal goal there
> Here a goal there a goal, everywhere a goal goal
> Bruce Arena had a team e i e i o

And finally:

> Poland! You're attacked from the East
> Poland! You're attacked from the West
> Poland! You are Europe's doorstep
> Even Mongols took you!

In replacement for our CONCACAF "Estados Unitos" cheer, we learned to chant "United States" in Polish for our final game, although not well enough I remember that barrage of consonants yet today.

We planned to meet with other Sam's Army people at a place called NASA Bar but once again had trouble finding the precise location for it based on our address and map (shakes fist at Korean address system). We flagged down a couple of Koreans who were kind enough to stop what they were doing and lead us to the bar themselves when we couldn't understand their spoken directions. We were so thankful for the help we gave them one of our soccer pins which they tried to refuse, but we eventually convinced them to accept. We'd been in the bar for about 15 minutes when we were surprised to see them return holding a Korean bamboo fan. It was far nicer than the token pin we had given them. Once again, we asked ourselves if we would ever learn that you cannot out-nice the Koreans. You really can't even offer a small token of appreciation without getting into a match of niceness one-upmanship.

The atmosphere at NASA Bar verged on celebratory. We were almost guaranteed passage to the next round. We were all in high spirits, singing and partying with people we'd just met not even two weeks prior who already felt like life-long friends. It had been a great trip so far. We were all thoroughly bonded, and we were so confident in our assumed victory. We sang non-stop for an hour on the bus and then an hour and a half before the game. We were pumped up and ready to receive our World Cup spoils for beating Portugal and tying Korea.

The game started and it was almost immediate disaster. We watched in horror as goalkeeper, Brad Friedel, and a defender had a breakdown in communication, got confused, and let a Polish player score on a loose ball to the left post in the 3rd minute. Dear G-d, this must be what it was like for Portugal in our game: having all the wind sucked out of our sails from practically the first whistle. Things seemed to almost immediately improve when Donovan scored, only to have our hopes dashed again as his goal was called back because of a foul that was clearly shoulder to shoulder tackle. Donovan just out muscled the other player. Then Poland scored again making it 2-0 in only the 5th minute. THE FIFTH EFFING MINUTE. Pushing us to near panic, we were inspired to sing even louder. I turned to Doug and asked "How could this be happening? This is not how it's supposed to end."

The American supporters section sat huddled in the corner end of the field. Our emotional state resembled a straight-jacketed, muttering inconsolable locked in a fetal position and banging her head against the wall. With the desperation and anxiety level soaring and about a half hour into the match, the Korean fans across the corner from us started going nuts. They were pantomiming to us, holding up one finger, but we couldn't figure out why they were so excited. We desperately tried to comprehend their message but could only take general solace that if Korea was doing well that was a good thing for us. If their opponent Portugal suffered, the more likely was our advancement. At halftime, we learned the one finger had been for a Portuguese player who had been shown the red card and sent off in the first half. Refereeing research taught me the strong statistics for a team with one red card rallying to victory, I wasn't comforted by the ejection. At least the score was still tied and perhaps Portugal would be worn down in frustration.

The second half started and there was no relief to be found on our field. The Polish team was in full defense mode and was shamelessly time wasting at every opportunity. I didn't have a sense we had what it took to win the day, and I only became more convinced as I watched our players get increasingly anxious as it came close to the end of the game. You could see it sink in: we would not advance. We had beaten Portugal and tied Korea, only to go down in shame against our group's sleeper, Poland, and whimper out of the World Cup. Just as I was about to slip into a full-on hallowed out depression, there was a surge of excitement from the Korean supporters section. They were jumping up and down shaking two fingers ecstatically. It took endless moments to confirm from the Irish behind our section that Portugal had just had a second player ejected from the match. A glimmer of hope: Portugal was frustrated.

As we watched the Koreans revel in their good luck, Poland buried another goal into our net, and we began to believe our only hope would come from the hands of our Korean hosts. In my mind, I re-imagined Princess Leia in an endless holographic loop of "Help us Korea, you're our only hope." Moments later, in the jumbled pandemonium of stadium confusion and misinformation, the Koreans started to celebrate in a way we had not seen yet. As Friedel stopped a penalty kick to keep the score from becoming ridiculous, we thought: Could it be? Had they finally scored on Portugal? We watched, desperately trying to sort out what was happening that would make the Koreans get so excited. Then confirmation came mercifully: Korea had scored and was beating Portugal 1-0. The stands became a riot of joy and celebration. The Koreans finally had a score they could gesture back and forth with us in mutual celebration. The Koreans, who had been pro-Poland, began cheering for the USA. There was one American fan who had an international-enabled phone and decided to throw all fear of expense to the wind. He called the US to get updates on the Korea game for us. Incredible, the 90-minute emotional roller coaster, intense and tumultuous, was not done yet.

Pregnancy shows no mercy for football schedules, so of course, when Donovan finally scored one for the US new mom, Ellen Flannigan, and I were both in the bathroom. Yes, the babies knew when the goal would come and made sure we would miss it. In the flurry of last-minute goals in both matches, we were left on pins and needles scrounging for any information on our fate for the second round. It became clear in injury time, watching all the players stop playing in our game, that the Korean game had finished and our result didn't matter. The ref had signaled four minutes of added time but called it after only two had passed when everyone stopped playing.

It was one of the few times I had been in a soccer stadium at the end of a match where everyone was joyful. The Koreans were elated that they had beaten Portugal to send both themselves and the Americans through. Poland was happy to be redeemed from a three-loss World Cup. The Americans were breathing a sigh of relief, thankful for having escaped the round any way we could. We chanted *"Kamsa hamnida, Corea,"* (Korean for "Thank you, Korea") in the stadium and all night long. Polish and Koreans began trading jerseys with the US in the stands, just like the commercial at that time. Our friend, Andy, traded USMNT stuff for Polish swag with some fans from Poland and took a bunch of pictures with fans from around the world.

We stayed at the stadium cheering, dancing and singing until 11:30 or so, then sang on the bus on the way to the shuttle drop, then headed to the bar. As we were leaving the stadium, one of the Korean volunteers asked to trade her Korean volunteer jersey for my knock-off Donovan jersey. I immediately agreed. A $10 fake US jersey I'd bought in Seoul in exchange for a sweet blue polo only available to official volunteers, something no one else in the states would have was a great trade for me. She seemed excited to have a USMNT jersey, replica or not.

Koreans were going bezerk cheering for both the US and Korea. Mass celebrations raged in the streets downtown. People were hanging out of cars, urban surfing on vehicles, waving flags, singing, dancing, and even burning things every once in a while. There wasn't an unhappy person around, although it was a little unnerving watching the ordinarily reserved Koreans rioting en masse in the streets. When the rioting started, we stuck together and made our way to the bar. There were rumors of the Korean fans flipping a bus over in the celebration, which we never did confirm. It was a wild time late into the night. We basked in the game afterglow for a while and then headed to the PC Bang to email friends back home about our experiences. Even when we left the internet café at 3 AM, the Korean celebration was still going strong but my pregnant body was more than ready to crash. Even in second-trimester elation, it had been a long and exhausting day. We walked back to our hotel, watching hundreds of Koreans dance in the streets.

Back at our room for the night, Doug and I had to have a serious discussion. Our planned departure flight was during the next USMNT. We had to decide if we were staying or going. When we emailed home to our friends, I said, "I guess we'll see how we feel in the (late) morning!" By the time we made it back to our room, reality had set in: we could extend a day and make the next game but we acknowledged that once we stayed on, we would be emotionally committed to staying until the end. We were set to play Mexico next and we were pretty confident if the right team showed up, we would beat them. Then we would have another four days until the next round. After all my bravery of the previous weeks, I had to admit I was absolutely exhausted from traveling, and while I wasn't worried about having the energy to get to the 17th, I had serious concerns about staying beyond that round. We decided then and there that unless things looked dramatically different in the morning, we would return to the states on the day the US played Mexico in the second round of the World Cup.

We spent our last couple days in Korea relaxing and sightseeing and picking up the last few souvenirs for our house-sitter, family and friends. I had thoroughly enjoyed the trip, but I had hit the wall and was ready to go home. My sleep deprivation from the night of our final game resulted in a deficit that took weeks to repair. In our final "love hotel," by far the sketchiest of the trip, I would wake up in the middle of the night thinking something was crawling on my leg, and then find myself unable to drift back off to sleep. When we returned to the US, it was impossible to change from Korean time, because with games still going on, I had zero motivation to nix my jet lag. I would wake up and watch games for the rest of the tournament. That was probably the hardest part of traveling to the World Cup pregnant: the lack of sleeping pill solutions for my formidable jet lag.

We did manage to sneak in one final match before leaving: Spain and Ireland in the Round of 16 match. It was played in Suwon, close enough to Seoul we could catch the game even though it was the day before we were leaving. We spent the morning and afternoon shopping in Itaewon, the discount center of Seoul. Most of our friends had already shopped there several times and raved about the bargains they'd found, but this was the first chance we had to experience it ourselves. We did some serious bargaining and negotiating on a new soccer bag for Doug and enough souvenirs and baby goodies to almost fill it. Our final day in Korea was going quite well as we headed off to the Spain vs. Ireland match.

We got tickets in the middle of a section of Irish and began enjoying the atmosphere and joined in the Irish cheering and singing. The Irish joy was short lived as Spain scored in the 8th minute and proceeded to go into a defensive shell. The referee missed penalty after penalty for the Irish until he finally called one in the 90th minute. Ireland scored, tying the game, only to face more defensive ugliness from Spain who defended the game into overtime period and forced penalty kicks. By this time the whole stadium was behind Ireland who'd so clearly gotten the short end of the refereeing for the night. To no avail, the Irish were sent home on kicks. After getting our fill of Irish-accented complaints, we headed for the hotel to finish our packing to return home the next day.

12

Homeward Bound

By the time we returned to the hotel and settled, it was 3 AM, and we only had a chance for a couple hours sleep before we had to head for the airport. We finished packing and walked out of our hotel just as a taxi was pulling up, as if it had been ordered just for us. That was where the smooth sailing ended. We'd been told via translator it would take 30-40 minutes to reach the airport, and we had padded that to 50 minutes. We got stuck in horrible traffic and didn't arrive until 80 minutes later. Then the line to check in was about a mile long, and we'd only made it through two thirds of it when they pulled our flight out of line and rushed us through check in. Next there were the endless customs lines at Incheon. Thoroughly frustrated as we were running to our flight, I couldn't help but think how angry I would be if we missed our flight and were stuck in Korea and NOT at the US vs. Mexico game. It would be more than my tired, pregnant, and emotional body could handle. The airport trials made us even happier to make our flight for home, taking a bit of the sting out of leaving the party early, knowing there was no way I could go on. I collapsed into my seat and most immediately passed out, as I'd hoped, to catch a nap before the US game kicked off.

Leaving before the US was eliminated was a bit like turning off a soap opera halfway through the show. Our friend Monty had a date with some woman. Uncle Jimmy had met an American named Amanda who was looking like a potential love interest for my hero. Yet here we were, headed home when our new family was going on with their lives in Korea. It was bittersweet leaving, but particularly after making the run for the plane, I was ready to sleep in my own bed and tolerate only getting updates via email. There was just one thing I really cared about receiving an instant update on: the USMNT Round of 16 game. Once I'd grabbed a few hours of sleep and the US game had kicked off, I became obsessed with finding out anything I could. I asked for updates a few times, but they either could not or would not update us. The flight attendant claimed the plane only had contact with Russia at the time, and the Russians were all business. I suspected if the captain had cared about the game as much as I did he would have found a way to get an update, but finding myself out of options, I tried to forget about the game for a bit and sleep for a while longer.

When I woke up, it was 6:30 p.m. Korea time, an hour after the game should have ended. I could not take it anymore. Most of the plane was sleeping at this point so I quietly went back and found a flight attendant. It was torture wanting to know the result but dreading what the news would be. It took several minutes of quiet self-therapy, telling myself that the game had already been played, and that our fate was already sealed. All that was left was to receive the news. As a supporter watching a game, you feel like you can impact the outcome of a game by sheer force of will, but the experience of knowing a game has been played and there's nothing you can do if it didn't work out was absolute torture.

I flagged down a flight attendant, and asked her if she knew the results. She didn't, but agreed to call the cockpit and get an update. I didn't even need to play the desperate pregnant woman card! She called the cockpit, and I suffered through the eternity it took for her conversation to take place. It could not have been more than a minute, but it seemed like half a lifetime had passed.

"Yes, I have a passenger here who would like an update on the US vs. Mexico game … (long, painful pause) … I don't think so …"

You don't think what? What? WHAT?

"OK, so 2-0?"

At least it didn't go to kicks, but for the love of all that is holy … WHO WON?

"That's the final?"

YES IT IS … TELL ME WHAT HE SAID!

"OK, Thanks!"

She did a beautiful job deadpanning the whole thing … completely preparing me for the fact we had lost. I was sure this message to the cockpit had taken longer than the 90 minute match. Just tell me. Tell me we're out. Kill me now.

And then, in a darkened, completely quiet, full plane of people, I became totally shocked and disbelieving as she said, "The US won 2-0."

I should not have been responsible for keeping my joyful shouts to a reasonable level. I tried (there was a plane full of sleeping people around), but I may have woken a few nearby people with my almost silent screams and jumping up and down. I hi-fived a few Americans who had gathered around the flight attendant and shared our little moment of pure bliss with them before rushing back up the aisle to tell Doug who looked stunned, then psyched, and then said "the absolute best place for us right now is on this plane." It really was given my exhaustion and knowing there would be no way I would have left Korea knowing the US was going on in the tournament. I walked around the whole 747 looking for awake American soccer fans asking "If you could know the outcome of the game, would you want to?" I got to have a mini celebration with about a dozen awake people. Not the stadium, but a memorable experience none the less. Over the past decade, I've had many moments of momentary regret for not being in the stadium for the US vs. Mexico and US vs. Germany games. Then I remember where we were in our lives, and I look at our daughter and cannot regret a single thing. It was the perfect summer and the best way to start our journey into being roadie parents for US Soccer.

We returned home to the US, although it took me weeks to reacclimate. I was reaching the point in my pregnancy when even my own bed was not easy to sleep in, and with jet lag on top of that, I struggled to re-enter my American lifestyle. More challenging than jet lag was adapting to the culture of American soccer apathy. People watched games, but it was so early in the morning, I didn't get the community feeling I had in Korea. We searched desperately to find a place to watch the USMNT vs. Germany game and found a watch party at a local bar in Des Moines named Wellman's. Not a soccer bar, or even a sports bar, but they had a kitchen and were willing to open for breakfast. We went for the 6AM Friday game and found the place jam packed with US soccer fans. The bar planned one cook and one person to take orders at the bar, but as the fans streamed in, they called in all the help they could find that early in the morning. The waitstaff did their best to keep up, and we were so grateful to have a place to watch the game we tipped 100% of our tab. It was my first experience watching soccer in an American bar with American soccer fans. So much better than watching at home by ourselves, it made me want to organize watch parties for all the games I couldn't attend.

When I think back over the 2002 World Cup and try to put into words what it meant in the greater scope of US Soccer history, I consider the press that was written regarding about Americans while we were in Korea. One of the major complaints in the foreign press was that if the US advanced out of their group (and supposedly sent the host home since no one expected Portugal to get sent), no one in America would care. An annoying sentiment in 2002, but I look back now and try to sense the validity in retrospect. In reality, there were watch parties, and many Americans did care, but there was a strange yin and yang to the ultimate result of the 2002 World Cup. Would we have as many 20 and 30-something USMNT fans today if the results had been different in 2002? Would I go on to form a local supporters group in Des Moines if I had not watched the US play Germany with so many friends and strangers at Wellman's? And yet, so many modern fans think the greatest moment in US Soccer history was eight years down the road in South Africa. For us, Donovan's 2010 goal pales in comparison to several 2002 moments. The 2002 World Cup was the moment when US Soccer pivots from the bottom of the qualifying nations to a legitimate contender for the Cup. As a nation thriving on superlatives in athletics, I am not sure if American fans would be where they are today had we not had such a strong showing in 2002. How many fans would have been watching in 2010 to see a goal pulling us from falling below expectation had there not been all those glorious, world-shocking moments in 2002?

13

Soccer Mama

My Dad called me late in my pregnancy to wish me good luck. He said, "The day your first child is born is the single biggest day of change in your entire life. You will look back on that day and you won't be able to remember what life was like before it. On that day, you can't imagine how different your life just became from the day before." It's the sort of statement you think you understand before you have children, but then you have them and it makes sense on an entirely different plane of understanding. It is the single biggest day of change, but not in the "your life is over, go buy a minivan" way that people think. There is a shift in the order of the universe, that when embraced, becomes a lovely opening to a layer of existence you didn't know was there. Children remind you of a world forgotten or one maybe you'd never known before, but it's stunning in beauty, complexity, and frustration in a way you couldn't fathom from the self-centered world of kid-free existence.

Our daughter, Aviva, was born around Columbus Day weekend, about a week and a half before we expected her. While it was a life-altering day (week, month, year) having the rhythm of soccer in our lives helped ease the transition. Even with the monumental disruption of new parenthood, we were in relentless pursuit of our dream of the American soccer lifestyle. We had the sensation that the Soccer World paused for Aviva's arrival. The WAGS Tournament scheduled the weekend she was born was cancelled thanks to the D.C. sniper. We laughed when we called the tournament director from the hospital to share our announcement, and she was in her office, clearly not running the tournament. We hadn't missed anything but the news of events captivating the rest of the world. From the beginning, Aviva was initiated into Soccer World. By the end of October, she had attended her first soccer tournament in Muscatine, Iowa, and she flew back to New Jersey to meet my family before she was three months old. Thus, by the time Gold Cup came around the following July, we were skilled travelers.

I can't say I was completely without reservation about bringing a nine-month-old into Gillette Stadium. By that time, we'd had our fair share of baby travel disasters, but we had also gotten better at stocking the diaper bag with the ridiculous amount of items it took to keep everyone in clean clothes and fed in almost any situation. There's always the "what if" of the soccer stadium, but like any other thing in parenting, you have to be attentive to what's going on and be willing to bail if the going gets rough. In preparation for "what-ifs," I made friends with security first thing and planned out elaborate fantasies of what I would do if there was a fight or riot in our section. This usually involved lifting the kids to the pitch and making an awesome escape/pitch invasion story out of it.

We went to the tailgate and had fun showing off the "Korea Baby" to many of our 2002 travel buddies and their friends. She was an outgoing little charmer and loved to be the center of attention. It helped my parents had moved to Boston by 2003 so we weren't base camping in a hotel room for the game. Aviva was happy and with her ears thoroughly stuffed with sound dampeners, she just cooed and smiled her way through the festivities.

We sat down towards the front of the supporters' section with Monty, Kaela, and the rest of the New England fan base. It was a triple-header day with a Gold Cup game first, New England Revolution playing second, and the US Soccer game third. We shortened that to a double header of the MLS game and the US game, not wanting to completely exhaust ourselves on our first attempt at a non-asterix cap for Aviva (we count her in-utero games in Korea as *caps from "obstructed view" seating).

In the end, Aviva loved the soccer game. She smiled at the fans, cooing at people who smiled at her. She laughed at the crazy antics of the

Sam's Army people and loved the clapping and singing. The highlight of my game came when someone a few rows behind us started a chant with a curse word in it. A few other fans started jeering the curser with "Watch your language!" and "C'mon man, that's not necessary." A half-hearted chant of "Family friendly! (clap clap clapclapclap) Family friendly! …" started up at which point I hoisted Aviva over my head and shouted, "Yeah, watch your mouth!" in a high-pitched baby voice. A cheer went up from the section and the chant immediately changed to "Soccer Baby!" for the next minute or so. I was in heaven. I was with my daughter, at my first game as an official soccer mama, and she'd scored her very own cheer. Pure bliss for us both.

We had such a positive experience with Aviva at the Gold Cup, I decided to take her to the Women's World Cup 2003 quarterfinal game in Boston. The tournament, typically held in the summer, had been planned in China but was moved to the United States at the last minute due to the SARS outbreak. We'd already planned a trip out East, and when the USWNT advanced to play their quarterfinal game in Boston I made plans to go. I remember talking to Aviva about the women that were playing, telling my almost-one-year-old girl about all the wonderful things she'd be capable of one day. My only source of frustration for the day was at the merchandise booth … as there was nothing there to buy for a baby. I bought Aviva the smallest thing they had: a youth medium t-shirt that finally fits her now as a fifth grader.

The next foray into our parenthood conversion would be refereeing at the WAGS Soccer Tournament over Aviva's first birthday in October. We'd talked briefly about refereeing the Warrior Classic over Memorial Day, but didn't have good family support to watch Aviva while we worked there. Over the summer, I had worked the Midwest Youth Regional tournament in Des Moines and had the extraordinary good fortune of meeting FIFA referee, Sandra Hunt. I had been struggling getting my running speed up to pre-baby levels. My top speed fell right around bare-minimum requirements for referee fitness tests before pregnancy so any faltering was unacceptable. Ms. Hunt was one of the very few people who could take one look at my refereeing and diagnose not only what was going on but also how to fix it. Female referee mentors were hard to find, finding a woman who'd refereed through childbearing years was more difficult than finding a unicorn covered in fairy dust. Once I was running on my toes and following Hunt's advice, I was back up to speed and ready for tournament life again so off to WAGS we went.

It was the perfect tournament for us. The tournament put us up in a two-room hotel suite, which allowed Doug and I to talk or watch television without disturbing our sleeping baby. Uncle Jimmy LaRoue, our friend from Korea, came out to meet Aviva and help watch her while we refereed. It was adorable watching him play with the Korea baby while Doug and I ran from one field to the next. When Jimmy wasn't available, referee friends were pleased to help with the new ref tent baby. Anthony Vasoli, a future FIFA Assistant Referee from Chicago, and Lee Tesdell, our Iowa referee/ World Cup travel buddy, both took shifts for us while we were refereeing. It was funny to see our friends with an infant for the first time and the transformation of the ref tent when Aviva was around. All referee business would cease and people would gravitate toward Aviva to coo at her and play peek-a-boo. Our girl loved all the attention, monopolizing whatever corner of the world she happened to find herself.

WAGS also allowed us to be on the East Coast for Aviva's first birthday, and she got to celebrate in style. Several childhood and college friends of ours gathered to join us for dinner on the night of Aviva's birthday. We had cake and presents at a restaurant with friends, which kicked off several weeks of Aviva's birthday tour. After her birthday celebration in D.C., we headed up to Boston and New Hampshire to celebrate with my parents and sister, and then returned to Iowa for her "home" party. It seemed to be a fair exchange of fatigue and traveling all over the country for the month-long celebration of her first year.

14

Somebody Stole My Sombrero

Our 10th wedding anniversary was on the horizon as qualifying for the 2006 World Cup began, and we had been parenting for two and a half years without a significant break. Our passion for soccer had become a game of one-upsmanship against ourselves. In 1994, we went to games without caring what teams we saw. In 1998, we went to USMNT games but none of the qualifying matches. In the 2002 cycle, we'd gone to domestic qualifiers but had yet to travel to away games outside the World Cup. Now, in preparation for 2006, we wanted to experience traveling outside the US to a qualifier. We looked at the schedule for the final round of CONCACAF qualifying, which is known as the Hexagonal or the Hex, for the six teams that must play each other in a home and away series. We'd set our sights on arch-rival Mexico to be our first away qualifier. The game was set for Easter Sunday. Not really a significant day for us as Jews, but seemed like a religious experience … going to go see one of the best teams in our region against our USMNT. Perhaps the most epic idea we could possibly have for our first away qualifier, we hoped exciting enough to blunt the trauma of leaving our baby girl for an extended period of time for the first time.

We got Aviva settled in with one of her best girlfriends, another Jewish girl she knew both from synagogue and daycare, for the extended weekend, with relief help from her Iowa Grandma and Grandpa. She was excited for the sleepover and not too sad about Mom and Dad leaving, so off we went, ready for adventure, but praying fervently we would make it home safely. I remember sitting in our Mexico City hotel room desperately scribbling a note to Aviva so she would have something from us on the fluke chance we were somehow permanently harmed in the stadium. Over-dramatic, I know, but it was terrifying to go into Azteca knowing there could be violence in the stands and realizing we were responsible for a small person so far away.

Our hotel was in Zona Rosa, the arts district of Mexico City, in a beautiful luxury hotel without the four star price tag, because it was in Mexico City and not a well-known vacation spot. The neighborhood was quiet and was even more so over the holiday weekend. Before we left, people warned us about Mexico City's infamous air pollution which turned out to be not bad at all. When we inquired, they told us most people leave the city for the Easter holiday, and the air quality quickly improves. How fortunate for us since the altitude made breathing difficult enough. There were other challenges integrating into the local culture. We wanted to call home to let Aviva know we'd arrived safely so we hunted down the calling procedure for the country. The pay phone required a calling card, which we purchased, but were horrified to see it was printed with a photo of Rafael Marquez, the Mexican Team's captain. These are the real-life decisions a passionate soccer fan must face: were we willing to use a photo of the leader of our worst enemy in order to phone our beloved daughter? True sports fans must understand the challenge we had to overcome. We checked in with Aviva and then never spoke of the card again, at least until the next time we had to call home.

Our hotel neighborhood may have been quiet, but the hotel rooftop certainly was not. As soccer fans began to arrive from around the world, the hotel rooftop became a gathering point for drinking and storytelling. There were several Sam's Army people we knew from around the US and a couple ex-pats who were stationed or working overseas and joined us for games occasionally. One English guy, a Manchester City fan who had come in for the game because he was curious about American soccer fans. He was a classic English football hooligan, drinking and cursing heavily with an obvious love for the game. I found his unpolished manner and tattoos absolutely charming and couldn't resist joining in any chant he wanted to get started. The feeling must have been mutual as he was having us swear oaths that if we ever came to Manchester we would look him up and let him take us to a City match. It was the life … rooftop party in Mexico City with a gorgeous, smog-free view of the city, while we prepared to face our arch-enemy. Exhilarating and terrifying, rallying up with our band of soccer brothers in preparation for a momentous match in the hallowed, storied grounds of Azteca.

We'd been interrogated about our vacation by our non-soccer friends who could not understand why we'd only visit Mexico City when there were so many more beautiful places to visit in the beach resort areas of the country. They spoke of the capital with disdain, as if it were an unsafe, dismal grey slum offering no joy or pleasure. Not being big beach people, we didn't really have any interest in languishing oceanside and the urban center fascinated us, at least from a Google perspective. We resorted to telling people it was a soccer thing … they wouldn't understand. To a soccer fan, seeing a game in Azteca was like a religious experience. The stadium was known as one of the greatest home-field advantages anywhere in the world and also one of the most intimidating places an American could go as a visiting fan. There were legends of Mexicans throwing things at visiting fans and players from the grossest of bodily fluids, to dangerous coins and batteries, which would do significant damage when hurled from the upper deck. Why would a person risk bodily harm for the experience of seeing a soccer game live? For us, it was the challenge and exhilaration of supporting our boys to the least friendly venue, to experience the passion behind these fans, and to have the chance to see the first USMNT victory at Azteca. That we might see our team defeat an opponent so few had beaten at home represented a huge opportunity in American Soccer history. What true-blue American fan would want to miss that, no matter what the cost?

We had a few days before the game to acclimate to the elevation and experience the local culture. Far from the dull, urban wasteland our friends described, Mexico City was a colorful explosion in Zona Rosa. The streets were lined with women selling hand-painted pottery and art, along with endless rows of beaded gifts and jewelry, all swirling together in a street market riot of color. The women, who ranged from young girls to old women, each had a face sharing a secret history of her own. They were friendly, spirited, and engaging in their negotiations for their wares. I would kneel on cobblestones, absorbed in the details of their pieces and trying to soak in the loveliness of the scene all the way down to the last bead, every swirl of paint. Interspersed with the markets was architecture ranging from gleaming modern office towers to beautiful old buildings in various stages of ruin and repair.

One of my favorite spaces was the National Art Museum, housed in the Renaissance style building formerly known as the Communications Palace, it was located in the Historical Centre of Mexico City. The building had the hallowed, holy feeling of an art museum but had an exquisite quality of daylight from the open arching walkways between the galleries. The gallery spaces were so open to the outside, making me wonder how they could maintain the humidity and temperature needed for the art pieces, but the airflow and sunlight was so divine, I stopped caring and just breathed it all in. It was sensory overload … the brilliant colors of Mexican art, the holiday-weekend cleansed air, the smell of fresh landscaping, and being away with my husband for the first time since becoming parents … it was a wake-up call for my soul.

Just as amazing, although much more physically challenging, was the tour we took to the Teotihuacan Pyramids about 30 miles outside Mexico City with a few other Americans from our hotel. One couple, Matt and Yezenia, bonded with us on the drive out to the historic site, partaking in the roadside souvenir and tequila shopping with us. We shared stories of soccer and our lives back in the states along the way. The city, whose name means "where man met the gods," was built between 100 BCE and 250 CE and remains a series of pyramids connected by tunnels and walkways with examples of ancient art, architecture and writing throughout. As one of the largest cities of its time, it was fascinating to walk among the ruins and imagine what life was like in an ancient holy city of Mexico. As part of the experience, we climbed the Pyramid of the Sun, a steep structure more formidable with every step higher into the thin atmosphere. I hadn't planned for hiking on this trip and was outfitted in cheap sneakers I'd purchased in a Mexico City mall for this excursion. My shoes were barely proper for walking so by the time we summited the Sun Pyramid I was thankful to still be breathing and feeling about ten years older than I had at the base. After the requisite "the Mexicans are already beating us" jokes and top of the world panoramic photographs, we climbed back down and collapsed on the bus for the return trip to the hotel.

That night, we went bar hopping but forgot to leave word for our friends Matt and Yezenia as to which way we were headed. Doug volunteered to run back to the hotel and leave a message for them, and we would meet him along the route. In the madcap world of international travel on a holiday weekend, our gang of soccer fans stopped along the way to the bar to get tacos and somehow missed when Doug walked right by us. In the pre-international cell phone days, we had no way of reaching him and he spent a fair amount of time wandering Mexico City looking for us while lacking the tequila we had to dull our worry about him. To be honest, I struggled to remember he was ever missing. Time passed quickly for me drinking with my best mates. However, the terror of not being able to find us was quite clear to him, even years later. (Sorry, honey!) Fortunately, he managed to catch us and drown his sorrows in tequila and street tacos soon enough. On we went, creating a scene of rowdy American soccer fans everywhere we went, breaking into song and chant at times, chatting and laughing between drinks.

Our last cultural stop of the trip was to the Basilica of Our Lady Guadalupe, housing the icon of Our Lady of Guadalupe, a major pilgrimage site for Catholics according to our Catholic travel buddies. Of the millions of pilgrims visiting each year, several thousand come through on Easter weekend. We braved the excruciatingly long lines to see the shrine and buildings. It seemed appropriate, even as Jews, to pay homage to our hosts and witness the devotion of those around us. Architecturally and artistically, the shrine was beautiful and I found it inspiring to be in the presence of awe, even if it was not my own belief.

My day of awe came the following day as we finally reached game day. We crashed the Sam's Army bus, which fortunately had a few seats open for us to hop on and avoid the trek through the game day subway snarl. With a bus full of some of my favorite supporters from around the US, we were sure to enjoy the ride to the stadium. It was even better than expected. We pulled up next to Mariachi guitarist who were playing the tune of our song "Somebody Stole My Sombrero," so of course, we had to serenade them:

"Ay, ay, ay, ay … Somebody stole my sombrero
That dirty old rat, has stolen my hat,
And now I have nothing to wear-o … wear-o … weeeaaarr-O!"

It was met with expressions ranging from surprise to amusement to laughter as we continued on our way to the stadium singing loudly out the open windows all the way. Happily ensconced in the safety of two busloads arriving hours in advance of the game, we hoped to avoid major confrontation with the Mexican fans who had officially shifted from host to opponent. An impressive security detail greeted the buses and escorted us into the stadium through a narrow tunnel of shoulder-to-shoulder police in riot gear. Once in the stadium, we were moved several times until security was satisfied we were safe enough in a corner of the lower deck, barricaded from neighboring Mexican fans by fencing on one side and a row of tightly packed stadium security on the other. The Mexican fans communicated quite clearly their feelings for us with chants of "Osama Bin Laden" and a banner about the Twin Towers. We answered the "Osama" chant with our own chants of "Cortés!", the Spanish conquistador who led to the fall of the Aztecs (it's important to travel with at least one history buff). We were still in the age of US Soccer fandom when we were a small group of people who took pride in coming up with funny, obscure references for our chants. While I love the present day supporters sections of thousands, if not tens of thousands, it does take away from the atmosphere of a tight-knit family of soccer geeks we cut our teeth on. The creative stuff we used to be able to chant over our whole section, albeit a tiny section, has been relegated to the pre- and post-game parties of die-hards who cannot be satisfied by chanting the same six things over and over again for 90 minutes no matter convenient that may be for a united front in the stadiums of today.

Before the game started, we noticed Drew Carey, television star and well-known soccer fanatic, was in the press section off the edge of the pitch directly in front of us. We began calling out to him and chanting "Drew Carey" and "Cleveland Rocks" in reference to the Drew Carey theme song. He turned and started snapping photos of us, as did most of the journalists in that corner, appearing thrilled he'd been recognized and called out at the game. In turn, we became ecstatic to be acknowledged for our efforts. It was a mutual admiration which took place for several minutes and remains documented in the archives of Yellow Card Journalism photography at http://www.ibiblio. org/footy/2005a/0327_mex_usa_ycj.php. After a few hours of hanging around the stadium, talking with each other and joking around, we were ready for the game to start.

Excited and singing through the game, the feeling like we might finally beat Mexico at home lasted until the 30th minute when there was a cross our keeper Kasey Keller had covered until he fell backward in preparation for a shot that never comes. Instead it's tapped in front of the net to Borgetti who buried it in our net. We barely had a chance to get ourselves refocused on getting back to a draw when less than four minutes later Borgetti tapped it over to an impossibly wide-open Naelson who scored easily. Now Mexico is up 2-0 in the 33rd minute, but I was sure it was possible we could eke out a draw. After halftime, the US came out strong, attacking and almost scoring in the 52nd minute with a great series of passes and a shot that was deflected and almost regrouped into another attack. Then in the 58th minute, Landon Donovan dished the ball to Eddie Lewis who shot through the tiny window of space between defender, keeper, and post to make it 2-1.

Let me pause here to say when you tell people you're going to Azteca, soccer fans drop into the hushed tones your grandmother used to use when she talked about "the cancer." "Oh, you're going to Azteca? Have you heard about the things they'll throw at you there? They pee in beer cups and throw it at you. They throw batteries. They throw coins."

While I love the US Soccer team, I wasn't too jazzed about getting pee thrown on me. Despite having a very young child and being perfectly accustomed to all the gross bodily fluids involved with infancy, that was not the same as some grownup stranger hurling their urine at you. But I also knew most "what happens at soccer games" horror stories were exaggeration which I filed under "things people say to stop you from being more awesome than they are" and ignore it. That said, I made sure everything I wore was disposable or washable, and the hotel had a VERY hot shower, just in case. Mexicans did not just like to win at Azteca, they like to shut teams out at Azteca. Thankfully, there were no bodily fluids raining down on us when the USMNT scored. We did get small projectiles thrown at us. A coin broke my sunglasses after the goal was scored before we could pull the Baby Ass Flag over our section for protection. I could deal with broken sunglasses with no permanent physical damage … a sore nose bridge was the price of doing business as far as I was concerned.

Now that I had experienced my first US goal at Azteca and lived to tell about it, I could taste the blood in the water and desperately wanted another goal. Mexico felt the same way, pressuring on the attack. Kasey Keller made brilliant saves to keep it 2-1, but there was nothing left in the US attack to level the score, and the game ended in favor of Mexico. We traded flags and banners with some of the Mexican fans while we waited for the crowd to thin out a bit. Security escorted us back out of the stadium with riot police, and we made it back to the bus and head back to the hotel. After a break to get cleaned up, we headed out with a group of Americans including Rishi, Kyle Lindsey, Brent Gamit, Vince Stravino, and others we'd met in either Korea or elsewhere along the road. We hit a remarkable number of bars considering it was Easter Sunday. We drank and smoked cigars before finding our hangout for the night: a great bar playing 80s music. We sang along to the music, sans karaoke machines, while getting stares from the wait staff who couldn't seem to figure out why we were so happy. The looks on their faces said "don't you know you lost?" That's the thing about traveling to US games overseas: it's almost always a great time because of the people you're traveling with … wins were just icing on a already fantastic cake.

After a few hours of getting silly to 80s classics, we got in two cabs and headed back to the hotel. Doug and I got in a cab with Rishi and another guy, but several blocks from the bar we got pulled over by a police car. The officer wanted to see our passports, and lucky for us, Rishi spoke up immediately.

"We all left our passports back at the hotel." The cop was agitated, demanding to see our IDs, but Rishi was calm. "It's fine man. Follow us back to the hotel and we'll get them for you. No problem."

Finding no opportunity for a shakedown, the cop finally gave up and let us continue on our way to the hotel, all our cash still in our pockets. Just one more time I was grateful to be traveling with people who were quicker to recognize trouble before I did.

The next day was our last in Mexico City, and we spent the day walking around the city with Vince Stravino, an American who lived overseas and traveled to as many US games as he could. I'd seen him a few years earlier at a DC United game and remembered him because he had the greatest fleece that he had embroidered with all the caps he'd gotten with US Soccer. So cool to see his history displayed like that, I eventually made one modeled after his for Doug and then one for myself. I bought sunglasses from a street vendor to replace the ones broken during the game. I got a pair nicer than the ones I'd brought with me for $4, which Vince said was a rip-off, even though they were half the price of American shades, and I didn't have the heart to barter with her. It was a nice end to the trip, spending the day sightseeing and market shopping, before heading back to the states the next morning.

15

Timbers Army Initiation

While we considered Mexico our 10th wedding anniversary trip, our real anniversary wasn't until May 28, 2005. We probably wouldn't have done anything huge to celebrate, having blown our budget on the qualifier, but I wasn't planning on being home alone either. Doug was working on his laptop one day and let out an uncharacteristic expletive as he peered at the screen. "What's wrong?" I asked, concerned what he'd read to inspire his little outburst.

"I screwed up." He said. This was a bad sign. My husband is not one to leap directly to apology mode unless he really jacked something up good. I gave him the "Oh really?" eyebrows and waited.

"I didn't even think about it. I just forgot." He stammered. "When I was blocking my referee schedule, I didn't think about blocking our wedding anniversary and I got scheduled to referee … in Portland."

Deep, calming breaths were required. Doug was trying to break into refereeing Major League Soccer and getting an assignment in the Portland Timbers' A-League, the division below MLS, was the big break before the big break. It was not an assignment you turned down if you wanted your career to go any further. I wasn't about to even ask him to turn it back, although the thought of spending my 10th wedding anniversary home alone sounded super lame. Intolerably lame, in fact. It took me about ten minutes of cursing and then an additional ten minutes rationalizing the expense before I proposed I should just come with him. My proposal sounded something like "[long stream of cursing] Well, fine. But I'm coming with you." USSF would pick up the hotel room and the per diem would cover dinner. Paying my airfare seemed a reasonable price to pay for marital happiness.

I didn't know anything about the Timbers in their pre-MLS days, but I was excited to see the city of Portland for the first time. We arrived in Portland and got checked into the hotel, which had upgraded us and sent up champagne in honor of our anniversary. It was setting up to be a great little trip as we headed over to the stadium before the game. The referees had to be at the stadium hours before the match, so I dropped Doug off and took the rental car to check out some of the local boutiques. The city was full of adorable little shops and lovely people, but as game time approached, I decided to head back there and find my seat.

Referee tickets were usually pretty sweet. My reserved seat tickets at midfield were probably pretty close to the field. I never found out where my seat was, because as I walked into the stadium, I heard the most amazing sound … a completely legit supporters' section creating a ruckus long before the game kicked off. So stunning to hear organized singing at what I had anticipated being barely a step up from Des Moines Menace games in fan support. I was mesmerized. I abandoned my search for my reserved seat, and started walking around the mid-level deck towards my people in the supporters' section.

I filtered my way down to the middle of the barely-controlled riot taking place and soaked up the atmosphere. The chants were easy enough to pick up as I started to meet some of the people sitting around me. Most people were quite curious what I was doing in the section without a single stitch of Timbers merchandise on. When I explained my husband was the ref and it was our 10th wedding anniversary, I became an instant honorary member of the Timbers Army … complete with my own patch with crossed timber axes. When the Timbers scored, human masoct "Timbers Jim" ran down the sideline with his chainsaw and cut a huge slab of wood off a giant tree trunk as part of their goal celebration. I was completely enthralled. It seemed impossible this was an A-League game. The atmosphere was so intense, and unlike anything I'd ever seen. I was still a little sore my beloved hadn't blocked our anniversary, so I sang "Blue Bastards" with gusto when Doug called a penalty against the Timbers. Once the game ended, I went to one of the Timbers Army bars, the Cheerful Bullpen, and drank beers on the patio out back while I waited for Doug to get out of his debrief. I met Timbers Army supporters and completely forgot I was at a lower league match. It was such a great experience it made me a lifetime member of the Timbers Army.

Doug's night, unfortunately, didn't go as well as mine. He called a good game, but in an attempt to make the leap to the next level, he took some of his usual personality out of the game, when (in my opinion) he needed to have more personality than usual. It's tough to make the leap from one league to the next, and you only get a handful of chances at the most. I thought his game merited continued appearances in the A-League, but his assessor and I didn't see eye to eye. May 28, 2005 was the end of Doug's pursuit of refereeing in the MLS. He completed 10 seasons as a US Soccer Federation National Referee before retiring from the National Program at age 41. We both continued to referee youth, high school, and college games, but our passion turned full time to supporter culture and the joy we found in that world.

We rounded out 2005 with caps number 7, 12, and 13 for Aviva, Doug and I respectively at Crew Stadium in Columbus, Ohio, on September 3. The USMNT was in the final stretch of the Hex and it was our turn to host Mexico. The ten hour drive to Columbus was one of the shorter (well, at least it was a distance we could drive) trips that we could make to see the US play soccer. Kansas City had not gotten a game since 2001, and while Chicago received games more frequently, that five hour haul now involved a hotel room if Aviva was joining us. Columbus was the next best thing.

Off we went, road tripping our way across the Midwest, stopping to let Aviva out to run around with a soccer ball occasionally, and otherwise going full steam ahead to Ohio. (No, it is not the same as Iowa, or Idaho for that matter ... but I digress). My only memory of this road trip: we'd stopped somewhere in Indiana for lunch and to let Aviva stretch her legs. She was about to turn three, and she was doing great on the road trip but needed to burn off some energy if we had any hopes of getting a nap out of the afternoon. We got sandwiches and made a roadside picnic on a small lawn next to the lunch place. We got out the soccer ball and let Aviva run around, playing keep-away from her parents. She was doing her toddling run after the ball, blond hair streaming out behind her, laughing hysterically at our attempts to trick the ball away from her. She was so full of joy and sunshine; it was one of those perfect family moments.

We got to the game and had a fantastic time beating Mexico. Steve Ralston was in the right place at the right time as a free kick cross bounced post to keeper to Ralston's head to the back of the net in the 53rd minute. About five minutes later, DaMarcus Beasley took a short corner, and before I could gripe about wasteful short corners they'd converted it to a goal and the US was winning 2-0. US supporters agree 2-0 is the best score to beat Mexico with as it allows us to continue the chants of "Dos a Cero" all night long. We were in high spirits, and having had her nap, Aviva was quite happy to join us at the after party bar with Kaela, Monty, and the rest of our travel buddies. We ate dinner, drank a couple rounds, and reveled at our qualification. We were headed to Germany for Weltmeisterschaft 2006.

16

Weltmeisterschaft with Brucesliga

I have always loved learning the soccer language of the countries we've traveled following US Soccer and four years of high school German gave me a head start in 2006. I love how World Cup sounds in German: Welt (World) Meister (Champion). It just sounds better than World Cup. There are many social media memes that agree with my opinion that things that are meant to be shouted typically sound better auf Deutsch. Our coach, Bruce Arena, had a name that lent itself to incorporation into the German league name, Bundesliga, nicknaming Yanks in Germany Brucesliga.

Of course, qualifying was just half the battle, now we needed to get tickets. We had not won the FIFA ticketing lottery as we had in 2002, and had been unsuccessful in the next round of ticketing as well. Doug had the idea to purchase TSTs for a likely qualifying team who had a good chance of playing either the US or Germany. We gambled on a purchase of Ecuador first-round TSTs, which we'd only be obligated to if they qualified. That ended up being the brilliant move of the 2006 ticketing venture when Ecuador drew Germany, which left us holding three very valuable World Cup tickets.

The next round of US Soccer ticketing was a complete fiasco. In the purchasing round, you had to fax in your five-page application, no hand delivering, emailing or any other method allowed. As soon as the lines were open for faxing, the fax lines jammed and crashed, the discussion boards at BigSoccer.com blew up, and there was panic and chaos throughout US Soccer fandom. Doug was working at Maytag at the time, and his passion for soccer was so well established with his employer they allowed him to stand by the fax making dozens of attempts throughout the day. In addition, I was working at my store, attempting to serve my customers while hitting resend over and over. It was incredibly frustrating to get so many failed transmission messages, all the while wondering if we were already too far down the list. We read about people who started faxing to other US Soccer fax numbers, hand delivering applications, and sending them via express shipping. Our friend and fellow referee, Tony Vasoli, offered to walk our application into Soccer House for us, but then we were worried that they would reject it because you weren't supposed to hand deliver them, which was kind of stupid … what Federation is going to turn down a hand-delivered application from one of their top referees? We decided the best option was to get FedEx Early AM Delivery for the next day and send our application the next fastest way to faxing it.

Then, we waited. We read about people getting tickets on BigSoccer, so orders were getting fulfilled, but we still had not heard anything. Finally, after a few weeks, I couldn't wait anymore. I called. I wasn't about to wait until all the tickets were gone before I made a little noise. I took a deep breath, sat down in my office with the door closed, and dialed. It was intense trying to stay calm, but I focused on the idea that I was not hanging up until I knew I had tickets coming to me.

"Hi, this is Tanya Keith calling from Des Moines. I'm a USSF State Referee and I'm sorry to bother you, but my husband, Doug Jotzke, who's a National ref, and I have been waiting to hear about out ticket application." Heck yes, I'm calling in my "I'm a referee for you people" marker. I had suffered enough through my referee career, it better be worth something!

"Yes, hi Tanya. I was just looking at your application." Squee!! That can't be bad. "The trouble is, we're limiting tickets to two per application, so I can't fulfill Doug's request for three" (my heart lies splattered on the floor for a moment) "but I think I can make it work, because you have different last names." HOORAY FOR WOMEN'S LIB and not wanting to spell Jotzke for the rest of my life! US Soccer set us up with tickets for the first and third opening round games leaving us to fend for ourselves for the US vs. Italy game, which was fortuitously held in Kaiserslautern, where the Trommers live. Aviva could stay with the Trommers, and we would only need two black market tickets.

I've never been happier I kept my maiden name! I couldn't believe that's what it came down to, after all our years of service to USSF, we were going to get tickets because we had different last names. Or maybe because of our years of service we were getting a break, and the names were just the method. Either way, it happened. We had tickets for our family to two out of the three games, and the third game was in the town where I'd lived for a summer in high school. If there was a place for us to get lucky scoring tickets, it would surely be in Kaiserslautern. We were off to Germany!

As the tournament approached, Doug's work situation went from bad to worse. Maytag was in the process of being sold, and we knew it was going to be a rough road, but we had hoped he would still have a job in Newton, Iowa, at the end of it. Then news came: Whirlpool was buying Maytag. We still thought there was a chance his job would stay since Whirlpool didn't have a Research and Development Lab, and there was an excellent one in Newton. It seemed to make some sense they would leave R&D in Newton and save us from a job change. Then the final word came: no jobs were staying in Iowa.

Doug briefly considered moving to Michigan, but Whirlpool made him an embarrassingly low offer. It was equal pay for a 7% cost-of-living increase. This after he had told them that we didn't want to move because the store I'd opened was just getting off the ground, and I wasn't interested in running it from out-of-state. Doug had been considered for promotion before, so a lateral move for all the trouble of moving was like a slap in the face. The joke of us never going to a World Cup both gainfully employed was starting to not be as funny as we prepared for another World Cup unemployment.

A few weeks before we left, I met a guy at a Passover Seder who was opening an industrial bakery in nearby Boone, Iowa. We talked about business ownership and his plans, and when I mentioned I knew a soon-to-be unemployed manufacturing engineer, he was interested. By the time we left, Doug had a tentative job lined up, but he still enjoyed bragging about his "soccer bum" status all over Germany. We had several weeks severance from Maytag, so it wasn't so bad as long as we didn't spend too much time dwelling on it.

Doug decided to terminate his employment before we left, which made sense, but meant he had to go do his exit interview on the day we were flying out. He went in, did the interview, said goodbye, cleaned out his desk, came home from Maytag for the last time, immediately headed to the Des Moines Airport, and flew to Chicago for our flight to Frankfurt. While it was sad to leave a job we had thought would take him into retirement, there was no time to be depressed about his job ending. We were once again off to the World Cup and to a country I loved and spoke the language. We were too excited to be down for long.

Aviva had flown before but never internationally. We weren't sure how we'd keep a 3-1/2 year old occupied for the 7-8 hour flight, but we crossed our fingers her domestic travel training would be enough preparation. It turned out keeping her busy on the plane wasn't the problem. It was convincing her to ever fly domestic again that was the challenge in the end. Aviva was fascinated with the huge plane, the personalized-pick-your-own-movies in the seat back, and the full meals. She spent the entire flight in wide-eyed amazement and happiness. The challenge for us was trying to explain the concept of time zones and that she should probably go to sleep for a while, even if she hadn't yet watched all 20 movies that caught her attention. She was so enthralled that we joked that her future career would have to involve world travel.

We landed in Frankfurt in the morning and headed to the subway to our hotel. We were all so exhausted, but we knew the key to beating jetlag was to not nap, and the only way to not nap was to drop our stuff at the hotel and get out into the city. We found our hotel after a train ride and long walk. The front of the hotel didn't look like anything special, but inside was remodeled into a modern display of efficient European hotel design: no wasted space and sleek little features that made my designer's heart happy. We got settled and I barely escaped the call of my bed when Aviva and Doug drug me out into the sunshine for a walk by the river in old Frankfurt. It felt so good to be back in Germany, my second home. Aviva was so excited to be somewhere new. We walked across bridges and found little playgrounds and watched Aviva try to absorb these children who could not understand the language she was speaking. She managed to negotiate a teeter-totter play date in short order while I stumbled through my German language reintegration with the parents of the other child. So unfair—to even attempt foreign language jet lagged and stone cold sober, but I did the best I could.

We soon got hungry and headed to the center of the old city to find a pub. With it, we found soccer fans gathering from around the world. We grabbed a table between a couple groups of fans from England. They started arguing back and forth about their football teams and were delighted and entertained when our family jumped into the conversation. Most groups of fans at the World Cup are groups of men with a few women sprinkled in here and there. Family groups like ours stood out and were a hit almost everywhere we went. Pretty soon, Aviva had charmed the surrounding crowd including the English soccer fans, dome-helmeted policemen, and the other diners into watching her dance and sing. She posed for photos like a celebrity with her new-found fans as any fears I had about taking my preschooler to the World Cup quickly faded away.

After a night in Frankfurt and our first German breakfast, albeit a hotel breakfast, we headed out to Kaarst outside Gelsenkirchen for our homestay with Micky and Detlef for our first couple games. We had some confusion in finding them as the directions to their house instructed us to take the train to the "Terminus." We had a heck of a time trying to find the Terminus station when we should have been just heading to the end of the line. It was a lesson in not trying to translate too much.

Mickey and Detlef were as much ice hockey fans as we were passionate about US Soccer. Talking to them was like meeting a German ice hockey cartoon of our own sport obsession, which made our conversations entertaining and enlightening. Aviva was more interested in their cats, although the feeling was far from mutual as the cats were not accustomed to the … let's call it "love" … of a small child. This homestay marked our first chance to stay with people who were as sports obsessed as we were. Even though it was a different sport, they understood our lifestyle and were even nicer hosts with their grasp on the ultra fan lifestyle. We had great talks with them about hockey and soccer, but they understood our need to obsessively watch every match in real time.

We went to our first WM match, Poland vs. Ecaudor, in Gelsenkirchen. The German rail system struggled under the strain of so many additional passengers, and our 1.25 hour trip took 3 hours, marking the first time in my life I've been late traveling German Rail. We made it in time for kickoff and got to see a fantastic upset of Poland, who I was still a little sore about from the 2002 World Cup. On the way, along with the local Germans, we met many great fans from Scotland, England, Ecaudor, and the US. My informal poll convinced me there were more "Polish" fans from Chicago than from Poland. We sat next to some fans from England who made me realize how well my cultural immersion was going as I struggled to speak English with them. I kept wanting to drop into the German that surrounded us and infiltrated my thought process with increasing frequency.

One of the first things we noticed was how serious the Germans were about their recycling. Years before public recycling started in the US, Germany had ubiquitous recycling containers for plastic, paper, packaging and miscellaneous. Every house had all that, plus composting. There were bottle returns, and in the stadium, they even had reusable plastic cups in place of paper or Styrofoam disposable cups. Stadium fans were supposed to return the cups for deposit refund, but the deposit was far more than weak American style nickel per cup. Beer and water bottles were .25 to.50 Euro, or 30 to 60 cents, and stadium cups were 1 Euro. We passed up the chance to finance the trip on returned stadium cups, even taking a few Coca-Cola cups with the World Cup trophy printed on them. The cups made a nice souvenir for a buck twenty each.

We sat amongst the Ecuador fans, and Aviva was a very popular girl with them. She got popcorn and high fives as she danced and celebrated with enthusiasm when Ecuador scored and went up 1-0 in the 24th minute. Aviva was in love with the World Cup and insisted we sing US cheers during the game, which prompted the Ecuadorians to fully adopt her as a mini mascot. They taught her their songs, which she performed with pleasure. We were feeling like soccer parent professionals until our sweet girl passed out in a heap of exhaustion in the 69th minute, prompting the family photo essay, "Aviva Sleeps Through the World Cup," as she would continue to pass out mid-pandemonium throughout the World Cup. She was so fatigued, she slept the entire way home on the train, and set a new family record, sleeping until 11:25 the next morning. We were now completely convinced bringing a 3-1/2 year old to the World Cup was pure genius … she was sleeping better traveling than she ever did at home, and she was so charming at the game no one could resist her. Ecuador was able to prevail without her support and finished the game 2-0 against the favored Polish side. It was strange to go to another team's game, but the Ecuador game only reminded me of the US vs. Portugal game in 2002. I was watching the Ecuadorians go nuts understanding exactly how they felt and enjoyed their win vicariously. It made me even more excited for our opening game three days later.

We woke up and had a great German-style breakfast with Micky and Detlef. In my opinion, there was no breakfast better than German breakfast. There were rolls of thick, crusty breads, some with grains and nuts and others with tasty yeast flavor. There was quark, which we can now finally buy in the US marketed as a spreadable cheese but so much better than that description. Quark, a cross between cream cheese and yogurt, sweet and tangy, and absolutely amazing on nut bread with honey drizzled over it. And I haven't even begun to talk about the meats and cheeses! There was salami and cured meats that were salty and savory, cheeses that blend with the meats perfectly, and coffee that was strong and flavorful. I could live forever on German breakfast.

We took our "break day" to travel to nearby Köln (Cologne as Americans call it). It was one of our favorite cities in 1998, and we thought Aviva would love the Rheine River cruise. After our lazy morning, we took the train into the city center for the afternoon and headed down to the Rheine. We made a reservation for the cruise and had enough time to get a traditional German dinner of Wiener Schnitzel and bier in one of the Bier Gartens on the river banks. It was delicious and relaxing, and it made me so happy to be back in the familiar sights, smells, and tastes of my second homeland.

The river cruise was a hit with Aviva, who had never been on a boat before. Oh, my poor land-locked daughter. She was glued to the bridges and "castles" along the banks and adored having her parents' undivided attention. The cruise was a beautiful look at the city including Köln's most famous landmark, the Dom. Doug explained the engineering of the various bridge designs (never too young for physics in this family!) and Aviva chatted with us and the people seated next to us until we were back on dry land.

We headed to the Köln Fan Zone after our cruise to watch the games and meet other soccer fans. As we walked through the city, I showed Aviva the old city's Mikvah where Jews from the 1400s would go for ritual bathing. We showed her the Dom and let her dance with the street musicians in one of the pedestrian malls. The streets were full of colorful flags, music, and celebration. Aviva loved it, and the soccer fans and performers were equally thrilled with her. We headed back to Kaarst well worn out from a great "rest" day.

The following day Mickey and Detlef offered us a guided tour of Düsseldorf's sights. We went up into the Rheinturm TV tower, allowing us a great view all the way to Köln on our perfectly clear day. We walked around the wavy harbor buildings that were designed by Frank Gehry and saw the Wilhelm Marx house, which was Germany's first high-rise. We discussed the Düsseldorf hockey team, our hosts' team of choice, and shared stories of sports fanaticism. They also introduced us to the local liquor, Killepitsch, a liquor made with 90 herbs, fruits, spices, and berries. People say it's like Jagermeister. While I could see the similarity to Jager's kick, Killepitsch has a smoother and more delicious flavor.

We walked around the city until the afternoon games started then found a pub to sit down and watch the match over late lunch. Now it was Mickey and Detlef's turn to watch us obsess over soccer the way they loved hockey. We had fun hanging out with them and watching the Serbia and Montenegro vs. Netherlands. We ate and drank, enjoying the World Cup in a place where work essentially stops while games were on. There were huge courtyards set up with televisions for people to watch while they ate, in addition to TVs in every café and bar. It was heaven to be surrounded by people who were all glued to each and every World Cup match.

After the afternoon game, we tried to go to a cool shopping area Detlef and Micky liked but we were delayed along the way by a fire somewhere on the tracks which diverted our train. The delay was of little concern to Aviva, who was wearing her US team kit, and discovered a boy her age wearing a Croatian kit. The two of them started making faces across the train which developed into increasingly silly faces. Aviva went over and said hello, and the two became friends as they ran around a little open area of the train. Soon, they were running around the hanging poles and had an absolute blast turning the train into their private playground. Away from the other passengers, they were only a small nuisance to people getting on and off on their sweet international soccer play date. We finally gave up and got off the train at 7 PM, abandoning the mission of getting to the shopping center. It took until 9 PM to make it back to Kaarst, but at least it was in time for the late game, Angola vs. Portugal. We grilled dinner, and afterwards, Aviva was so tired she actually went to bed by herself without being asked! We watched replays of the day's game and went to sleep dreaming of the following day's opening game for USMNT.

17

Reality Czeck for USMNT

We traveled to Gelsenkirchen by train, and with each train closer to the stadium, there were more and more Americans, building anticipation with our approach. The last train was almost a full car of Americans singing and joking, jubilant to be at the World Cup. We were on the upper level of a double-decker train, and I'll never forget the glorious sight of Aviva in her "Don't Tread On Me" dress (custom made by Dad), as she led the entire car in the Sam's Army call-and-response song "Everywhere We Go". Priceless, and a proud moment for us as parents having a 3-1/2 year old not only brave enough but sharp enough to lead the whole song all by herself. The crowd loved her, and she positively glowed in the attention.

We got to Gelsenkirchen and saw hundreds, maybe even thousands, of Americans flowing out of trains from all points into an endless stream of red, white, and blue from the station to the designated American bar. We must have outnumbered all others by at least 100 to 1. At the bar where Americans were gathering we were stunned by the number of fans already there. It was absolutely fantastic to see many of our buddies from the Korea and Mexico trips back together again. You could tell the people who had been travelers with US Soccer for a while, because we all had the same look. Our faces all read some version of "Finally, Americans are getting it. They travel, they party, they sing … it's all coming together." When we arrived, Americans filled the bar, inside and out. As game time approached, US fans spilled into the square mobbing the surrounding area and creating a moment that felt like the beginning of something amazing for US Soccer. We were so happy as we walked to the stadium together, smiling and singing the entire way, never imagining what was to come that day.

Everything changed at the stadium. The Americans were spread over several sections which seemed great at first. As soon as the team took the field, you could feel disaster looming. With the core of Sam's Army spread all over, there wasn't any organization to get cheers started. When we were all in one section, it was easy to keep chants going, but spread out, all those newbies just didn't know the songs well enough to carry it throughout multiple sections. All the pregame energy drained away and with it, the feeling of impending victory.

It did not take long for the life to be further sucked out of us when we were scored on in the fifth minute and then again ten minutes before the end of the first half. It was terrible to watch the US. You couldn't even call what we did playing. It was standing, or being pathetic, or I don't know … it was so frustrating to finally have the attention of international football and most importantly, to finally have additional American fans traveling to games and then look so pathetic. Particularly frustrating when we knew what it felt like to beat Portugal on the world stage. A huge leap backwards and at what felt like the worst possible moment.

The only consolation for us was we were with our friends from Korea. Kaela summed up the night crying out "Please tell me I did not just fly all the way to Germany just to have my team not show up." Usually, I would roll my eyes and make reference to her reputation as US Soccer's hardest fan to please, but this time she was right. She likened their performance to parenting. The play from our team was like raising a child who had some talent. He gets good enough that you invite all your friends to see his performance. Then, when it's show time, he won't even get on the stage. But it's almost worse than that. Your child maybe you could forgive, but they talk about supporters being the 12th man, so this performance was actually more like a teammate who refused to perform. We showed up, brought game, and did our part for the team, but we had eight or nine teammates who did not even show up for the big game. Inexcusable.

After the game, we stayed at the stadium for a while huddled amongst our supporter family. We got back to the city at 10 p.m. with one tri-fold wish: a place that with 1) the Italy game on TV, 2) food, and 3) beer. Do you think we could find all three at once? No. We found a place with food and the game, but no beer. We went on the street and bought a case of something that was supposed to be beer but was actually alcohol-frei, fake beer. We had been beaten badly. We were tired, hungry, and thirsty, and now, the joke was on us. The Americans could not even score a real beer in Germany.

The quote of the night came on the way back to the train station where we walked into Gelsenkirchen Hauptbahnhof and looked up to see, unbelievably, Dunkin Donuts! Yes, Ladies and Gentlemen, in 2006 you couldn't get the best donuts in the world in Iowa, but you could in Gelsenkirchen, Germany. Finding Dunks on that long night in Germany was like running into your mother's arms after a bad day. After photos with all the club banners in front, we all went in and waited in the long line to place our orders. While we were waiting another fan came running in with a desperate, wild-eyed look. He stopped in the middle of the room and shouted out at the top of his voice in relief, "Is this the American Embassy?!" It perfectly captured the dispirit of the night and had the Americans present hysterical with laughter making "the American Embassy," our permanent nickname for Dunkin Donuts around the world.

18

You Mighta Won if We Only Had Seven

The next day we kept up our tradition of barely making our train by almost missing the 7:34 AM train to Kaiserslautern to visit our friends, the Trommers. We finally mastered the art of sleeping on the train, Doug and I … not Aviva, and nearly missed our connection in Mannheim. Pretty sure we're setting Aviva up for needing massive amounts of anxiety therapy, as she now panics every time we say we have to get off the train. After repeatedly witnessing our "Holy Crap!" pack-up after oversleeping or just general lateness we could hardly blame her.

We arrived in Kaiserslautern in the afternoon of the 13th for our first visit with the Trommers since the 1998 World Cup. Seeing them for the first time as a parent brought back a flood of memories of all the parental advice I'd gotten from them over the years. It made for a nostalgic reunion and introduction of Aviva to her "Germany Grandma and Grandpa," even though I was sure I'd hold back on sharing the infamous but useful advice Jutta had given us on our first trip as teens. She told us, "Don't get so drunk that you can't find your way back to the youth hostel, and don't get pregnant." Words to live by, with the obvious exception of producing the occasional grandchild.

As we were traveling Germany in 2006, my parents were packing up my childhood home, the house they bought when I was a baby. It was a difficult summer trying to keep up with all the changes in my family: Doug's job changing, my mom retiring from teaching, and my parents

127

selling their house along with most of its contents with no regard for what I might want to grab before the big garage sale. Adrift without anchor was the perfect time to come back to Germany and my second home with the Trommers for our beloved World Cup. I did not realize what a touchstone the Trommer house would be for me, but just like always, soccer brought me exactly what I needed.

We arrived in time for Wolfgang's birthday celebration with his department at the Universität Kaiserslautern. It was wonderful to greet the family once again particularly at a time of celebration. We met some of his friends and colleagues, but I was exhausted from traveling and struggled to understand the new accent. We got back to the house and I fell asleep on the couch for a few hours. The fastest way to recover German speaking skills is to drink beer or sleep, but why not try for drinks after catching a few Zs?

The Trommers house is on the edge of a residential district and has a great backyard on the edge of the Black Forest. Aviva loved running out every morning to see where her favorite snail and pile of silk worms ended up overnight. She picked wildflowers in the backyard and collected an extensive set of pinecones, looking like a blonde version of my sister and I as children. We grilled out in the backyard our first night there and had a great night talking out on the patio. It was lovely seeing more and more similarities between Wolfgang and my father, and having my first chance as a parent to spend time with a family that had added so many pivotal moments to my personal development. Even though I hadn't been there in years, everything with the house and family felt so familiar … a welcome break from our first overseas travel with little Aviva.

The next day we slept in until late morning then headed out for lunch on the downtown Fan Mile. There were kiosks set up for food, beer, and play things for children. There was plenty of football merchandise except what we were looking for … merchandise from the local Bundesliga club, FC Kaiserslautern. Aviva found a two-story kid hamster tube with a ball pit and slides and all sorts of wonderful entertainment. It was a miracle we ever pulled her out of there.

That night, the Trommers took us to a local Biergarten, although German Tanya claimed it was not a "real" Biergarten like the one she would take us to in Munich, but it was acceptable enough for us. Jutta, Aviva, Doug and I all left the house together, and Wolfgang met us there. We had settled in to our table and Aviva was exploring the playground when Wolfgang arrived and stopped at another table to talk with some neighborhood friends. Jutta and I were joking about how long he was taking to come join us when she told me to go bring him back for dinner. I walked up to the table and said "Deutsche Pappi, wie gehts?" (German Daddy, how's it going?) So colloquial and familiar, we later agreed it was a good representation of our quasi-father/daughter relationship. Later in the game, Aviva ran right past me and jumped onto his lap. I said "Well, Deutsche Grandpa is here, so mom macht nichts" (doesn't matter). Wolfgang replied, "Oh Tanya, I remember you running past your Dad to me to do the exact same thing." There are so few people in the world who get to know you through your life. There's something sacred in friends who have known you as a child and can still talk to you once you become a parent.

The Biergarten food was delicious as their Heffeweisen bier, and it's always more fun to watch a game with true fans of one of the teams. Wolfgang and I sat up front with some of his friends, alternating between German and English. One of his friends started off a conversation asking me "So, do you understand the rules?" We chatted about how funny this question was now on my fourth World Cup trip and talked about my refereeing experience as well as our Sam's Army adventures. By the end of the conversation, I had thoroughly established myself as an atypical American. In retrospect, it would have been fun to tease him a little and pretend I liked soccer, but it's kind of boring with so few goals. In reality, the US was still at a point where the ignorant-to-soccer American was too true to be a funny joke, as if I could have played a straight face saying it.

Germany's play was a little shaky, but they were able to score at the very end of the game only increasing the anticipation of my trip to Berlin to see them play in person. Although it also meant the Berlin game was only to ascertain if they would advance in first or second place. It's never a bad thing for the host to get their advancement ticket punched early. Happy hosts make good hosts.

The next day was the 15th of June, and we had three tickets to the

Ecuador vs. Costa Rica game. With a five-hour train each way between us and the game in Hamburg, we decided Aviva and I should stay in Kaiserslautern and have a rest day. Doug took our tickets with him to sell at the stadium. He had a great time at the game while Aviva and I had a nice, relaxing day with the Trommers. We slept in, I went running in the forest, and then walked Aviva to a beautiful little playground I found on my run. She had a great time running around, picking up different types of pinecones and playing. We walked back to the house in time to see Ecuador vs. Costa Rica. We looked for Doug since he was in the eighth row right behind the goal, but we couldn't find him in real time.

We had a fantastic dinner outside on the Trommer's patio. We had salad with duck and steaks that were absolutely divine. My love of quark expanded to quark with chives and spices on baked potatoes … so much better than sour cream. Doug joked about writing a blog about German food called "If You Don't Love Sausage, Go Home," but there's more to German cuisine than meats and beers, and quark will always reside at the top of my German food list.

Even better than the food was the chance to talk with Wolfgang and Jutta once Aviva had gone to bed and it was just the three of us. The World Cup had developed into a checkpoint of sorts for me, and I wasn't sure where to head following this one. I had drifted apart from my American parents, torn apart in the sale of my childhood home. My mother's enjoyment of the 1999 Women's World Cup never really took root, and my father felt increasingly comfortable expressing his distaste for my passion for soccer. One after another, the safe topics of discussion with them had dwindled, as they became clearer about their disappointment in my life choices. It left me feeling emotionally orphaned, and standing in the middle of a life that looked successful but seemed like a fantasy. I had created a company that was growing as fast as my own family, but not really in the direction I had intended. I was terrified by my own high-wire act of running a company while trying to raise kids. We had been talking about having a second child, but I was apprehensive after suffering a miscarriage earlier in 2006. I was creeping ever closer to the "advanced maternal age" status in the obstetrical world and was beginning to feel like I was standing in the eye of my own hurricane, unable to move in any direction without getting blown to bits. Talking to Wolfgang and Jutta gave me the moment to pause and reflect on what I really wanted out of the next four years of my life. They were the parental sounding board my parents couldn't give me and gave me the grounding I needed to move forward and brave the storm of my own creation. The World Cup had now become more than a sporting event, it was the quadrennial reminder to not let my own life pass me by unnoticed.

The USMNT vs. Italy game day had finally arrived, but we were still without tickets to the match. While I was completely confident we'd find a way into the match, I did have more than my fair share of butterflies about the task at hand. We got up and immediately (which in parenting a three-year-old world means after about two hours) headed into Kaiserslautern to look for a few new books, eat lunch, and start the US pre-game party. We found some German books for Aviva and some English books for me, and we sat down to lunch with Jutta. While we were ordering, one of the cafe workers was talking about our ticket situation. He thought it would be impossible for us to buy tickets, and if we could get them, we would not be allowed through security. Germans were so afraid of FIFA security, it was quite charming. In all of our World Cup experiences, we had never seen FIFA check match tickets to passports. We were not concerned, but many Germans worried for us.

This conversation did, however, get me thinking that more valuable than any cash we could afford to part with was our three tickets to Germany vs. Ecuador. I REALLY wanted to see this game. It was in Berlin, and I never get to see Germany play when I can cheer for them in person. It finally occurred to me we only needed two tickets to US vs. Italy, because it was a late game and we planned to leave Aviva with German Grandma Jutta. I proposed to Doug that we return to the house and get his and Aviva's tickets to the Germany game as an extra bargaining chip for US tickets. He agreed he would rather see the US, and we went back and got them.

Jutta was kind enough to drop us at the train station, aka black market central, and took Aviva back to the house for some quality time with her Germany grandparents. We started negotiating for tickets with various brokers and quickly found ourselves priced out of early selling.

They claimed our Germany tickets were useless (ha! Maybe to them!) and they had Cat 1 for 500 Euro and Cat 3 or 4 for 450 Euro. EACH. Not even our love of the Nats was worth $1200 for one game! We headed into downtown with our sign like everyone else: "Need 2 tickets." There were so many people who needed tickets, it was depressing. We've had to do this before, and as it approaches game time, the prices usually drop dramatically. However, we were so far from being able to afford what we wanted, I was starting to really become concerned we would not see the game. There were too many buyers and not enough sellers.

Desperate times called for desperate measures, and I finally convinced Doug to write "Have 2 for Germany game, will trade" on the bottom of our sign. That quickly drew attention. One guy stopped us, took our cell number, and said he would call in a half an hour. We said OK, but if we got another offer, too bad for him. Then a guy and his girlfriend stopped us. Here was a devoted woman (or a woman who really doesn't care about football—I'm not sure which): She couldn't go to Berlin for the Germany game, but she offered to give up her US vs. Italy ticket so her husband and his friend could trade for our tickets. The only problem: the friend was off shopping in a store. We ordered a couple beers while he tracked down his friend. They came out moments later with his friend yelling in German that he was crazy to turn his back on us and why hadn't he already made the trade? Of course it was a good trade! I wish I had a photo of the look on this guy's face when he saw us and realized he'd get to go see Germany play. We traded the tickets, and all were blissfully happy. It remains, by far, the best way we've ever gotten tickets to a match.

We stopped in the FC Kaiserslautern Fan Shop to pay a little homage to our home field and got a T-shirt and bracelets from FCK (yes, I'm a second grader and snicker every time I see the FCK logo; and yes, it has raised a few eyebrows back in the USA). We walked down the fan mile to the stadium with other US fans singing all the way. Everything was great except Doug almost got pick-pocketed in the crowd but caught the guy fishing around, created a scene, and got an undercover police after the wannabe criminal all in true "never-a-dull-moment" World Cup style.

Kaiserslautern's Fritz Walter Stadium is definitely my favorite. The walk up the hill to the stadium through the trees is beautiful, and I love the steep slope of the stands that cozy up to the field, plus … it's loud! We got to the seats we had traded for and were pleased we were in the German "locals" section right behind the American section. The locals were none too happy we intended to passionately support the USMNT for the entire game. Fortunately, we found a German couple stuck in the American section who were thrilled to trade seats with us so everyone could better enjoy the game. It was quickly clear that the US was far more able to create a lot of noise for the same effort we put in at Gelsenkirchen. We had a better position as a group and a better drum disbursement. That sounds ridiculously Sam's Army Ultra geeky … worrying if our drums were properly spread out through the section, but it makes a big difference! We sounded great, and I was starting to feel like we might pull something off as our boys took the field.

Italy scored in the 22nd minute, and while it was brutal, I felt the fans and the team didn't fall to pieces like the first game. When we scored moments later (well, really, Italy scored an own goal, so technically when they scored, only more favorably), it was pandemonium in the stands. Finally!! Such relief. I could exhale for the first time since arriving in Germany. The curse of scorelessness lifted. It felt like anything was possible. Italy had a player sent off in the 28th minute edging us closer to that elusive three-point win against the Italian soccer powerhouse.

Alas, the Uruguayan red-card-happy referee worked harder against us as he had for us, and we had two players, Mastroeni and Pope ejected in the 45th and 47th minutes. Now we were really under the gun and praying to hold onto the one-point tie. The end of the game was intense, but the players persevered as the fans kept singing, chanting and cheering our collective heart out. It felt more like the family we became in Korea. Maybe the new Sammers are growing up a little. I don't know. It just clicked, and we escaped the Italy game with a tie and a point.

We were jubilant on the hour walk back to the bar we Americans had rented. We serenaded the Italian supporters the whole way. We sang "You mighta won if we only had seven [players]" to Yellow Submarine, as well as "Nine men! We only had nine men!" to the tune of "Blue Moon." Then, to the tune of "That's Amore," we serenaded them with "When your league is a mess cause you paid off the refs, that's Azzurri" referencing the recent Italian league scandal with referee bribes. There were chants of "It's called soccer!" and "Nobody likes us, we don't care!" and the Team America standby call and response "America … "F--k Yeah!" It was shocking to hear at first, with so few F-bombs in our chants of the day, but we rationalized that a line stolen from the Team America movie … heck, at least it's an American original and not stolen and/or bastardized from England. Finally, the long wait for mass transit away from the stadium inspired us to serenade our usually-punctual German hosts: "It's Not Very Efficient Over Here."

The downtown Kaiserslautern bar was about as far from the stadium as possible. They sold out of wristbands before we arrived forcing us to rely on friends to get beers for us as we spilled into the street singing and chatting with our soccer family and friends. There was a young man playing a drum harder and better than any supporter I had ever seen and was surrounded by appreciative fans of his playing. Doug had the State of Iowa flag draped around his shoulders which attracted the attention of a guy from Des Moines who I recognized but had never really absorbed his name back home. Corey Dickey had traveled to Germany without knowing that others from Des Moines were also going. It was strange to bump into someone from Des Moines, but strengthened the bonds of local soccer for us. Corey, leader of the Red Army supporters for our local PDL Menace Soccer team, became our gateway from sitting with the referees to sitting with the Red Army and expanding our supporter culture horizons. Together, we sang and partied until 2 AM, then waited until almost 3 for the 2:15 bus ("It's Not Very Efficient Over Here" was not nearly so funny at 3 AM), and got to bed around 3:50. Totally worth it, but our 3-1/2-year-old alarm clock was a rude awakening the next morning.

The next day was our day at the Gartenshau Kaiserslautern. As Jutta told it, the Neumühle Park hosted a garden show that was intended to be temporary, but it became so popular they made it a permanent exhibition open annually from April to October. We could have easily spent the whole day exploring the gardens interspersed with 80+ replicas of dinosaurs that thrilled Aviva to no end. She ran around checking out every bloom and dino model, and enjoyed being surprised when Daddy would make sudden prehistoric roars as she approached one.

There were huge playgrounds with giant basket swings and rocket slides, sunken terraced soccer fields and water spraying features ... basically preschooler heaven.

That night, it was just us and Jutta for dinner as Wolfgang had to leave for a business trip. He left specific instructions to take us to a specific restaurant in Kaiserslautern (Wolfgang's very serious about food). The ambiance was small-town quaint, but the food was delicious and savory. We feasted over several courses, including everything from an aperitif, appetizer, salad, main course, dessert, and a great wine. When Tanya and I were traveling around Europe together as teens, there were days when we had so little money we survived on yogurt, oranges, and Coca Cola. By 2006, I'd graduated to primarily street foods of curry wurst, or any sort of wurst really, and Doner Kebabs (Turkish wraps with meat and veggies), and Fanta soda. In the midst of budget-cuisine existence, our last dinner with Jutta was an oasis of decadent, rich flavors ... only Aviva was happy to return to simpler meals.

19

Wir fahren nach Berlin!

Berlin is the home of the Bundesliga championships and the host of the World Cup final. So the cheer "Wir fahren nach Berlin!" (We're going to Berlin!) was the ultimate expression of hope and wish for soccer fans in 2006. Personally, Berlin is one of my favorite places anywhere so I was ecstatic to reach this stage of our trip. After seeing the city's transformation from 1989 to 1998, I was eagerly anticipating the scene after eight more years of rebuilding progress and craving the impact I knew Berlin would bring to me as a parent and as an artist. I was ready to continue my ongoing love affair with Germany's capital city.

Doug had pre-arranged a homestay with 22-year-old Tim and his mom, Ines. We knew next to nothing about them when we arrived but immediately began to make connections. Tim was studying mechanical engineering for his Diplom, a degree similar to our Masters, so he and Doug hit it off professionally, and Ines' beautiful garden entranced Aviva and I with its beautiful flowers and fragrant strawberry patches.

Initially, Ines intimidated me as her limited English-speaking skills required me to step up my German speech to a new level while Tim was at school. As we got to know each other, Ines became my best resource for German language recovery. We enjoyed each other's company, and we were equally tolerant of each other's language limitations as we engaged in "the slowest conversations known to man." We would get three or four words into a sentence and need to look up a word in the dictionary. Eventually, we would manage to complete a thought. Then

136

we would ask if we had said it correctly, and if not, received corrections. Finally, whoever was the native speaker in the other language had to share the correct translation into the other language. It was painfully slow, but was very helpful in acquiring new and useful words and phrases.

Tim and I also had long conversations, but most of our talks were about advanced level language acquisition. One of the big challenges in speaking a foreign language is the idioms, expressions, and colloquialisms, and I found myself challenged to come up with increasingly obscure and quirky phrases and words like "deer in the headlights," "cooties," or "suck it up," to ask Tim the equivalent expressions in German. We sifted through the pitfalls of each other's language, such as "Beer Stein" which literally translates to Beer Stone and the German "sympathisch" does not mean sympathetic, but "likeable." Similarly, when we say "gross" in English, we don't mean large as it translates from German. And I think most Germans don't realize we say "Gesundheit" just like they do for sneezes. Then there were hours of material to debate such as the various differences between American and German cultures. In 1989, I had seen a war memorial on Berlin's East side, that was a memorial to the World Wars. It had a plaque that explained it was a memorial to the millions of murdered Jews, gypsies, and homosexuals. With Tim, I finally had a German I could ask about how Germans felt about their national history, from the Third Reich through reunification. It was amazing I ever slept while staying with them.

Tim and I talked about young Germans and how they felt about Germany's role in World War II. Our conversation got me thinking about how I felt as a Jew who really loves German culture. I had always felt that it was my obligation to face what happened there and not avoid it. Germany was having a surge of national pride. I enjoyed being a part of positive German nationalism and seeing their ordinarily reserved culture revel in face painting and flag waving. This country has so much to offer the world, and while I don't suggest or desire to erase their history, it was good for Germany to grow through the World Cup.

As much as I enjoyed showing my favorite city to my husband in 1998, it brought me even greater joy to share it with our daughter. We took her to the Pergamon Museum and watched her swoon at the huge Babylonian gates and Greek Temple frieze. She loved the rivers and bridges, and she was struck silent (at least for a few minutes) by the Berlin Dom cathedral. My most treasured memory was watching her race across the lawn in between the Berlin Dom and the National Art Museum. It seemed time suspended in that courtyard and I was simultaneously the 17 year old having lunch in a communist style luncheonette, the 26 year old woman having coffee on a terrace café, and the mother watching her daughter joyfully running. It was as if a piece of my soul always resides there. The broadcast tower that served as my directional beacon as a teen was now decorated as a soccer ball, delighting Aviva as it popped in and out of the skyline from various vantage points. It all reinforced the sensation I've always belonged in Berlin.

On the day of the Germany game, Doug and Aviva went off in search of adventure at the Fan Fest while I made my way to the stadium. It was doubly strange for me, finding myself without my daughter, and on one of my first solo trips to a soccer stadium. Any nervousness I felt in my mission disappeared as my train arrived at the stadium stop and thousands of German fans streamed toward the game. As the energy level rose, my nerves settled as I soaked up the electric atmosphere and became immersed in German football culture. I milled around the stadium grounds and watched German fans gather, decked out in country colors and sometimes in more ambitious costumes. There were lederhosen and crazy hats but mostly people in German jerseys and t-shirts. I bought some mustard-flavored sausages and a beer, collecting another 1 Euro souvenir cup.

All too soon, it was time to leave the carnival atmosphere and head into the stadium. I found my seat and the guys who had traded tickets with us. We caught up on what a great time we had at the US vs. Italy game and how thrilled they were to see Germany play. We chatted until the teams walked out and then settled in to watch our common German heroes. After watching Germany play the US so many times, it was refreshing to enjoy watching the Germans throttle someone that was not us, particularly with my new authentic-German supporter friends.

We said goodbye after the match, and I left the game feeling elated and only mildly apprehensive about my next task: finding Doug and

Aviva again. As I made my way through the maze of subway lines that would bring me back to the east side of Berlin, my happiness waned and my anxiety waxed. What on Earth made me think I would be able to find either my family or our host house? I was kicking myself that I hadn't paid more attention to the directions back to the house when there on the platform of my final transfer was Doug and Aviva! By some miracle, we had ended up catching the same connection. I hadn't realized how much I missed them until my heart swelled at the sight of them standing on the train platform.

We spent the next day walking Berlin's art galleries and finding interesting little places with creative interpretations of the beautiful game. We bought some placemats with soccer inspirations printed on them and trinkets with "Ampel Man," East Germany's famous crossing walk guy who had become a graphic design icon. We found a gallery that had silk screens of abstract painting with German words that I fell in love with. They were captivating. We had made a tradition of buying art on our trips, so we purchased a stretched painting from the artist and somehow managed to get it all the way home without tearing it.

From Berlin, we took the train to Nuremburg to watch US Soccer's final match of the opening round vs. Ghana. A win against them would put us through to the next round. We got into the city on game day and spent the day walking though the city center checking out the architecture. Of all the German cities I'd seen in my life, the only place that made me uneasy was Nuremburg. I had the sensation of dread all through the city and hoped it was only due to the historical significance of the city and not a sense of foreboding about the game. It did not help to tour cathedrals that boasted in their literature they had been built on top of old synagogues. I tried to shake it off as we headed to the game.

The stadium was over by the parade grounds where Hitler had delivered his more famous speeches. The parade grounds still stood and reminded me of photos I'd seen in the Nazi party address. I stood on the parade grounds holding my blonde-haired, blue-eyed Jewish daughter and tried my best to convey my flipping off to whatever Nazi spirit was left there before heading towards the stadium.

The party atmosphere was getting started as we approached the stadium and said hello to friends along the way. We met up with new people and were enjoying the company in our corner of the stadium, but I could not shake the feeling that something was off. My worst fears were confirmed when 22 minutes after kickoff Ghana scored. Dempsey tied it in the 43rd minute only to have the referee call a PK against the US in stoppage time before halftime, which Ghana converted to a 2-1 win. There were chances in the second half, several convincing, but the score ended with Ghana winning 2-1. That close … only to fail to escape the group on a PK and so many missed opportunities.

We walked back to the bar and drank, depressed and angry. All of us, except Aviva, who was thrilled to find ducks in the river that flowed by the bar. She entertained herself with the ducks and by dancing in circles dangerously close to us, the morbidly upset zombie look-alike soccer supporters. It was nice to have someone remind us that life goes on and there's happiness all around but really, most of us wanted to drown our sorrows and grouse about what might have been.

With the time we had anticipated spending at the second-round match we were able to travel a bit to see family and friends. We headed to Munich to visit with the Trommer's daughter, Tanya, and her boyfriend. We hadn't seen each other since the 1998 World Cup, and we were looking forward to seeing her new home and new beau. It was lovely to catch up with my namesake and tour downtown Munich, home to the famous glockenspiel I remember racing to see with my parents when my little sister was Aviva's age. We enjoyed walking around the city even if the pre-K set wasn't into the endless walking. She was much more in favor of Munich's authentic Bier Garten.

Tanya was serious about introducing us to a real Bier Garten as opposed to the facsimile her parents had taken us to. We took the subway and then walked to her favorite place where they had large screens set up to show the World Cup matches for the day. There were big open seating picnic tables and a bar where you could order beer and drinks. You could buy food there but we did the traditional German thing and packed a picnic dinner supplemented with purchased beer by the liter. I'm not talking a liter pitcher but individual mugs were liter and half-liter size. We spent the day in perfect weather watching World Cup games on outdoor big screens drinking great German beer and eating fresh picnic food. It was one of the most perfect days of my whole life. The beauty of German beer is that it is so much better than American beer. I drank 3.5 liters of it over the course of the afternoon and was not hung over the next day.

Aviva's attention was captured by the huge playground where the kids could go play while their parents ate. After lunch Aviva scampered off to the swings and sandbox and had a blast playing while doing her best to teach all the German children to speak English. We were finally able to explain that she had to use gestures to communicate or the other preschool-aged children wouldn't understand her.

From Munich, we rented a car and took the Autobahn to the HABA toy factory in Bad Rodach and then drove to my cousin's place in Weimar. I sold HABA toys in my store and wasn't about to pass up the opportunity to see the factory first hand. Our reserved car was a tiny European thing that had zero chance of hauling us with all our bags. We upgraded to a far superior Audi diesel A4 wagon, a vehicle worthy of Autobahn travel. Driving the famous German highway made Doug so happy, but unfortunately, Aviva was not nearly so fond of the drive. We were not far into the trip when the dreaded "Mommy, I feel sick" struck. I was able to get her a bag before she started puking ... initiating us into parenting carsick children.

We made it to HABA and Aviva was much happier as we toured the toy factory while enjoying the colorful design and collecting more than her share of sample toys and beads. We got to see the inner workings of the factory and then bounced outside on the giant dome trampoline in front of the outlet store. I enjoyed the stories of how the company had progressed through the transformation from West Germany through reunification. HABA was located near the former border so they had a front row seat for the transition of East Germans re-entering the job market of the west. It was a great history lesson in the middle of a toy factory.

From Bad Rodach we set out for Weimar to visit one of my cousins who had moved to Germany from his childhood in the northeastern US. I hadn't seen Jason Keith since we met randomly in Times Square at New Years Eve 1996 and it seemed only appropriate to get together in another random corner of the world. We got to meet his wife Conny and tour Weimar. They showed us the Kahla Ceramics factory and outlet where we made our big souvenir purchase of the trip: place settings for eight in their asymmetrical Elixyr pattern. We somehow managed to get all the pieces home without breaking a single piece. Using them brings me daily happiness.

We arrived at Haupt Bahnhof Frankfurt at around 11 PM, and the station was dark, peaceful, and sleepy. I love train stations and Frankfurt Haupt Bahnhof was one of the greatest ones I'd visited. It's huge with the long tracks stretched out in rows. I used to think it was so exciting as a child. I would watch the trains pull in and out, friends meeting and parting, students with impossibly huge rucksacks struggling to race to one place or the next … all the commotion punctuated by the railway schedule flipper board. My favorite thing was to watch the black board with white letters that flip across the board announcing all the fantastic places you could go. My anticipation would climb as I watched my train creep closer to the top of the board. Most of the schedule boards are computerized now … a sure sign of how computers are taking all of the adventure out of real living and replacing it with sterile, soulless communication. I still hear that clicking sound as I glance up to look for my train on the giant projection screen.

As I stood looking at the departure board on my last night in Germany I felt a panic tighten in my chest. My train was coming and I didn't want to get on. I wanted to stay with my soccer family, those of us crazy enough to leave our lives once every four years to follow our obsession with soccer. Where "This was my fourth World Cup" was met with respect, not "Why would you do that?" Part of my heart always resides in Germany but it felt like too much of it would be there until the final on July 9th. As we walked through the train station that night it seemed like we were getting the chance to say goodbye to our fellow soccer fans one team at a time. Aviva fell asleep on the train so we decided to leave our luggage at the station so we could get her near-lifeless body to the hotel safely. At the luggage lockers we ran into four drunken fans from Argentina. They made a horrible racket before seeing Aviva sleeping in her stroller and then seemed quite amused by our little family caravan. We smiled and they left to go find their next adventure for the evening.

We walked out of the station to a rhythmic, pulsating drumbeat emanating from the Fan Mile. We walked down the street to find three Ghanans playing their hearts out for a growing group of fans from around the world. Ghanans, whose team had just been eliminated that day, were dancing, smiling, and doing everything they could to get everyone else excited. We got on our tram and sat down with four guys from Australia and struck up a conversation about the games of the day: how Aussies got robbed, how the US just stunk it up versus the Czech Republic, the differences between Korea and Germany as hosts, and of course, our expectations for 2010 in South Africa. We had a brief but spirited debate on the SoccerRoos now officially calling the sport "football." We got into our hotel and met two Americans in the elevator on the way up to our room. They were from Minnesota and South Dakota … where else but the World Cup do three Iowans, a Minnesotan, and a South Dakotan end up alone in an elevator in the middle of Frankfurt, Germany? It was a moment waiting for a punch line.

Finally in our hotel room, we put Aviva on her "bed" of folded up feather blankets. She barely opened her eyes and said "Where am I?" As soon as she was reassured we were safely in our hotel room, she drifted back to sleep and was out for the night. She had been melancholy all day asking repeatedly when she will be back in Germany to visit her Germany Grandma and Grandpa. German MTV was playing a soccer music video about every other song. Does US MTV even play videos anymore, let alone know that soccer music exists as a genre? What made me fall in love with the World Cup twelve years prior continues to grow every year. It's a chance to be with people who love soccer, from every corner of the world, and live your life 24/7 to the ebb and flow of game on and game off. Whether you watch at the stadium, fan fest, the local bar, Biergarten, or friend's house, this was where four years of pent up soccer passion exploded into the world, where anything could happen.

I would have a few more days to watch games back home and then the World Cup cycle would reset to start the wait for 2010 South Africa World Cup qualifying. Once the final had been played, we took up the business of coping with Doug's unemployment and detoxing Aviva from the thrill of daily travel. Depressed, stressed and numb, but I was just getting back into the swing of things when I got a terrible email from Kaela. One of the Sam's Army ultras, Dave Gonzales, had been in a fatal boating accident on July 3rd. Dave had been in Korea and in Germany with us. He wasn't a good friend of ours, but since he stayed at the Mill in Germany with all our friends, we had spent some time with him. When we got stuck beerless without a wristband in Kaiserslautern, Dave had brought beers out for us. The few conversations had with him left me with the impression that he was a great friend. We decided to road trip to Chicago to honor our fellow supporter at his funeral which gave us a chance to glimpse one of our travel buddy's hometown lives and offered me the deepest sense of family amongst our travel friends. We came together with his family of origin, his local drinking buddies and friends to honor his life, lending to my growing suspicion that this group of friends who gathered every four years to follow the US National Team through the World Cup was more than just a group of friends. Somehow, in a very short amount of actual time together, we had become a bonded tribe, people who would have your back against all odds, around the pitch or not.

There were moments of brevity amidst our mourning. As we drove from one event to the next in a car with Monty, Kaela, and Brock, I got a call from Doug's parents who were taking care of Aviva. They wanted to tell us that she'd been playing in her pretend kitchen and had found a can of soda which she determined to be beer. Doug's parents thought it was hilarious that our child was pouring beers in her play kitchen (although after her summer abroad, I suppose we should expect no less). We were a bit embarrassed as we relayed the story to our friends.

"It's not like we're alcoholics or anything!" I said amidst the laughter of our best drinking/soccer buddies.

"Of course not." said Monty in a gleefully mocking tone "Alcoholics go to meetings, you're drunks."

At least we have friends who know us.

20

And Then There Were Two

If our Germany trip proved one thing, it was that our parenting and soccer lives were compatible, and by the following fall, I was expecting kid and store #2 (and thankful I was NOT planning any flights to Asia). After a previous miscarriage, I was pretty nervous about … well, everything. Only US Soccer could pull me back from the brink of pregnancy-induced neurosis. Doug was already in California for National Referee Camp allowing a family game at 33% off. Aviva was born on the same day as her second cousin once removed and her "twin" cousin was living in LA, upping trip value while cutting expenses further. Off we went to our seventeenth cap, which was double digits tenth for our four-year-old and the soon-to-be Raphael's first "obstructed view" cap. We brought Aviva's twin cousin, Kathryn, and Kathryn's mom, Donna, to the game. Donna, who is 12 years older than I am, joked she and I looked like the grandmother and mother of the "twins" while Aviva enjoyed showing her cousin the ropes of early supporter culture. The US won the friendly 3-1, and I got to shake the sense of doom from my pregnancy once and for all.

That was our last game before Raphael was born since his July due date knocked out any travel plans over the summer. Raphael went a couple weeks past his due date, and in the end, I had to pick the day he was born. I was given the choice of the last week of July through August 2. I have forever considered this decision one of my great failings as a soccer parent. I did not yet know US Soccer's August 1st cutoff for youth soccer makes a July 31st baby the youngest kid on the team. Had I known, I could have held off one more day after 42 weeks, but I was so upset he hadn't come in July and I didn't want an August birthday reminding me forever of that summer. Alas, my son Raphael was born two hours and four minutes before the best birthday in youth soccer.

We didn't know about the cutoff because Aviva didn't begin playing youth soccer until she was eight, mostly due to supporter-parent problems. We knew she loved playing with us and she loved going to games, but whenever we asked her about joining a team, she became upset enough we stopped asking after a while. We did not want to push her into hating soccer (which would have been a huge problem in our family). I finally asked her one day why she didn't want to play on a kid's team.

"I don't want to play because players get hurt playing soccer." she said.

"Not very often, and usually when kids get hurt, they are okay in a minute after they dust off. It's just like when we play in the backyard …" I replied, wondering where she'd gotten this idea.

"No, Mom, sometimes the guys run on the field with the cot and carry the hurt guy off." said my deeply concerned Aviva.

Now I got it. "Honey, those are professional players. And even when they get hurt, it's usually not for long, they just stretcher them off the field so the game can keep playing. Kid's soccer isn't like that."

Aviva looked relieved, if not a little skeptical. Communication taken care of, we were able to convince her we had her safety at hand and she started playing rec soccer. She soon moved up to an academy developmental team and then select soccer, requiring three, then five or more trips across town a week to various practices and games. Encouraging her to play was clearly the better parenting move even if it did multiply the time and money we throw at soccer annually.

The year 2008 started as a blur of soccer with children. Just before my son was born, I expanded my company, a children's store called Simply for Giggles, into a second retail location. When I made the decision to expand, I had two great managers who could each run a store efficiently, so having them run their own location made sense. Only within a few months, one was hired away from me and the other was pregnant and would eventually decide not to come back to work. Suddenly, I had two stores, two kids, and no life. I ran from my company to the kids and back again, never feeling satisfied with anything. The economy was crashing down around me but somehow I kept everything going ... if for no other reason than to get to the next soccer game.

Enter the American Outlaws. February 29, 2008 my husband came home and told me about a supporters' group he had found online called the American Outlaws. I emailed their contact, Korey Donahoo, expressing my interest in a Central Iowa chapter. He wrote back that there was no Iowa chapter, but he would make me the contact for Iowa and as soon as there were 25 members here, we would become official AO Des Moines. At the time, 25 members sounded ridiculous to me. Sure, we had four people in our house, but I thought I knew all the soccer fans in Des Moines. I doubted there were 25 to round up, but heck, by all means, post my email and have them contact me. Over the next 18 months (and beyond), I was shocked at how many people would email me and ask where we watched games. Turns out I didn't know all the soccer fans in Des Moines after all.

Raphael's made his first out-of-belly appearance at a soccer game shortly after turning one at the USMNT vs. Trinidad and Tobago game at Toyota Park in Illinois in September. The following February, we found the pull of US vs. Mexico in Columbus to be too strong and road tripped 12 hours to get there. Totally worth it to finally introduce Raphael to many of our East Coast friends. Summer of 2009 brought the return of CONCACAF World Cup qualifying and the Hexagonal with three more games for our family. In June, we went to US vs. Honduras in Chicago. We met up with the Flannigans and their daughter who was a tiny baby while I was pregnant with Aviva in Korea. It was so fun to see the girls playing together as six- and seven-year-olds, just as we had dreamed they would. They played and ran around the tailgate like they owned the place, and I painted faces for beer money. We were having a blast.

Gold Cup 2009 marked two important shifts for me: I started traveling alone to games that the family couldn't make and I helped move tifo banners around the US for the first time. I flew out to Washington, D.C. to visit my Korea buddy, Andy Gustafson. We went to the Gold

Cup game together and tailgated with DC United supporters from Barra and Screaming Eagles. It had been so long since I had visited DC United's home field and the growth of the supporter community there was impressive. DCU fans had always created a great stadium environment, but now there were buses and trucks tricked out for soccer tailgating and road tripping, a food festival's worth of international fare, and soccer fans chilling out all around the stadium. Watching the match from RFK's bouncy seats, where the fans got rowdy and bounced the entire section while singing and jumping, was just what I needed from the insanity of running two stores and raising two young kids.

I took the train from D.C. to Boston carrying the Sam's Army banner which was a huge leap forward in my supporter world: my first time as a tifo mule. I could not have been happier except if more people asked what was in the huge awkward box that I was carrying then I could have been the religious zealot proselytizing about my journey around the country … "let me tell you a little about US Soccer." I met up with the rest of my family in Boston, and we went to the Gold Cup match versus Haiti. While Doug and the kids played at the tailgate, I stumbled across US Soccer's leader Sunil Gulati. I introduced myself and chatted with him about the team and my travels around the US and the world supporting US Soccer. I told him I was getting nervous about not being able to get tickets to the South African World Cup. He told me that if I didn't get tickets in the draw to send him an email and he would make sure I was taken care of. It was the best news I'd had all summer. While it didn't remove my fears, I at least felt like I had options beyond the means that had previously delivered four consecutive World Cups of tickets.

21

South Africa 2010

As it turned out, I did not need to call in any favors for South Africa ticketing as we were selected for tickets in one of the later rounds. The day the letter arrived, stating we're set for tickets to the World Cup is such a rush of excitement, anticipation, and relief. It's better than winning the lottery. Waiting to hear if you've gotten tickets or not is the most stressful part of World Cup travel. I console myself every time that one way or another, it always works out. With each consecutive World Cup, the pressure to continue our streak mounts. Hopefully, the day never arrives that I'm not able to buy tickets legitimately, or if it does, perhaps I'll be able to afford hemorrhaging enough money into the black market to get myself into the stadium.

For South Africa, the issue was not obtaining tickets, but trip budget. Ironically, the first World Cup that we were both gainfully employed we were coming up short on travel funds. We thought that South Africa would be similar to South Korea: expensive to get there but cheap in country. The closer the trip got the more expensive our estimates became, and the less we had in our bank account. The first change was to cut our tentative plans to bring the kids with us. We had enjoyed bringing Aviva to Germany, but two kids to South Africa meant an additional $3500 in airfare, plus the hotels charged per person instead of per room which made bringing the kids too painful.

Leaving the kids with the grandparents made sense on several levels. We had been concerned the trip might be a little too dangerous for a 7-1/2-year-old and almost 3-year-old with issues about security in Johannesburg and safety of our planned safari. They probably would have been fine, but safari in South Africa was serious business. Besides that, we were at a crossroads in our relationship. Doug and I had been married for almost fifteen years, with two demanding careers in the family. After leaving Maytag, Doug had taken a job with a manufacturing start-up company that seemed like a good idea at the time but ended up going bankrupt without tipping off their employees. This left us owed over $50,000 in back pay, bounced paychecks, and unpaid medical bills. My company had flourished in its first few years, but I had spent two years under the strain of understaffed stores caught in the firestorm of new baby, new store, and abysmal economy all converging on me at once … plus one husband's career crisis were enough to push me to the brink of insanity. Everything was a mess, and there were many days the only thing that kept me from throwing my hands up and declaring bankruptcy was the thought that if I could just hold on until the South Africa World Cup everything would magically be alright. I downsized my expansion store in 2009, and had my former manager back in place by 2010, since it turned out glamorous mall pay wasn't worth the crappy mall hours. It also marked the end of a string of really bad hires. It finally seemed like I could see light at the end of a long tunnel.

However, months of chaos left our marriage on empty in Spring of 2010 and things were not going well for us. I had been so focused on our baby and my business, I had lost track of my marriage, and my husband hadn't spoken up and voiced what he needed from me. Ordinarily, I'd notice the silence, but I was constantly putting out fires and oblivious to how dangerously close to the brink we were. By the time either of us realized how bad things were, Doug had hurt me deeply and we'd walked ourselves right up to the edge of divorce.

I was so angry with him for betraying me, and the fact that it was a World Cup year made a sting a thousand times worse. There were days, weeks even, when I didn't think I could forgive him … but what was I going to do? Was I going to leave my marriage and then immediately pack up for three weeks traveling in South Africa with someone I was in the middle of divorcing? If we split up, who would get all our soccer friends in the break up? Neither of us, and that would make for miserable trips for the foreseeable future. For the time being, the only path forward was to try to work things out at least until we could get through the trip to South Africa. I'm sure there have been plenty of marriages wrecked by soccer obsession, but our story is rare if not unique: a marriage saved by soccer obsession.

We flew into Johannesburg over June 11th and 12th on the longest flight I had ever taken. We dropped the kids in Boston with my parents, then flew to Dubai, and then Dubai to Johannesburg, for a total of over 24 hours of flight time. The flight to Dubai was long, but it passed quickly with hundreds of movies on a personal player and not entirely terrible food.

Our Dubai layover left us time to see a few sights and experience a tiny slice of culture. Even traveling as a couple, we had to take a lady's taxi, to protect my femininity in a way I did not quite comprehend. The cab driver took us to the Dubai Mall where you could shop, eat, and … ski. There was a built in ski slope where you can rent skis (and I assume winter coats in the middle of the desert) and go skiing on indoor slopes. It was a weird to see people skiing indoors, but okay … I get snow as an attraction in the middle of extreme heat.

Our next cab driver was kind enough to point out some sights and took us to a cool hotel with a huge aquarium built into it. She showed it to us for the fish, which were impressive, but for me were wildly overshadowed by the stunning lobby. There were soaring, carved white columns around an atrium with a tower of blown glass swirls forming a trunk that seemed to writhe with pent-up energy in a suspended explosion of color climbing from a saturated turquoise blue to flaming yellow-orange. The design of the buildings, inside and it, was staggering. There were towers that earned their skyscraper status with ease, and interiors that were torture to rush through. There was so much to see. It seemed utterly disrespectful to view in an American drive-by fashion. Heartbreaking to me, with my BFA in Interior Design calling out to me to stay and drink it all in, however the airport and the last leg to South Africa pulled me back to reality and we hopped the flight to Joburg.

The last leg of the flight was "only" eight hours, but it seemed like time suspended. It was like we were in school and waiting for the final bell and the hands on the clock refused to budge. After what seemed like forever, we landed in Johannesburg and found our hotel. We'd planned on staying with friends at a guest house called "Africa Grey House," but when we were booking, we weren't sure when we were flying in. Therefore, the days before the first match, we had booked rooms with Kaela at the Tree Top Bed and Breakfast, a more expensive but gorgeous place near the Johannesburg Zoo. Our room overlooked a little courtyard that was lush with plants, flowers and birds. We got settled and began working on acclimating to South Africa before meeting our friends at the Grey House the next day for the road trip to the first game versus England.

The Grey House was the best and worst of things. It was wonderful to be back with all our friends, but we were about to learn of the amazing marketing skills, along with wide angle photography and salesmanship, that allowed the Grey House to convince us it was a luxurious oasis of relaxation when it was really one step up from a youth hostel. We took one look at the bunk beds, smallish common areas, non-functioning WIFI, and the total lack of privacy and ran for the hills. Fortunately, Tree Top had a room available for the days we'd be in Joburg. We'd met the family of innkeepers and could not pass up their hospitality and the huge upgrade in accommodations … well worth spending a little extra money. Tree Top was owned by an Afrikaans husband and wife and their young boys offering prime time South African hospitality, culture, and ambiance. During our stay, we became friends with Joey, the woman who ran it, and her family which allowed us to become deeper involved in the local culture than we would at a mass market hotel. Staying with them renewed my interest in one day opening a guest house of our own.

Almost immediately, it was time to load the vans for our road trip. There was beer stacked waist high and piles of bags of ice all ready for the several-hour drive to Rustenburg. We thought we left early enough to make the drive with time to grill out pre-game prior to the 8:30 PM kickoff, but the drive was several unpredictable hours long. The vans were a rolling pre-game party, with supporters singing for the guys from One Goal who were shooting a documentary about American fans at the World Cup. There was plenty of beer to drink, good friends to catch up with, and gorgeous scenery screaming "holy crap, we're in South Africa!!" Still jet lagged, taking a long road trip on the other side of the world was a little surreal. I found myself repeatedly looking out the window and thinking I had fallen into an alternate universe of awesome.

We had plenty of time to acclimate to our new surroundings as the closer we got to Rustenburg the more insane the traffic became. The highway traffic was bad enough, but once we got into the city, it became almost impossible to drive; the closer it got to game time, the more frustrated we became. The ride had already been far too long, but now there were discussions of "well, we could do this, or that, but I'm not really sure where we can all park." At our wits end, we decided to abandon our plans for stopping somewhere together for a bigger tailgate. We decided to abandon ship and head out with a few of our friends to the stadium. While the van was stopped (again), we grabbed our beers, jumped out, and started walking along the residential streets and dirt fields to the stadium. More cultural shock moments followed as we walked past businesses marked in various languages ... or perhaps initials for something? ... and no real clear American-marketing directions of what business was conducted there. We found a spot outside the main entrance where we made camp in the middle of the road for a little primetime media whoring.

It seemed like we were at the crossroads of the world with fans and/or media from almost every imaginable country walking by us, shouting or filming as we drank our beer and painted our faces. There were fans dressed in every possible color combination with various creative displays of fandom expressed in face paint, hats, traditional dress, and banners. The news media loved our happy band of US supporters, We looked like the love child of a Fourth of July Parade and an American political convention had thrown up all over us. We had superhero capes with red sparkles, a few red, white, and blue tiaras and what I liked to call "the Ugly Eagle" shirts. These shirts were so over the top ... post 9/11 Americana that one might find in a store and think "who would buy that?" My friends, ladies and gentlemen, that's who. We seek such atrocities of fashion out and proudly sport them for international media. We did interviews with Brits, Chinese, someone in Arabic, and we greeted Americans from around the US. We ran into some friends from the Minnesota 1st Volunteers who were a group of guys I'd seen around a few times. We greeted them shouting "Midwest Represent!" as they walked up. They came to this World Cup selling what was quite possibly my favorite scarf of all time, the "Total Jackassery" scarf. South Africa, particularly down by Robben Island and Cape Town, is known for its Jackass penguins. In Germany, the "gotta have it" item was the Brucesliga shirt, a nod to our coach Bruce Arena, with the logos of the three Bundesliga teams in our round robin host cities adapted to look like US team logos. It was one of my favorite fan generated items, and when I saw the "Total Jackassery" scarf, I knew it would be a new classic. I bought one right away and had one of our Minnesota friends send me another after the Cup.

Once we had our fill of mugging it up for camera crews around the world, we decided to walk a few blocks to find some food and a restroom. We found a place that had a braai (barbeque) going and a few "bathrooms." There were facilities for the ladies, but we had a good laugh at the guys lined up at a trough urinal practically in full view of everyone. We did our business and snapped a few photos of the backs of American fans draped in flags and assorted Americana lined up at the urinal trough, then made our way back to the stadium for the march into the match.

I love walking into stadiums at night. The floodlights shine down through the dust and mist, making the stadium look like an alien spaceship landed, with thousands of the fans draped in all sorts of colors walking willingly to be assimilated. There were US fans in Mexican wrestling masks, draped in US flags, Americana track suits, and all sorts of patriotic costumes. It was a steady riot of red, white, and blue, punctuated by singing and chanting with various antics of American (and English) soccer fans.

We got up to our seats in the upper deck and set about the business of hanging the American Outlaws Des Moines banner and setting up the stadium flag. I was so happy to be sitting in my lucky spot at the corner of the flag. Doug thought I was a little silly about this, but humored me with a photo of me blissed out and kissing the corner of the flag. It was part of the reason we bought our own stadium flag: so I would always be able to sit with the flag since I would be the one bringing it. Once we had our seats, we headed to the railing to hang the AO Des Moines banner, which would become a beacon throughout the World Cup, as fans from around the Midwest would see it and come over to introduce themselves. We ended up banner neighbors with our friends to the north: Neal from Minnesota 1st Volunteers supporter club. It's funny bumping into friends from the next state hanging banners halfway around the world.

When we go to a game outside the States, we typically go into the stadium about 60-90 minutes before kickoff. At games in the USA, we are allowed inside four hours prior in order to hang banners and set up tifo displays of flags and banners. However in foreign countries, you have to carry flags and banners in and pray you don't get stuck at stadium security with an overzealous gate guard that doesn't want to think about whether or not your banner adheres to stadium policy. In all our travels, I've had a few tense moments while waiting for approval to come down from management, but usually it works out. Entering early leaves a fair amount of time to entertain ourselves prior to kickoff, so I used the time to explore the stadium amenities.

The concession stands were very TIA (this is Africa): Not enough employees, not organized, limited options, and huge lines. The wait was far too long to count on getting a snack at halftime, so Doug went to get drinks while I further explored our stadium world. In the ladies room, I was surprised to find two women in police riot gear who were not using the facilities but guarding them. These were two of the most bad-assed looking women that I've ever seen, and apparently, there was need for them in the women's restroom, a thought I tried not to dwell on.

The atmosphere was exciting prior to kickoff and only became more electric and emotional when England scored in the 4th minute. I always believe we will win, and atat this point in US Soccer's history, we often played better when we were behind. I was almost relieved when England scored early, perhaps it would settle the boys down and get them to focus on the task at hand. We were starting to have some control and chances when in the 40th minute Clint Dempsey took a shot that should have been an easy save for England keeper Rob Green. Instead Green fumbled the save and let the ball roll into the back of the net. We were tied with England! The US Soccer supporters section went nuts, singing songs and taunting the drunk England fans around us to the verge of a stadium brawl.

The US had a few chances to upgrade our tie to a win in the second half, but we were only able to hold the tie. For the US, it was something to celebrate. We took a point from England who was considered one of the top teams in the tournament. After the game, we hung out in the stands, rallying up with Americans who had been scattered around the stadium and celebrating the victory by taking photos and singing. Our voices echoed through the concrete stadium structures, amplifying our celebratory chants and taunts. We danced and sang until we got too tired and hungry to do it anymore and headed back to the buses.

For England, the tie was almost more than they could stand. As we walked out, a heated discussion developed between our friend, Prairie Clayton, and a few English guys regarding the merits of the American soccer program. The English guys were saying they couldn't believe the US had earned a point from England, since we didn't even have any stars on our jerseys (national teams get a star on their jersey when they win the World Cup). Prairie countered she indeed had two stars on her US Soccer jersey (she was wearing a women's team jersey). The English guys thought this was a ludicrous idea and claimed women's team stars didn't count … about the most aggressive fighting words they could have used with Prairie. I had one of those moments where your brain goes into narration mode of your own life: "Huh, funny. In a game where I could easily be getting into a brawl because our team upset the team that outranked us, I'm going to battle stations defending Prairie and the USWNT. Hilarious."

We escaped without fights breaking out, and made our way to where the buses were parked. We grilled food and drank, waiting for everyone to make their way out of the stadium. The guys from One Goal were shooting post-game interviews with the supporters in our group. Once all were accounted for we headed out on the long ride back to Johannesburg feeling satisfied with our first day of action in South Africa. The return trip took until 3:30 AM so it was nice to be able to rest peacefully on the way home, sleeping well with the satisfaction we were off to a good start to make it to the next round.

The next day we slept until 11 AM (so thankful for late breakfast!)

and then hung around the house until early afternoon. Then Doug, Kaela, Christina and I all went for a walk around Tree Top's neighborhood looking for a place to watch the Algeria vs. Slovenia match before heading down to Cape Town. The neighborhood was residential, but every home was gated by a high stone or metal fence with serious-looking sliding gates, protecting the inhabitants from a danger we never saw but often heard about. We walked through a park and stumbled upon the Zoo Lake Bowling Club, a private lawn bowling club, but non-members can eat in the clubhouse and watch the giant TVs set up for the World Cup … good enough for us! We ordered lunch and sat down to watch the day's games. We ate and discussed our opponents' strengths and weaknesses. The food and company were good, and we found Castle Milk Stouts and Savanna Ciders to keep us going until it was time to head to the airport for our Cape Town flight.

We headed to the airport for our flight to Cape Town and enjoyed going through an airport that didn't involve TSA. There was security enough to make you feel safe but not the circus we're forced to endure in the US. Our flight was late and we were disappointed the airport was not broadcasting Germany vs. Australia. We sat eating our fast food dinner at a table with a South African also on his way to Cape Town. He struck up a conversation with us over my t-shirt, a red shirt with black block lettering that read "DES MOINES, HELL YES." It was from a store in the East Village neighborhood of Des Moines called Raygun, a store full of shirts and gifts printed with funny or ironic things about Des Moines or Iowa. It's one of the few places with the same sense of humor about living in Iowa as I do. Iowans typically do not find humor in the fact that they live in Iowa, but let's be honest, living in Iowa is hilarious, particularly when you're the polar opposite to the stereotypical Iowa girl. I love traveling in shirts that proudly proclaim my Des Moines residency, because it's the perfect way to strike up conversations and spread my love of the city. Rarely has such a conversation paid off so nicely and in such short order. Within minutes of hearing about our World Cup trip and my frustration that I was not watching the Germany game, he produced a laptop and began streaming the game for us. We were able to watch the game live and enjoy Germany destroying the Socceroos until boarding.

We arrived in Cape Town late and met Kaela and Christina for our Cape Town apartment share. We picked up our rental car and Christina slowly remembered how to drive stick shift. In South Africa, rental cars were all standard transmission, and South Africans drove on left. Even knowing how to drive stick still leaves you with the task of shifting lefty and then master driving on the left side. Turning left meant staying in the near lane … not as easy as it sounds. Furthermore, not seeing out of my right eye, I have never had to deal with the distraction of seeing my passengers in the US. In South Africa, I was suddenly forced to cope with my passengers constantly moving around in plain sight of my highly-developed peripheral vision. I have no idea how two-eyed people do this on an everyday basis. It made me feel like I was completely relearning how to drive with people in the car with me, even though my car in the US was standard transmission.

Christina, on the other hand, knew how to drive stick shift, but her regular car was automatic. So there we were, late night at the Cape Town Airport, with her trying to take a crash recertification in manual transmission, preferably without actually crashing. She figured it out and soon enough we were on our way to our rented apartment. As we got closer, the neighborhoods appeared to be getting more and more sketchy until we finally reached our address and decided it would be not-so-affectionately referred to as "Dodgyville." There were a few questionable-looking people, and the apartment was another example of creative advertising on the part of South Africans. While there wasn't anything completely false in the online ad for this place, through the use of creative wording and photography, the landlord had made it sound like there were two bedrooms when really it was a studio with two sleeping areas and no privacy, a problem for two women and the no-longer-all-that-happy couple. After our initial disappointment, we mutually agreed we were too tired to do anything about it that night and passed out in our not-so-great room.

The next day I woke up for my first day in Cape Town with a bit of dread. Now we would see exactly the situation we were in and if daylight at all improved the sketchy appearance of the place at midnight. Doug took a shower, went out for coffee and breakfast, and brought back some very promising muffins and coffee. There was a moment of amused confusion when he handed me my coffee, a mocha, which I tasted and loved. I asked why he had gotten it for me since I usually get plain coffee or lattes. Doug looked at me surprised and a bit perplexed. "You don't drink mochas?"

I smiled. "It tastes great, but I've maybe had 3 mochas in all our years together."

Some people find it romantic that "he" knows exactly how "she" likes her coffee. I found it charming my non-coffee-drinking husband had no idea how I wanted my coffee, but still manages a pleasant surprise for me.

Coffee consumed and showers taken, Kaela and Christina left before us so they could scope out the internet cafes and places other than our possibly sketchy, definitely-too-small apartment. It was nice to have a little time alone with Doug at the apartment so we could have some time to sort out our day's plans and discuss the room situation. As much as we wanted more space and privacy, we were already splurging on the bed and breakfast in Johannesburg and to find a completely new place in Cape Town would further annihilate out budget. After a brief powwow, we decided to see what the ladies came up with as a plan, but otherwise resolved we wouldn't be spending much time in the room anyway. I was anxious to see the outside world, so I got dressed and we headed out to explore.

My fears about the neighborhood were set aside as soon as we stepped out the door. We walked out facing the Company Gardens where the Dutch settlers once grew their food. It had been manicured into a beautiful walking garden that was lush and picturesque, refreshed from the rain the night before and full of singing birds and darting small animals. As we turned up the street, we caught a breathtaking glimpse of Table Mountain wrapped in a hazy veil of mist … so lovely. I was immediately put at ease that we had picked a totally acceptable residence for the next few days.

We turned down Long Street and I was pleasantly surprised to find all sorts of interesting places to shop and eat. There was hardly a store that we walked by that I didn't want to look in for one thing or another. Suddenly, the apartment my husband had found was quickly climbing from "total disaster" to "seems OK" and on its way to "great idea." It reached "great idea" status when we started to ask around what people had paid for their rooms. Prices ranged from $100 and up for a hotel room to $60-70 for a hostel-type accommodation, all significantly more than our rental.

The sad thing was that South Africa should have been a very affordable country, but many places were jacking up prices into the stratosphere and taking advantage of World Cup travelers. It started with the airline tickets … ordinarily $1200 but got as high as $4000+ (we got a "bargain" flight at $1750). Hotel rooms were three to five times as expensive as the normal off-season rates. We spoke with one South African who said bus fair before December was 3 Rand (38 cents), then it jumped to 8 Rand ($1.00), and now was 15 Rand. No one was saying that $2 was unreasonable for bus fair, but it was five times what they were paying, and as one resident put it, "it's not like we get to show our ID that we're residents and pay the old fare." The few times we got to pay the non-inflated prices we get a painful glimpse into what could have been an affordable trip. The point these price gougers were missing was there would be no return business many South Africans hoped for if we all went home broke.

The people of South Africa were so charming and kind though we quickly forgot how fast we were burning up our checking account. Shop keepers and other shoppers were happy to offer advice about things to buy, eat, drink, and do while in Cape Town. I found a small silver necklace in the shape of a hollow soccer ball. It looked an old school pentagon/hexagon, black/white ball, only the black parts were open and the white parts were silver panels. I have purchased a necklace at every World Cup, and this one seemed a perfect way to avoid spending a fortune on South African gem stones. We shopped for a while then joined Kaela and Christina for the early game over lunch. The place we found, Long Street Café, would become our regular hangout for the Cape Town part of the trip. A wide bar beckoned from the right side wall with the dining area broken into two rooms connected by walkways. The seating was mismatched wooden tables of different sizes which made the place seem casual and welcoming. The food was delicious, and they had decent beers and liquor, plus large televisions that always played the games. The crowd was casual during the day while night brought in an eclectic mix of swanky cocktail drinkers and casual diners. It seemed to be a nicer place that would not ordinarily have television on, but during the World Cup had to play the games. I enjoyed watching World Cup culture infiltrate a place like this and enjoyed spending game times at Long Street Café for the remainder of our time in Cape Town.

We spent the afternoon wandering through galleries with exhibits of World Cup art. One had a display of photographs of handmade soccer balls from around the world, showing the diversity of handmade street soccer balls and telling a photo-journalistic story of ghetto street soccer from around the world. I was relieved to find the exhibition book in paperback, expecting it to become a favorite coffee table book when we returned home, although it has ended up sequestered in our soccer shrine room … too much a favorite to leave out just anywhere.

As afternoon turned to evening, we walked down to the stadium via the culture walk, a promenade designed to feature the sculptures and paintings of local artists while funneling World Cup travelers past musicians, art and food vendors. There were parades of street performers and soccer fans trying to out-do each other in colorful displays and singing all on the way to the Italy vs. Paraguay match. We wandered around the courtyard outside the stadium trying to buy black market tickets to the match, but they were so expensive, even as game time approached. We ran into a friend of Doug's from his college soccer days, and found ourselves with four people looking for not-too-expensive tickets but only one ticket among us. As match time approached, we decided there were too many people with deeper pockets than ours and sold our one ticket for enough money to buy the first round at a tavern across from the stadium.

That ended up being the best place to watch the game anyway. Much cheaper beer served faster than in the stadium, better food, and far better company. After catching up with Doug's friends, we grabbed a table next to some English soccer fans who were entirely entertained by my soccer knowledge and passion. They regaled us with tales of their travel following the English soccer team. By the end of a 1-1 tied match, we were quite drunk and sore from laughing so hard all night long.

Our second day in Cape Town started with a muffin/coffee run followed by wandering around the gardens across from our apartment and exploring the Jewish Museum and a local synagogue. The museum offered an interesting history of Jewish settlement in South Africa, and we enjoyed the small but beautiful synagogue still used for worship services. Our morning exploration was interrupted by our landlord at the apartment calling and threatening to take all our stuff if we didn't complete payment for the rest of the week. We had considered moving out once we found out it was a studio, but a quick search of Cape Town lodging did not offer up any better options that weren't crazy expensive. We walked back across the garden, confronted our psycho landlord, settled our bill if not our differences, and headed back out to explore.

We walked down the idyllic Government Road past several houses that seemed to echo apartheid from their architecture. You could visualize the segregated South Africans living in their isolated world of colonial white buildings, gardens, and sculptures. It was interesting to see how apartheid could become so intrinsic to a culture you would see its remnants in so many corners of their world.

Continuing the theme of the day, we met up with Christina at the Slave Museum. In yet another TIA moment, we accidentally toured the museum backwards and saw the Nelson Mandela exhibit in reverse. We'd asked for directions but apparently didn't understand the guide. South Africa was a little backwards and sometimes we did the wrong thing for lack of understanding or due to our would be guide's reluctance or apathy in setting us straight. We ended up with the full story of Mandela's life, only we had to re-order it in our own minds.

We walked through a marketplace of African crafts ranging from cheap vuvuzelas to amazing and beautiful works of art and artifacts. The one constant binding all the merchants together was the aggressive bargaining that took place at every booth. If you dared make eye contact, they would approach you with the bargain du jour: "very lucky for you" "buy one, get four free." My favorite promise was the guy talking to me about masks who said "I guarantee it for three years. It will not break. If it does, you just hop on a plane and come back here and I'll replace it for you." That's the South African sense of humor. We did find a cool petrified shell which we purchased, but decided not to carry vuvuzelas for the entire trip.

At this point, it was 3 PM and Doug was starving again as we were approaching lunchtime of our World Cup routine: wake up around 10, breakfast at 11 or noon, late afternoon lunch, dinner at 9 PM. We stopped for lunch in a local café before continuing the long walk to the V&A Waterfront. As we approached the waterfront recreation area, we came across a ferris wheel offering views of the stadium and shoreline, and since we still hadn't found a clear day for Table Mountain, we decided to take a ride. The views were stunning. We could see the QE II ship docked in the harbor, the city, the shipbuilding yards, and the stadium, which looked magnificent at sunset.

As we got off, we received a pissed off message from Kaela who had a business appointment earlier in the day and wanted to know "where the hell are you guys?" She had been trying to reach us for hours with texts, emails, and phone calls, none of which reached us. This struck me as very TIA/South African … as if their network said "Yeah, I'll get that delivered, eventually." Kaela was none too happy with us (although, really, it's not like we were ignoring her intentionally), but she was able to settle down after a beer in a very cold and damp outdoor bar. To all those people who told me Africa would be hot, I told you so. June was winter in the southern hemisphere and it really was chilly and rainy almost constantly.

We found a place with heaters for dinner and settled in to watch Brazil vs. North Korea. The Brazilians never really got excited about the match and left themselves tied at 0 at halftime. The first half was mostly dull, but we did get to have a funny, ongoing conversation about travel wives and travel husbands. Doug and I travel together as husband and wife, but many of our friends travel away from their married spouses (or are single) and travel with friends. We have noticed that these travel partnerships have developed into mini-pseudo marriages. Christina was Kaela's travel wife, Sean was Brock's travel wife, etc. The travel wives did all the little planning things and arrangements while the travel husbands kicked back and enjoyed the travel (so technically, Doug was my travel wife). We were cracking up that Kaela had a rough day at the office and was coming "home" like the belligerent husband, all grumpy and upset because (s)he had a bad day at work. The running joke of this year's trip was Brock couldn't come with us to Cape Town because his wife (Sean) wouldn't let him. It was moments like this that made me love our dysfunctional soccer family all the more.

After dinner (2-1 Brazil over North Korea) we took a cab back to Long Street. Christina (now playing the role of mom and wife) wanted to go home, but the rest of us went out for one more round at Long Street Café. It wasn't as much fun without the other wife to talk to, and we left after our one drink. We stopped for a soda at the gas station on the way home where Doug was too excited to find Mountain Dew for "breakfast" the next day. As we walked home, we noticed there were police officers on every block. So many we started to get concerned that perhaps our neighborhood was as dodgy as we thought the first night we arrived. The cops were all very nice and greeted us along the way. As we approached our apartment, one of the officers broke off from the rest and started to walk with us. He asked where we were going and we told him. I asked if he was our escort and he said, "Yes, I'm here to make sure you get home safely so you can come back and visit South Africa again." It was sweet and with a fair amount of pride in his town and country. He said goodbye once we reached our apartment building, and any fears I had about Cape Town were once and for all set aside.

We had heard really good things about the wine country in the mountains surrounding Cape Town, and not ones to be shy about drinking, we had to check it out. Since we were on World Cup time, it seemed totally reasonable to start drinking at 10 AM. Of course, we didn't realize most places wouldn't open until afternoon. Never too early to start drinking at the World Cup, but apparently no one told the wineries this. We finally found an open place in an absolutely gorgeous setting. They had a fountain with a ceramic orb floating in the center of it and a porch where you could sip wine overlooking their garden. It was beautiful, but the wine really wasn't impressive and we left without purchasing.

On we went to the only other winery we'd seen open before 2 PM and drove up to it with a sense of impending disappointment. It was modern and sterile, and if the gorgeous winery wasn't tasty, how good could this place be? It turned out to be the most pleasant surprise of the trip. Their tasting was free, and their wines were mind blowingly good. We bought cases, aggressively calculating how much we could drink in country and still skate under the import limits to bring back to the USA. As we were wrapping our tasting experiences the owner of the vineyard sent over a tasting of their not-for-sale-or-tasting private collection of reserve sparkling wine. It was so incredibly good and the perfect end to our midday tasting trip. If you're ever in Cape Town, I highly recommend making time to go up to Stellenrust Vineyard (and bring some delicious reds back for me!)

We returned to Cape Town in time to watch the night game which was South Africa's game against Uruguay. They'd played to a draw against Mexico in their first game and needed a win, a tie, or a loss by only one goal to remain in contention for the second round. To advance out of the group stage, teams had to accumulate points (three for a win, one for a tie) to be one of the top two of four teams in their bracket. The tie breaker for points ties was goal differential, a combination of goals for and goals against; therefore, if a team cannot win or tie, it's important they don't lose badly.

By the time we got down to Long Street, the pre-game celebration was already in full swing. The sidewalks and bars were full of people from all different countries, but most people were draped in South African flags, colors, or wearing the yellow Bafana Bafana jerseys. The team's nickname, Bafana Bafana come from the Zulu for "the boys, the boys" or "Go boys! Go boys!" They use their nickname almost exclusively, far more than you would ever hear an American refer to the USMNT as "The Yanks" or (worse) "the Nats." We searched for a bar where we could watch the match, but Long Street was so packed, it seemed hopeless. People were starting to spill into the street and blocked traffic down to one lane. You could hear the constant wail of vuvuzelas interspersed with car horns of angry taxi drivers trying to weave through the throngs of supporters. We finally found a bar with a TV on their second floor balcony. Slower service, yet offered a bird's eye view of the happy riot below while we watched the game and cheered the host on to victory.

Unfortunately, it wasn't meant to be for South Africa. Up against the team that would eventually become the fourth place team, in the 24th minute the top scorer and player of the tournament, Diego Forlan, racked up one of his five tournament goals. South Africa had chances, but they never converted any of them into goals, and in the 80th minute, they had a penalty called and scored against them. From there, it was all over. A third goal scored in extra time meant they had a heavy disadvantage going into their third match, and would ultimately become the first host to not advance out of the first round. It was a sad day for all of South Africa, and so we finished our drinks and headed back to our room to pack for the next day's flight back to Joburg.

For our last day in Cape Town, the fog finally broke, clearing Table Mountain from the mist. We didn't have time to hike to the top, but we did drive up the narrow switch back roads to the mid-level lookout to take photos of the valley below. There were soccer fans from all over also taking advantage of the weather. We talked to a few people from Spain, Switzerland, and England, and enjoyed the touristy sightseeing with World Cup flavor. It was a gorgeous view: rocks and graceful South African trees juxtaposed against the urban landscape below, overshadowed by Robben Island floating in the distance ... the perfect way to end our time in Cape Town.

The other bonus of the fog disappearing was that tours of Robben Island resumed. Robben Island is the prison where Nelson Mandela was incarcerated and it was something we were really hoping to see. We bought tickets and lunched at an amazing, sun-drenched Ethiopian café before the 2 PM tour. The tour was another stark glimpse into South African Apartheid, as we toured the prison cells and heard the stories of suffering, strife, and imprisonment without cause. It was difficult to imagine Nelson Mandela, world leader, sitting in his tiny cell or working endlessly at the mines and enduring forced labor. Our tour guide was a former prisoner and gave a personal edge to the painful stories he told, which were a far cry from the beauty of the morning views, but a powerful experience of South African history.

We flew back to Joburg on a plane with a Puma Soccer nose cone. I have to say, flying on a plane dedicated to soccer made my day more than I'd like to admit. Shortly after takeoff, the sun slowly sunk below the horizon, and we had a bird's eye view of the stunning South African sunset. A gorgeous flight, and when we returned to the Tree Top B&B, we were moved into the honeymoon suite for our regular room rate. It was across the courtyard from the main house. It was a beautiful room with a tiled bathroom that had a high window facing the zoo, so you could hear the lions roar greetings back and forth. It was about as perfect as I could imagine a room to be, and it was ours for the rest of our time in Joburg.

USMNT Game Day #2 in South Africa started out with breakfast at Joey and Eric's working out the plans for the tailgate. After talking to Joey about our various parking options, we decided the "Park and Walk" lot was the best plan. Parking at the stadium would be nuts, and we could park free in the outlying lots and walk up to the stadium through the surrounding neighborhoods. That settled, I went up to get ready for the game. My South Africa uniform consisted of Southern Hemisphere inspired layers: jeans, my Wolf Pack red tee, sparkly cape, and tiara. I did my game day makeup (the newest addition to my game day routine) of hand drawn eye mask of red, white and blue drag queen eye shadow in stars and stripes.

We went downstairs and found the cars getting packed for the stadium with beer and snacks. Sean and the rest of our travel family from Texas had arrived from the airport, and in no time, we rounded up the people from Africa Gray House and were off in our two cars to the Park and Walk.

When we arrived at the parking lot, which was really just a grass field, we parked on the far end and opened up the trunks to tailgate. Doug rigged our AO Des Moines banner across the two cars' open trunks so it created a tent over the food, and became a billboard for our group. We had Savana Cider, Castle Milk Stout, sandwiches, and chips, and we were soon joined by other nearby Americans. There were three guys that had gotten American flag style palazzo style pants made with a corner of blue with white stars on their right hips and red and white horizontal stripes flaring around their legs. Combined with thrift store jackets detailed with USA across the back and vintage hats, they were pretty fabulously costumed.

At about an hour and a half before the game, our group was still entrenched in face painting and tailgating, and I was getting anxious about getting into the stadium to put up the banner. I don't think there is a diagnosed condition for the stress I feel if I'm outside the stadium an hour before kickoff, but it's serious business, and I prefer to avoid it if at all possible. The flag pants guys were headed in and we decided to walk with them. We walked out and almost right away hit a family selling food on their front lawn. It smelled delicious so we stopped and bought some of the pastries filled with meat or cheese and corn and a few of the little fried sugared donuts. It was out-of-this-world good food, and we ate as we walked on to Ellis Park, talking and joking along the way. One of the guys stopped to get a wig colored like an American flag. We stopped, when asked, to take photos with South African children along the way. We must have seemed really outlandish to them: five Americans dressed in the wildest cacophony of red, white and blue Americana. Even some of the less dressed up soccer fans were giving us glances. One of the guys facetiously quipped, "Next time, we really should dress up for this."

By the time we reached the stadium, Kaela, Brock, Trent, Sean and company had caught up to us and we all walked in together. We headed to Block 30 to our seats and found a place to hang the American Outlaws Des Moines banner. Our official seats weren't bad, about two-thirds of the way up in the lower deck in the corner. As soon as we got in, we headed down with the Angry Eagle shirt guys to the front where all the press was shooting to do a little media whoring. We realized that no one was fighting us for the seats and decided to make it our permanent camp for the game. We had a great time posing for the cameras and watching the team warm up.

The game started and Slovenia scored not once but twice in the first half. It was demoralizing and sickening to think that we had fought off England for the tie, but now we were struggling to even look respectable against Slovenia. I couldn't believe it and felt like I was going to throw up at any moment. I wondered if I had come all the way to South Africa just to see my team get eliminated before the third game in round robin. I'm hardly a fair-weather fan, but to have the expectation of advancement only to be on the verge of virtual elimination two games into the tournament was so upsetting. I was practically dry heaving before pulling myself together and willing the American team to do better in the second half.

Thankfully, mercifully, they did. First a goal from Donovan (Landy Cakes as my husband mocks, although he knew Dempsy was my 2010 favorite) then the equalizer from the coach's son, Michael Bradley. I often wonder what it's like coaching your own son at the national team level. When Michael scored, was it extra exciting/satisfying for his dad, Coach Bob Bradley? I have dreamed of the day my kids are playing in their version of the big leagues and watching them excel in their chosen arena. What must it be like for the coach of the national team to have his son come up through the ranks and earn a spot at the highest level of American play? But I digress.

It was tied 2-2 with less than 10 minutes to go. Miraculously, Maurice Edu flew in and buried the winning goal into the back of the net. But wait, you soccer fans must be thinking ... that game ended in a tie. True, the referee from Mali (they play soccer there?) took a look at the five fouls Slovenia was committing in the penalty area and perhaps the one foul the American player committed and called the play dead with a foul going OUT in favor of Slovenia before the goal was scored. We were literally tackling each other and jumping for joy when we realized that the goal had been called back. It was Doug who noticed first and started shouting they'd called it back. At that moment I had one of those irrational hatreds humans come up within moments of fury. I thought "Shut up, Doug. Stop it. Do not ruin this amazing victory with your referee realities!" Unfortunately, he was right and it wasn't a goal. I'm not usually one to blame the referee, but in this case, I made an exception. Our only hope at this point was for the US would force justice to be served by advancing on their own with a victory in the next game.

The game ended and the players showed their appreciation for our support. Finishing in a tie had been an impossible dream at the end of the first half when we were down two goals, to a lackluster "meh" finish in the light of our winning goal being called back. We hung out for a while getting pictures taken in the concourse area of the stadium before heading back on the road to the cars.

The hierarchy of photo taking at the stadium has always cracked me up. There were people who did not come dressed up, who thought our face-painted, crazy-outfitted group was a must-photo opportunity. Then there were the people whose outfits were totally over the top who were my coveted photo ops. At this game, there was Evil Kinevil and a group of three people dressed up like NASA astronauts. Then there was press, with US press and AP wire trumping foreign broadcasters. We kept score in a friendly battle of who got published where and in which media. South Africa triumphs included MSNBC, ESPN, Nightline, and several print publications. A woman who saw me in line for food at the first game asked Doug why I was wearing a cape and tiara to the game. Doug answered, "Because she can" but really I do it because it's more fun going to the games and completely letting go of the fact you're crazy psycho for USMNT. I love this team so much, and the tiara, make-up, and dressing up are just an expression of that love, like a teenage boy doing stunts to impress a girl who wouldn't give him the time of day. I mean, once you've followed them all the way around the world, is a tiara really that big a stretch?

We started the trek back to the cars cold, dejected, tired and hungry. We found a lovely little preschool along the way having a fundraiser grilling sausages for fans. We stopped and had the most delicious South African sausages and drinks. Most people got cokes, beers or mixed drinks, but I found more of the South African liquor Amarula and had to buy it. Between the South African wines and Amarula, I was starting to lose hope I'd be able to drink my way through my stash fast enough to clear customs, but dammit, I was willing to try! The sausages, which fell under my "don't ask, don't tell" policy of pork awareness and consumption on World Cup trips, were comforting and tasty. Besides, knowing South Africans much prefer beef to pork, my policy was far safer there than in Germany. As we ate, drank, and talked with the South Africans along the block, our spirits lifted and I began to feel better about the night with my faith slowly restored that somehow we would still advance to the next round.

A bit further down the road, we were attracted to a front lawn cookout advertising Bunny Chow. I had read about this South African treat in the guidebook and really wanted to try it. It was a specialty of Durban, but we were only planning on going to Durban if the US did not advance. Attempting to devour my fears and break the trend of us heading to Durban, I went to investigate. The guy eating there, wearing an American flag which did nothing to hide his South African accent, said it was the best food in all of South Africa. Gotta try that, right? Bunny Chow was a short loaf of bread hollowed out and filled with chicken or beef curry. The center part of the bread was used as a scoop to dig out the deliciousness. I can still taste the warm, delicious, soothing spices as I write this years later.

We continued on our walk aware we weren't in the best of neighborhoods. However, as 11 Americans, people were more interested in saying hello and shouting a few pro-USA comments our way than starting any trouble with us. People were typically friendly and interested in greeting us or perhaps taking a photo with the crazy Americans. The most aggressive comment we got was from one disgruntled soccer fan who was upset when we didn't respond the first time to his thickly accented request for the final score. I thought, "Hey, sorry dude. None of us want to think about the final outcome right now."

In preparation for this trip we had all been told varying degrees of "don't go to South Africa, it's not safe." While I'm sure there are shady neighborhoods in South Africa (as there are everywhere), I'm also sure it's not nearly as bad as most people made it out to be. Part of it was the World Cup: rumor had it there had been a pact among criminal elements to leave World Cup fans alone since crimes against soccer fans would make the news and hurt future tourism. South Africans we met were friendly and outgoing and wanted very much to share their culture with us. It gave me the impression South Africa's reputation for being unsafe was much like that of the New York metro area when I grew up in the 70s and 80s. It's about being careful and not being careless where you were and what you were carrying. Don't be stupid, and you'll be fine.

We got back to the cars and I swear every single guy had to find some creative way of relieving himself by either peeing by the side of the car or over in the bushes about 50 yards away. It wouldn't surprise me if the following week there were outlines around where all the Americans parked where the guys burned/fertilized the grass. Eventually, we piled into the cars and heading for more civilized facilities for eating, drinking, soccer watching, and bathrooms. We were going to look for a place close to the stadium, but when the lead car couldn't find anything fitting the bill, we headed for the Zoo Lake Bowling Club where we had lunch a few days prior.

We got there a few minutes after kickoff and were caught off guard by how totally different Zoo Lake was between the day and night crowd. The day crowd had filled one-third of the tables, with one table of blacks among all the whites. The night crowd was jammed into every conceivable corner and table, and the racial percentage had flipped to heavily favor blacks with a few whites throughout the crowd. We grabbed the last table all the way at the front right under the TV screen and settled in for drinks and food for those who had not found good vegetarian dinner options along the way. Prairie was not happy with the place, but the thing about the World Cup was once we had found a place with beer, the game, and bonus food and a halfway clean bathroom, it was time to suck it up … we were not going anywhere until the end of the game.

The 8:30 PM game was England vs. Algeria, the other half of our group. Given our two ties with Slovenia and England, and Slovenia's victory over Algeria, we were hoping for Algeria to win (impossible) or a tie (next to impossible). We sat down and started drinking, but after a while I couldn't watch any more. No one had scored and it was getting too intense for me. I went from our "last table available" at the far right front of the room to the standing room area at the back half of the bar and joined a conversation between one of our guys and two white, but not Afrikaan, South Africans. I got the crash course I had been looking for in cultural terminology. Afrikaan means Dutch-descended, white South African, but does not connote racism, although they may or may not be racist. Afrikaan was also the language they speak which was very similar to Dutch. The intricacies of differences and cultures between the various cultural groups in South Africa were staggering, leaving me wondering how people ever kept it all straight in the complexity of interwoven, interconnected cultures.

With that interesting tidbit tucked away, I really wanted to find out the black South African's take on the World Cup. I had talked to so many white South Africans about how they thought the World Cup had forced whites to deal with the impoverished areas where most World Cup venues were located. They talked about how soccer fans were typically black and whites usually follow and/or play rugby or cricket, but the World Cup had started to break down those barriers. What I didn't know was how blacks felt about what the World Cup had done for South Africa and race relations in the country. There I was in a room full of opportunities to learn answers to my questions with the bonus of lowered inhibitions to spur me onward.

I walked up to two twenty-something black men engaged in conversation, greeted them, and joined in their conversation after introductions to Peterson Khumalo and Ayanda Sibandze. We chatted about the World Cup and the US's performance. We talked about kids and what we did for a living and then I finally worked up the nerve to get down to the nitty gritty. I asked what they thought the World Cup had brought to South Africa. At first, Ayanda replied not really much, but then he corrected himself.

"Well, like EVERY road I travel on has an extra lane now." We laughed and talked about infrastructure and what the improvements meant for South Africa, then I asked what it had meant for race relations in South Africa. He said it had definitely helped but talked about South Africa as a country that was two generations behind so many other cultures in race relations. He said the World Cup had pushed together the whites and blacks of South Africa in very positive ways, which we could witness firsthand watching soccer in the first racially mixed crowd we'd seen in South Africa. I found it comforting that soccer was bringing good things to this beautiful, culturally abundant country.

It was interesting to note that the conversations we had with blacks were completely different than the small talk white people made with us. Blacks wanted to know if we were going to Soweto (a black ghetto) and if we were willing to eat culturally black food there without asking what it was. It was a completely different conversation, but the common thread was that South Africans were very proud of their country and their unique cultural heritage. Both blacks and whites were proud of the fact that there were many different cultures and languages represented by their country.

Back to reality, because there was a very important game going on. I had become so engrossed in the conversation I was a little startled when I heard the whistle blow to end the game. In disbelief, I read the 0-0 score line and it began to dawn on me the nearly impossible had happened! England had allowed Algeria to pass with a tie, leaving the playing field miraculously wide open for the Americans in our third and final game. As this revelation spread through the heavily pro-US crowd, you could feel the energy in the room start to crackle. Excitement skyrocketed. The DJ turned off the TV sound and shouted "Are you ready to wave your flag?" the place erupted in an electric burst of euphoria. He cranked up the "Waving Flag" K'Naan, the unofficial anthem of the World Cup, and people started dancing on tables and waving flags, scarves, and whatever else they could find to dance along with. Prairie forgot the limited vegetarian options and started dancing on top of one of the beer kegs. It was the World Cup equivalent of prom in a John Hughes movie. The anthem blared, surrounded by my friends, I danced and shouted along to the song, celebrating our new found hope for making it to the second round. I tried to lock every second of the night into my memory forever.

As the party simmered back down to a nice, respectable good time, Doug and I found ourselves with Peterson and Ayanda, who had turned to less serious topics of discussion as the party amped up. We were dancing American style when they asked if we knew how to dance Zulu. We said we hadn't learned it yet, and they set out to teach us Zulu dance moves. It wasn't too difficult: a knee swivel started at rocking your hips. It was fun and we were having a great time diving deeper into South African culture when Ayanda said "Have you had Zulu beer?"

"No, I haven't seen it anywhere … but I'm game. Let's go to the bar." I replied, already heading up to order.

He caught my arm and explained, "You can't get it at this bar. You can only get it in Soweto."

Ah … Soweto. That district that all the guidebooks said not to go to, and if you do, only go during the day with a paid guide from a trustworthy source. The guidebooks were not very clear on meeting two professionally dressed Zulu men and trusting them as your guides to Soweto, but I was guessing the answer wouldn't be "no." It would be more like "Hell no, do you have a death wish?" But here it was, the chance for a really authentic Soweto experience. A chance to see a side of South African culture Americans were typically not privy to see. So I trusted my gut about Peterson and Ayanda and said "When can we go?"

We made plans and exchanged phone numbers. The more we talked and danced the night away, the less I worried and the more I hoped this Soweto tour would really happen. I had wanted to go see Soweto, but the tours were expensive, and I figured they would only give us a fishbowl, touristy look at Soweto. I was not really interested in spending money on an inauthentic experience, but this was a chance to see real Soweto. If it came with some level of real risk so what … it could be the experience of a lifetime. Plus, Zulu beer. They had me at Zulu beer. For now, we would have to be satisfied with drinking Castle Milk Stouts and getting to know our new friends at Zoo Lake Bowling (Night) Club.

22

Safari Adventure With My South Africa Husbands

We woke up at 8 and ate breakfast with everyone downstairs in the main house with Eric and Joey. We were headed up to safari at Mapungubwe National Park, and it was a long drive requiring an early departure. We had to be in the park by sunset, when the gates would close. We packed and headed out armed with maps and intermittently functioning phone GPS. The beginning of the trip was pretty uneventful, even fun. We had Prairie and Mike in our car and we were making good time through little towns. Little did we know how quickly trouble can find you in South Africa, ever deepening the meaning of TIA.

Somehow we missed a road sign and turned off the road we were supposed to be on. With limited signposts and a map only marked with the roads we needed, not the surrounding area, we soon realized we were not where we should be. We stopped for directions, but only got misinformation. In defense of the guy who delivered the poor information, he looked pretty shocked to see a car full of white people in his part of rural Africa, let alone asking him for directions. By the time we realized we had to stop again, it was sundown and we were at least ninety minutes off course. We were in the middle of nowhere, a place where you stopped for gas at every station, because you might not see fuel again for a hundred miles or more. If we broke down, there was no telling if people or large destructive animals would find us first. If we found people, we had no way of knowing if they would help or rob us. It was not a safe situation.

Panic slowly set in, as we tried to find someone to ask for help. We found a police station, and with it, a flood of relief and gratitude. That is, until we realized it was behind barbed wire and looked very closed up for Saturday evening, allowing our fears to come flooding back with a vengeance. We drove a little further and found a gas station and decided to stop and ask for directions, feeling very much at our own risk, but out of options.

The gas station attendant was in appropriately dirty clothes with very crooked teeth in between spaces where he was missing teeth altogether. He spoke a simple, accented English, and it looked dubious at best we would get good directions from this guy, but where else could we turn at this point? We had to throw ourselves on his mercy and hope he could help us out of this jam. We showed him where we were trying to get and started working through the communication of where we were in relation where we were trying to get. It was at that moment he did one of the most startling things he could have done: he pulled out the latest model Blackberry.

It's difficult to describe just how out of place a Blackberry looked at the roadside gas station with pumps I haven't seen since the 1970's with the attendant, who looked far from techie. It was as if a time machine had dropped either the phone or the setting from another era. It was even more magical, because my smartphone hadn't had a data signal for miles, but somehow, he had a fast connection at the ready as if he had some secret decoder ring attached to the back of the phone. It was definitely a defining "this is Africa" moment for me, and a lesson in not only willingness to help but also how technologically advanced South Africans are, even in little Baltimore, South Africa.

We got ourselves some old school turn by turn directions … the kind written on a piece of paper. We bought some gas, because you don't pass up night time working gas pumps from a guy who just saved you from dying on the side of the road in Africa, and headed off into the night. Driving in South African countryside at night is not really something I recommend. It's pitch black dark and very few places along the way you could ask for help if you ran into trouble. We had gone so far out of the way West we had to chose between three hours on dirt roads or seven hours on highways. We were already getting in past dark, but getting in at nearly dawn didn't seem very wise. We were one flat tire away from the scariest horror movie script I could imagine but if you could suspend the ever present adrenaline response, it was beautiful. We never did see anything deadly, but we did come across a huge menacing porcupine who made his displeasure at our presence quite clear. As if Mother Nature said, "You might want to get home, there's more where this came from."

We finally found the park and realized from the main gate we had to drive 30+ kilometers to drop Prairie and Mike at their place. Then there was another 40 kilometers to our hut. At this point, we were so exhausted and fried from the drive of terror, but what could we do? We finally got to our hut around … I don't know, it felt like midnight or later. I sat up, trying to write notes about our adventure, as my husband tried to coax me to bed. He finally got my attention long enough to score a kiss and I have to admit, he smelled super delicious. I asked what he'd put on, because he knows cologne is like a drug for me. He said "Nothing, just man driving across Africa, with a hint of Stellenrust Wine … that's what I put on." Well, you just can't argue with that, now can you? South African plains … terrifying, but pretty damn sexy.

The next morning the world appeared to be much less threatening and we could finally see the beauty surrounding us. We were staying in a small round hut with a living room, kitchenette, large bedroom, and bathroom. Breakfast could be served on our porch, which was fortified with high walls allowing safe view across the plains, which were scattered with bushes and low slung trees to the hills of rock and dirt. The porch had rough wooden slats to block the sun and give further sensation of snug security in our own little world. It was the perfect place to recharge and reconnect, away from the larger group.

Doug and I headed to the main gate to meet the rest of our friends around 10 AM for the safari tour of the Mapungabwe Park Memorial site. When we arrived, I went into the reception area to look around and one of the staffers saw me and told me I would have to talk to my husband in a tone that expressed deep concern for his safety.

"Oh, ma'am, you cannot let your husband walk up here in the morning. There are leopards, he will be killed." I was confused, but I thanked her, and went into the ladies room.

When I came out, another staff person cornered me, explaining it was imperative I convince my husband not to go walking along the road in the morning, he would certainly be killed, or at least injured. She took my confused head shaking for a lack of seriousness, and doubled her efforts to terrify me with how many ways my husband would be maimed if he continued his alleged misbehavior. I assured her I would talk to him about it and went out to join Doug as our friends arrived. I found Doug and told him about the warnings and asked if he'd been walking around at all? Of course he hadn't, so we figured there must be something lost in translation, and joined up with our friends arriving from the other side of the park.

The comments remained a mystery until we were introduced to Scott Sanger, a guy from D.C. who had traveled with our group for years, but somehow managed to miss meeting us until that day. We were introduced and soon discovered he was staying by us in a hut just down the road. He told us he did not have a car so he decided to go for a run to get up to the main gate early this morning. Mystery solved! I exclaimed, "So you're my husband!" I told the story of how the staff had all assumed he was my husband and I was responsible if he was to die walking along the road again. Thus, Scott became my South Africa husband. From then on, we'd pick him up for breakfast on our porch and then head over to the other side of the park where the rest of the people were staying. We wouldd hang out there until late at night, then drive back to our place again; a strange pseudo-family unit.

The safari tour started at an architectural site but for me, the best part of the tour was climbing steps built into the side of a rock cliff. The steps climbed to a plateau overlooking an expanse of plains dotted with rocks and trees. Close inspection revealed animals hidden in their natural habitat, riveting and striking in how breathtakingly beautiful it all was. Looking around and seeing so many soccer friends I care for so deeply gave me a sense of profound inner peace. This was how the World Cup became so much more than just the greatest soccer tournament on Earth. A grand adventure, a family reunion, and a chance to reconnect with your forever friends, all taking place at the greatest soccer party every four years.

We wanted to watch the sunset at the river confluence, which we almost missed while enjoying our "morning" tour. We drove out to the spot where you could walk up to the lookout cliff over the confluence, and hiked up with our cache of wine from Stellenrust. Or it should have been hiking, but was more like sprinting while carrying wine (there's an Olympic sport I could win … sprint hiking with booze). As we watched the sun setting over the rivers, we heard sounds of animals coming to the river to drink. We saw elephants at least a mile or two away trumpeting so loud it had the power to startle us from so far. It was hard to imagine how it would sound standing next to them. It was as if time slowed down … the universe begging us to notice how perfect everything could be in natural order with animals in their habitat and soccer family sharing delicious South African wine. Looking back on South Africa, I was astounded I was allowed so many profound moments in such a short amount of time. I've heard people say that when you're in Africa, you feel closer to your ancient soul and the beginnings of life. There was a transcendent feeling of peace and tranquility I have yet to experience anywhere else on Earth.

We headed back to the main cabin where everyone (except me and my two husbands) were staying for dinner and a bonfire. Most of our group had hired local women to cook, but Kaela writes a cooking blog called "Local Kitchen," and the idea of passing up a week of her cooking seemed insane. We opted out of the meal plan and prepared our own meals with Kaela, which made the trip double as a cooking school. I learned more about the basics of preparing and cooking food in that week than the rest of my life combined. Plus, we had the bonding experience of working in the kitchen beside the local women and got to talk to them about life in South Africa and their impressions of our group of travelers. It seemed to tap into some ancient lineage of preparing food I missed growing up in a home where my mother cooked but never taught cooking.

After a day of adventure the food tasted amazing, and once it was cleared, there was a bonfire to gather around. We would gather every night around the campfire and tell stories of what we had done that day, drinking cider, amarula, or scotch, smoking cigars and lounging around the fire. We invited the kitchen staff out to join us, and they shared stories about South Africa. We sang soccer songs for them and asked them to return the favor. They sang the South African national anthem, which includes four languages, and the miner's song Shosholoza, which is South Africa's unofficial second anthem. Their music was so deep and haunting that understanding the words wasn't required for the song to captivate us.

The campfires were my favorite part of the day, where we could wind down and catch up, full of good food and great booze. I'd never been to camp as a kid but it seemed like if someone designed a camp for grownups, this was exactly what it would look like. Days were spent exploring the park and checking out the nature areas and walks. There were pools that would have been beautiful for swimming if it hadn't been so chilly. A boardwalk among the treetops allowed us to walk and watch monkeys playing all around us, a few even daring to jump right across our path. We explored the huge trees called baobobs, so huge our giant AO Des Moines banner didn't even cover one side when we posed for photos in front of it. Our seven-foot-wide banner only covered about 1/3 of the tree trunk's side. It dwarfed us like a natural-grown building. We would stop alongside the road every once in a while to watch animal herds. My favorite were the giraffes who were completely different in the wild than zoo-kept giraffes I've seen. They run in an undulating movement rippling vertically through their body in one fluid running motion so completely graceful and breathtaking it made them seem a totally different creature from zoo giraffes.

There was a small town, really just a group of stores, where we would go to get supplies and connect to a cell tower. There wasn't a cell signal at our camp. A reliable signal was either over an hour into town or you could climb a hill near camp for a spotty cell signal with no data. A few friends made one trek up, returning with stories of poisonous snakes they had to avoid. That was the end of me considering climbing a hill for a cell signal. At least on the drive I could at least buy more booze and whatever food we needed without fear of a deadly snake bite hours from a hospital. One thing became crystal clear in South Africa: if you made a mistake, you were dead. There was no margin for error … don't mess with animals that can kill you, stay far away from snakes, and watch your step.

Even everyday tasks became dangerous. In the process of the our daily drive over to the lodge in virtually off-road conditions our low profile rental car tires lost a total of three hubcaps, only two of which we were able to recover. One night it blew a flat, fortunately not too far from the main lodge. We got the spare on but the nearest town didn't have a service station, so my two husbands and I headed out in the other direction towards the larger but further town. We were warned it was more sketchy, but we were able to find a place to fix the tire. We took the hour to shop at an open air grocery that was unnervingly foreign and alienating, but after search, yielded items we hadn't been able to find at our "local" shop an hour away. Not really how we wanted to spend vacation hours, but yet it was another cultural adventure augmented by the company of soccer family.

Towards the end of our time at Mapungabwe, a few of the guys in our group went out on the eco-trail in the four-wheel drive truck they had rented to do a serious safari excursion. When our kitchen staff heard this, they laughed heartily and said "Oh, so they want to die." It's times like this that it was difficult to tell if the women were being serious or just amused with the crazy Americans. As the afternoon wore on and the guys weren't back, I was starting to get a little concerned. When they finally returned they were excited but pretty pale as they came up to the lodge shouting about an elephant they'd seen on safari. They flipped open their video camera and began to tell the story of their near-death experience.

They'd been driving along the trail, came upon an elephant in the distance and simultaneously got stuck in a rut requiring four-wheel drive mode to escape. As the elephant approached, trumpeting with increasing aggression, the urgency in the video voice-over ramps quickly from "Check that out!" to "Time to go … Time to go, man. TIME TO GO. TIME TO GO TIME TO GO TIMETOGO!!" Off camera, the driver struggled in his panic, groping for the shifter on his right instead of the South African left. As he grabbed the left side shift, he knocked the vehicle out of four-wheel mode. The more he fought to get it back in proper gear and drive the closer the elephant got. I'm not an expert in elephant behavior, but the elephant, now perilously close to their vehicle, seemed confused why they were still there. In the few moments the elephant paused in disbelief, the truck finally got in proper gear and drove away from elephant smash zone, allowing our friends to return to us, and thankfully, turning our kitchen staff's comment from a doomed prophecy to a charming quip.

We went up to the confluence for the last sunset of our safari, flipping back and forth between the Bafana Bafana vs. France game and the Uruguay vs. Mexico match on the radio as we drove up to the lookout trail. We efficiently enjoyed the sunset, then raced back to the game. We gathered in the main room of the lodge to watch the rest of the match with a dozen or more people gathered around a TV smaller than our home set. After the game, Sean welcomed newly-initiated people into our travel group, giving out official member pins to people who were on their first official Kennedy Kwiakowski International Football Excursions trip. Nerdy (and awesome) enough to have an official pin and spreadsheet of games attended so we can compare our own personal win-tie-loss percentages and cap counts. I love this part of my travel family best of all.

23

Once More Into the Breach

We woke up before dawn to leave for the drive to the US vs. Algeria game. We packed up our hut, picked up Scott, and sleepily drove the completely dark 7 km road to the highway to meet the rest of our group. I was zoning out in the back seat with my husbands talking quietly in the front, when I was jolted awake by the guys shouting a stream of terrified expletives. I looked up, but all I could see was a grey wall off the side of the road. Struggling to make sense of what's happening in the fog of sleep, I realized the wall wasn't moving and was not, in fact, a wall but an elephant we almost hit coming around a corner in pre-dawn darkness. We stopped to allow it to move off our path. The elephant was right next to our car at the side of the road. Struggling to think rationally, once the fog of sleep had been vaporized by a surge of adrenaline. As much as I wanted to capture the moment, a camera flash in pitch black seemed like the stupidest thing I could have done. I stood next to the car watching this magnificent creature a few feet away from us in the darkness, quietly lumbering into the brush. It was one of the coolest experiences of my life ... luckily ending with us driving away sans elephant car crushing.

Dawn came and the long drive to Pretoria was underway. After our near miss with the elephant, the drive was uneventful but offered the rare opportunity to photo-op the Tropic of Capricorn sign on the side of the road. The sign was misspelled Tropic of Capricon, much to our amusement. We arrived in Pretoria and settled into the apartment Sean had found for us. It was a clean place with enough bedrooms for all of us to find a place to sleep and located walking distance from the stadium and pre-game festivities. After exploring our new place we dressed for the game and headed out for some pre-game drinking and festivities.

Doug and I stopped by the American Outlaws bar as the crowd gathered and were able to sneak in a food order before the kitchen was overwhelmed. The atmosphere was increasingly energized, and we were meeting people from all over the US. My favorite were a group of guys from Wyoming who all had cowboy hats and looked reasonably authentic wearing them. There were a few guys from Algeria, a splash of green in a sea of Americana, who seemed comfortable good naturedly risking their lives, brutally outnumbered among the Outlaws. Singing, chanting, and a passionate rendition of the Star Spangled Banner made for an electric atmosphere but as the bar became packed and beer supplies dwindled, we decided to move on to the bar where our friends were pre-gaming a few blocks away.

Our bar offered a welcome break from the amped up AO bar. Crazy hijinx to be had, but a little less overwhelming … there was cigar smoking, funneling beer through vuvuzelas, and face painting en masse … with just enough breathing room and beer to take the edge off. Hanging out with my friends with the glow of the third game on us trying to forget if things didn't go well this would be our last game with everyone together for the next four years. Squelching negativity, we enjoyed our pre-gaming almost too long leaving only thirty minutes before kickoff to head to the stadium.

We got to our seats in the corner of the stadium, did a quick banner hanging, and rocked the media whoring as the teams finished warm ups and the lineups took the field. The happiness and glow of the bar ebbed as each minute ticked off tied at zeros. Thrilling opportunities for us and frightening chances for Algeria … all meaningless without change on the scoreboard. Both teams wanted it, but no one could put in that fateful, crucial goal. Ninety minutes dripped away, torture creeping towards the final whistle and still no goal.

I panicked … a tie. We were going home. The anxious voice in my head screamed "NO! This isn't how it ends." The stadium announcer spoke confirming four minutes of stoppage time left. I vividly remember opening a very personal conversation with G-d. Jews aren't really freestyle prayers by nature. We have our proscribed prayers for various times of day or for things we say at different holidays, but I'm not really one to sit (kneel?) down and have a conversation with a higher power. But as desperation set in, I pleaded, "Please, four minutes for one goal. We just need one goal. One. Just please … give us one goal" until "just one goal" became my mantra.

No clouds parting or sunlight streaming in to spotlight our fates changing, but there was Donovan and Altidore streaking down the field and mounting a last ditch attempt at greatness. Out of the jaws of defeat there was one last chance for heroism. Donovan passed to Altidore who passed back to Donovan who shot, hitting the post and leveling our hopes on the ricochet. The rebound fires back and Donovan strikes it into the net … launching the most epic, world-wide goal celebration ever performed by American soccer fans around the globe. An explosion of sound as the stadium erupted in jubilation. We screamed, jumping around and hugging each other in unbridled sheer joy.

But wait … minutes left. How many have passed? If we allowed Algeria to tie, we would never recover. We had to win. We must win. Each second took a minute, each minute an hour, but somehow time expired. Victory! We were through! We had won our group for the first time since 1930. Pandemonium. Security was too busy celebrating to care about Americans pouring out of the stands to run up to the boards surrounding the field. I went with the crowd and stood at the field edge celebrating with my fellow fans. The players made their victory lap. Seeing us at the boards, Jozy Altidore broke off from the group and ran over to us. He was one of my favorite players, and in my excitement, I stretched out my arms and screamed "JOZY!" Miraculously, one of my fantasies come true, I watched him jump the ad boards, ran directly to me, and wrapped me in his huge arms. Ecstasy … for about 1.7 seconds of a one-on-one celebration with my hero. Then I felt the crowd crushing in behind me with enough force to make me think, "Oh no. My mother was right. I'm going to die in a soccer stadium." This realization quickly followed by "… in Jozy Altidore's arms" as a somewhat irrational acceptance of my fate. Fortunately, my over-dramatized version of my imagined poetic demise never came to fruition as security rushed in and pulled Jozy away from me and the crowd, allowing oxygen to once again fill my lungs and adrenaline to surge back into my limbs. I'm not sure I'd believe this really happened were it not captured on Mike's video cam and uploaded to YouTube. There in his Jozy melee video was my shocking red hair clearly documented in the highest high of a stadium experience for me.

It quickly crashed into one of the worst experiences of my soccer supporting life. I returned to my friends, I saw stadium security people and friends huddled around a body lying on the ground. As I got close, I saw it was Kaela … she'd been knocked over, hit her neck on a seat arm and was in a great deal of pain. It took an agonizingly long time for the stadium to get an ambulance over to us to finally take her to the hospital. Fortunately, South Africa offered quality, affordable healthcare. She had to wear a neck brace for the rest of the World Cup and remained in pain much longer. Considering how bad it could have been, we were relieved there was not a more permanent reminder of the night our fates turned in "injury" time.

The celebration at the stadium continued at full strength for almost an hour after the game ended with singing and photos with the Americans and Algerians. We stayed inside the stadium as long as they would let us and then spilled out into the concourse for more celebration. We ran into a guy we'd sold a scarf to a couple weeks prior. He had arrived at the airport bound for South Africa with nothing to show his support of the US team. We took pity on him and sold him one of our scarves. Never expected to see him again, yet here he was proving what a small world Americans at the World Cup can be.

We made our way back to the biergarten-style bar where we'd met our friends for the pre-game and basked in the glory of our win. I smoked a cigar, drank more beer, and was deeply enjoying the moment, when Doug said, "I think that's Marcelo Balboa."

I sat up and whipped around. "Where?"

"There, at the bar," he said with guarded excitement.

Standing by himself was former USMNT captain, Hall of Famer, Marcelo Balboa just chilling out at the bar and watching the celebration. We walked over, said hello, and chatted with him about US Soccer history and his thoughts on the US in the World Cup. He seemed to enjoy hanging out with the fans, snapping photos with people who recognized him. It was low key with few people recognizing him in a bar full of soccer fans … we guessed most of the people at the bar were too young to remember Balboa's US Soccer days. We expected South Africa to be like Korea where only the nerdiest of nerdy fans would commit to travel. As it turned out, in addition to the nerds, there were many new supporters who decided to come to South Africa as their first World Cup, some with little or no game experience back in the States. It was fun watching the old guard talk to some of the newer people. The Wyoming boys in cowboy hats spent an hour talking to a few of our travel buddies about our adventures. They left the conversation saying they were going to do the same thing … every World Cup from here on out. The night ended a really cool mix of old school and new fans … and Marcelo Balboa.

24

Joburg Tourism

With our place in the second round secure, we were able to spend some time sightseeing around Johannesburg. We went exploring with Prairie and Mike, checking out the area in and around Soweto and shopping for souvenirs. Cultural mix-ups made finding Soweto more tricky than anticipated. South Africans call traffic lights "robots" which is pronounced more like "r'but," but even once we solved that riddle, we were still getting lost. We finally realized turn directions are given cumulatively in Joburg. For instance, "Go to the first robot, turn right, then left at the third robot." Following these directions in South Africa, you turn right at the first light, then skip one light and turn left ... because that's the third light. We finally figured it out after getting closer and closer to where we needed to go, but persistently overshooting the destination.

Eventually, we found Soweto and watched some rec soccer in front of a church. We talked to local artists and crafters selling their goods on the church square. There were photo-op-worthy newspapers posted on light posts which proclaimed "Landon Seals the Deal." We stopped by Vilakazi Street, the only street in the world where two Noble Prize winners grew up (Mandela and Tutu), and peeked at the Mandela House Museum, although it was too late in the day to go through it. There were murals on walls and on the giant water towers down the road. It was starkly beautiful, and made me look forward to coming back with Ayanda and Peterson.

Another day off was spent at the Johannesburg Zoo with Joey's kids. They were happy to show us around the zoo, and talk about the various animals there. Many of the animals were from the region and were new to us, plus the enclosures were huge giving more of an "in the wild" feeling. The zoo had a no-nonsense brand of South African humor, with signs like "Do not throw anything at the crocodiles or you will have to retrieve it." We finally got to see the lions we had been hearing from the B&B. While we watched them, my mom and kids called from Boston and one of the lions let out an impressive roar so loud I think my mother feared for my life momentarily. It was an impressive noise, in person or thousands of miles away by phone. Sometimes I think our best experiences of local culture happen almost as if by accident.

The zoo trip started as a thank you to our host for providing extras like helping us arrange with a street artist to make a US Soccer shield in the style of South African found metal street art. We had seen street artists weave wire, beads, and bits of tin cans into cool sculptural pieces, but nothing that really caught our attention. I wanted our art piece from the trip to be commissioned by a street artist but a representation of US Soccer in this found materials style. Joey agreed to take us into the shopping district and navigate the street artists and help negotiate a reasonable price. It was a fun side adventure, talking to artists and arranging the piece, which ended up even better than I imagined, and hangs next to our bed, so I wake up to the US Soccer crest every morning.

25

Soweto Inner Sanctum

We were soon headed back to Rustenburg for our second round match. We stopped along the way there for a photo-op of Kaela in her neck brace in front of the "Phokeng Trauma Center" The foreign languages turned English curse words meme never gets old for us.

On the flip side of seriousness, we stopped to hand out some soccer balls from Little Feet. LF is a charity that sells quality soccer balls and for every ball sold, they give away a ball to children in need. We drove through run down neighborhoods on the hunt for children playing. When we found them, we'd stop and hand them a soccer ball. Watching the stunned looks on their faces turn to pure joy as they realized we didn't want the ball back was an amazing experience for us, making the real gift ours to receive.

We met up at a local butchery business with grilling out back. We bought our meat and Doug grilled it while I procured beers and a free vuvuzela from a beer vendor who'd set up for the occasion. The place was swarming with Americans who broke into song at the drop of a hat, creating a raucous environment for our warm up to the match. So much red, white and blue, with eagles, explosions, and all sorts of Americana, it was hard to tell one person from the next, as their supporter fashion blended into one mass of patriotism, particularly as we all marched into the stadium together, singing in unison.

If only we could have won the game on passionate fans alone, but the curse of Ghana stayed with us. When the lineup came out, we were surprised to see Rico Clark listed, as he hadn't been playing well. Our concerns were validated in the 5th minute, when Clark got beat in the midfield and Ghana went up 1-0. We were heartbroken and frustrated, but had some hope in the 2nd half when Dempsey got fouled in the penalty area, and Donovan was able to equalize with the PK. We were feeling so hopeful when the game went into extra time, but our hopes were dashed three minutes in, when Ghana scored and we were sent home. This was the game that taught me how important coaching decisions are. I believe in my heart of hearts the 2010 USMNT team could have gone so much further save that one coaching decision to play Clark. It was a painful way to learn how important coaching is at the highest level of soccer.

It was awful to think we were so close from making it to the third round, particularly as you saw the teams we would have faced, and likely would have beaten, had we advanced. We were so close, but small mistakes send teams home from the World Cup. My parents' chipper attitude "Hey! At least you'll be home to get the kids on time!" was not at all helpful either. I doubt my parents knew how much temporary disgust I had for them wishing the US to lose just so we would be home on our scheduled flight. Once you've arranged your entire life around the World Cup schedule, from family planning and house purchases to career aspirations, getting home from a World Cup on time is no consolation in the face of the lost potential of an advancement that shoulda coulda woulda.

Even though the games were over, we still had our tour of Soweto to look forward to and/or be nervous about. We were getting mixed reviews on whether or not it was reasonably safe to go into Soweto with our new friends. Responses ranged from "It might be an okay idea" to "Well, I suppose if you want to die." At breakfast, the day after the Ghana game, we met a couple from Johannesburg and hit it off with them, chatting about life in South Africa. We broached the subject of the Soweto tour with them, and they seemed a little hesitant to endorse the idea until they asked more about our tour guides. When we mentioned the quest was for Zulu beer, they immediately relaxed and said "Oh, if you're with the Zulus, you'll be fine." We weren't sure exactly what that meant, and they wouldn't explain beyond "Zulus are respected." Good enough for us. Late that afternoon we headed off to Soweto, finding it much quicker now knowing the rules of South African style turn by turn directions.

We met the guys in the square just off Vilakazi Street as the sun was setting, trying to remain calm that we were in Soweto as darkness approached. Peterson and Ayanda had brought their friend Mpho with them, who was an even taller, muscular guy who further put our minds at ease with the thought that the only thing better than Zulu tour guides would be huge Zulu tour guides. They began telling us stories of Apartheid and South African history. We stood where the Soweto Uprising occurred on June 16, 1976, as our friends told us about the uprising and Hector Pieterson, one of the high school students who was shot by police while protesting the Apartheid practice of teaching Afrikaans in schools. Students protested the change, which had been instituted in 1974, with non-violent marches of an estimated 20,000 students in the streets of Soweto. Police started shooting student protesters, killing between 176-700 people. There is a famous image of Hector, wounded and dying, carried through the streets of Johannesburg in Mbuyisa Makhubo's arms to a clinic two miles away. That photograph was made into a sculpture in the memorial courtyard where we stood listening to stories of Apartheid and how Mpho's father had been imprisoned with little provocation. The uprising was a turning point in Apartheid, galvanizing the masses against white rule. It was inspiring, standing there and hearing first and second hand stories of South African history.

Once we finished exploring the courtyard, we headed over to meet Mpho's family, which was closer to where we could buy Zulu beer. We pulled our rental car into the fenced area around their small but inviting home. His mother came out to greet us, her face warm and glowing. We presented her younger kids with a Little Feet soccer ball, and we were invited inside to meet the family. We felt so welcomed, it was a necessary reminder when Peterson and Ayanda asked if we'd locked the car. We hadn't, since it was inside their gated yard, and we weren't staying long. "Lock it" was the response from our guides. Well, alright then … in Soweto, you may feel warmth and love, but still … lock the car.

After chatting with Mpho's family for a bit we said goodbye and walked over to purchase Zulu beer. We walked down the street not feeling too unsafe surrounded by houses that were certainly poor, but not frighteningly so. We turned down a smaller street, spiking anxiety just a bit as the street narrowed and darkened. Turning down an alley, I began to think if we somehow lost our hosts, we would be lost forever, possibly never to be found again, but we'd irrevocably committed to the beer quest, and fortunately soon found the back door entrance to our goal.

As I write this, I have been chatting online with Peterson, who was surprised I remember so much from that night. It was so emotionally charged, so profoundly terrifying and interesting, it will be forever burned in my memory. We stepped into this small room with cardboard milk cartons stacked to almost the ceiling and two men sitting in lawn chairs, waiting to take our money for the cartons. Not milk at all, but brewed Zulu beer, in some cases bubbling slightly out the top of the carton. The room was dimly lit and seemed better suited for back alley betting or drug dealing. This was certainly an experience you would never find in any guide book. The two men who were taking money were happy enough to pose for a photo with us, then we purchased our beer in milk's clothing and stepped back into the night.

Our next stop was a South African braai, where you can buy meat from a butcher, then walk around back and grill it and hang out and socialize. As we pulled up, Peterson and Ayanda explained this was a well known part of Soweto in the black community but most white people never came there. We had a side conversation about how Soweto had earned its nasty reputation, when we felt we were welcomed there. They explained "If you're white, and come to Soweto with an attitude you're at risk, nervously rolling up your windows and very defensive, people become upset you are treating them that way. But if you come openly, and want to meet people, it's different. Then people will respect you back." (And I thought, "but still, lock your car.") They warned us because white people never came this deep into Soweto, we should be prepared for stares from everyone. We were both wearing our US Soccer navy track jackets with bright white USA letters. We stood out like a beacon in the night.

We went to the counter and Ayanda tried to order meat. After a bit of back and forth discussion, the shop keeper produced what we were looking for. Ayanda explained she didn't speak the same languages he did, so they had to work out what he wanted with a little more effort. Amazing. I knew there were eleven official languages spoken in South Africa, but to come up against a language barrier in the middle of the city was shocking to me. Obviously they were able to work it out, but still, it was impressive to have such diverse culture integrated into one city. With meat and beer cups purchased, we headed around back to the grilling and socializing.

I may never know what it's like to be a celebrity, but I imagine it's something very much like the experience of being two white Americans at the World Cup in a part of South Africa white people just don't see. The guy working the grill was a man later in middle age, who was so excited to meet us it bordered on awkward. He was welcoming, greeting us and asking us to take photos with him. He grilled our meat, chatting away with us, trying to communicate how he excited and happy he was in our presence. There were people who glared and people who smiled, but there were very few people who did not take overt notice of our visit. We grilled and chatted, and when the meat was cooked, we took it to a table and poured Zulu "Joburg Beer" into red Solo cups. We ate our meat and drank our beer with our friends, as if we'd known each other forever and this was just another weekend hanging out at the braai.

Only this was no ordinary beer. We were warned it was very strong, but we brushed those warnings off. We'd just spent three weeks in training, drinking more than we could count … all day, every day. There would be no drink that could beat us now.

"Ha!" said Joburg Beer. "You think you can handle this?"

Printed on the side of every carton of Joburg Beer is a label taking up the entire carton. It says, in a font I believe is approximately 57 point san serif, "DO NOT DRINK AND WALK ALONG THE ROAD. YOU MAY BE KILLED." Joburg Beer ain't nuthin' to mess with friends. That warning label is not a joke. Doug got through about half a cup and handed it to me, saying, "I have to drive, there's no way I can finish this." First of all, it's not filtered, so it's like drinking the most delicious sourdough bread in the world. The flavor was wonderful, but oh my … the punch of the alcohol hits you with every sip, every gulp.

Even with our Herculean tolerance, we feel ourselves becoming more and more drunk with every swig. Every delicious drink brings you closer to oblivion by leaps. I finished my cup and the rest of Doug's, and felt like I'd drunk a six pack ... fast. It was the most serious thing I've ever had to drink. I completely believe you should not drink and walk. Forget about driving. You should take extreme caution drinking and WALKING. It was the perfect end to our time in South Africa.

The next day, we said goodbye to our hosts, and embarked on the long flight back to the US. There's nothing that takes away the pain of another World Cup ending. You know there's more games coming and another World Cup four years later, but the sadness of leaving a wonderful culture behind, especially one so lovely as South Africa, is profound. We have had amazing experiences in diverse cultures. We'd gotten handmade soccer street art with the help of our host. We had stories and photos but the experiences are irreplaceable and we were missing them even before we left.

26

A Whole Other Level

We'd seen things. The rise and fall of Sam's Army. The birth of American Outlaws. A World Cup halfway around the world, that drew more Americans than any other traveling fan base. How long could America sustain this growth? The best salve on my end of World Cup wounds was hearing that American Outlaws Des Moines had become an official chapter and had elected me President. My funny little chapter no longer existed for my own amusement ... we were legit, the 38th chapter of AO. It blew my mind that soccer was big enough for the Des Moines chapter to be an actual thing.

We traveled to Chicago for the US vs. Poland game and the two Korea babies finally met. The Flannigan baby and my baby bump hung out at the tailgate, just as we'd planned when they were tiny. The girls ran around the tailgate like they owned it (because they basically did). My son joined the kick around, excited to play with "big kids" who tolerated his intervention in their tailgate. It seemed like we were entering a new era, where soccer was normal and people everywhere were looking to join our merry band of tailgating rabble rousers. The weather was gorgeous and the day was idyllic from the dream tailgate through the game, where Aviva expressed more than a passing interest in the game, that is, between socializing and crafting things out of her program.

Further amping up soccer supporter culture in America, AO announced the AO Rally in Las Vegas on March 4th and 5th of 2011.

For $199 you got two days in a Vegas hotel with a few of soccer's craziest fans, along with Grant Wahl of Sports Illustrated, former USMNT player and soccer commentator Alexi Lalas, as well as reps from event sponsors Fox Soccer, Golazo, and Parlaid Clothing. With a trip already planned to Tennessee for later in March, and $200 to NOT see a game seemed like more than I needed to spend at first, but soon the rationalization started. It could be really cool … I'd hate to miss the inaugural year. By then, I was getting serious about writing this book, and I started to obsess about what this rally could mean in the history of supporter culture. In no time I'd rationalized that for under $500 it was on. Unfortunately, a Nascar race in Vegas meant all the direct flights between Des Moines and Vegas were booked or crazy expensive. Now I was stewing because (of course) I'd already decided to go and the budget restriction was now just an annoying complication in my need to bring my plans to fruition. I looked at which chapters were closest to Vegas and emailed AO LA on a whim, not knowing a single person there, asked if they had people driving. I promised to be a more interesting travel buddy than "mom from Iowa" sounded. John Santos called me, said there were people going to Rally, and there was room in their car. He sounded like a nice guy who would probably get me from LA to Vegas and back safely so I booked my flight and commenced worry about how good a character judge one could be by phone. But hey, we were all soccer fans … it seemed like a crazy idea but not one that was terribly dangerous.

I landed and the AO LA guys met me at the airport, and off we went to Las Vegas. I was with John and the Rodriguez brothers, Carlos and Richard, three Mexican-Americans who proudly support the US team. They turned out to be the nicest guys, and the trip passed quickly as we talked games, national loyalties for Mexican-Americans, and US Soccer history. The scenery was a warm, welcome change of pace from Iowa winter, and along the way they introduced me to the wonders of In-and-Out Burger. We got to the Rally just in time to check in before the night's activities. My roommate was Amy Swearigen, a woman from Kansas City, currently in Seattle, on her way back to KC. She was funny and smart, and charming in her sarcasm … a fine match for my first stranger roommate since college.

The Rally only got better from there. Alexi Lalas' keynote had me enthralled on the history of US Soccer and his experience traveling with the team in the 90s … back when US Soccer lapel pins on blazers were the big branding effort of the team. No one knew who they were except this tiny group of fans that would come out for games. He was describing my experience as a fan watching things change over the years, only from a player's perspective. It was validating to hear someone who played at the highest level having a parallel experience to us as fans. He integrated the US Soccer family … not just "us" fans following "them" players, but all experiencing this thing together. A decade later collectively looking back and reminiscing "Hey, remember back in the day when no one knew what soccer was? Those were crazy times." Lalas was entirely approachable, hanging out in the bar and the conference for the rest of the weekend, getting to know fans and sharing stories with us.

Grant Wahl, a writer for Sports Illustrated, related the experience of fighting his way to a full time position writing about soccer for a mainstream publication. Additionally, Grant had started a campaign for FIFA President in a tongue in cheek protest of FIFA corruption, and how the positions within soccer's highest governing body were technically elected, but functionally appropriated through FIFA politics. I was fascinated, listening to him talk about being a soccer writer, clinging to every word he said about the joys of working full time in soccer writing as an inspiration for finishing my writing projects.

I got the most out of those speeches and conversations with fellow supporters but the meat of the weekend was about American Outlaws and the strides they had made as a fast growing organization. Justin Brunken, Corey Donahoo, and others from AO National talked history of AO, where they saw it going, plans for travel packages, including World Cup travel charters. It was fun, watching these guys who seemed like kids when they started this group stepping into the spotlight and talking about their project growing up. I thought more in depth about AO's growth pattern, how Sam's Army had risen quickly then crashed and burned, unable to sustain itself under the weight of so many members' demands. I watched American Outlaws growth with guarded optimism I won't see history repeat itself.

Golazo Energy, a soccer-specific energy drink from the Pacific Northwest had a cell phone scavenger hunt as part of their sponsorship. Participants had to get photos of Golazo Energy with various Vegas landmarks and stereotypes. The winner would get two tickets to the next USA vs. Mexico game. Further opportunity to justify trip expenses! No way I was going to let someone else win those tickets. I relentlessly chased down taxi cab drivers, card flipping girl pushers, casino characters, and Vegas landmarks until I'd completed almost every task on the list, including a bonus stop at the Hoover Dam on our way back to LA. The other attendees were no match for my obsessive competitive drive for free soccer tickets, paying our way to USA vs. Mexico in Philadelphia in August.

My kinship with AO Rally people flourished through Facebook friendships and future games. I basked in rally happiness on the drive back via my first Hoover Dam experience, while getting to know my AO LA brothers a little better. We talked about the new Arizona immigration laws, and American and Mexican cultural differences. The whole trip was worth everything I spent getting there and then some. I keep waiting for them to host Rally 2.0, but so far, AO Rally was a one-off event.

27

Ch-Ch-Ch-Ch-Changes

2011 a year chock full of changes. It started with the house, one we'd been searching for since 2006. The home we'd purchased in 1996 with a 3-5 year plan of moving back East was five years past getting on my nerves. I'd been complaining about my fruitless house search to a new acquaintance at a Central Iowa Bloggers meeting, when she replied the exact dream home I sought was for sale right now in her neighborhood. Through the contrived way Des Moines real estate is listed her neighborhood, River Bend, had been completely off our radar. I took down the address and stopped by that night when my December retail work day ended at 9 PM. I stood on the front lawn peering through darkness at the massive three story Victorian in front of me, shining my cell phone flash light up the façade. Instant love before ever setting foot inside. I called the listing agent to show us the house, sure it was meant for me. I didn't realize was it would take 53 weeks of back and forth frustration with the seller's bank short sale department to possess my Victorian beauty.

We made our offer, listed our house for sale and started making plans for the huge renovation project before us. After four months of constantly cleaning our house for showings without a single offer, we turned our house into a rental property and had it rented in short order. We naively thought we'd be able to close in 30-60 days, and were caught off guard a couple weeks out from when we had to be out of our house with no closing in sight. Their bank lost paperwork, bumbling around with our full value of their appraisal offer, for delaying the process at every turn. We became increasingly convinced that the seller's bank was trying to delay the sale until they could foreclose on the property and collect the mortgage insurance they had taken out on the mortgage without the homeowner's knowledge. The national news was full of stories of people getting forced into foreclosure by big banking, but for most of 2011, we were living it from the purchaser side.

We'd started looking for apartments when I got a message from the seller who'd heard though mutual friends that we were in a bind. They were so grateful we were sticking with the process they offered us to live in the house rent free until closing in exchange for covering utility bills and lawn care. Worst case scenario, she said, if the deal fell through, we could stay until the Sherriff evicted us, since we were their last hope of staying out of foreclosure. It seemed like a reasonable gamble, so we moved in, and became professional squatters for the next six and a half months, perpetually 30-45 days away from closing.

Moving into the Hatton House brought my whole life into focus. Suddenly it was clear there were things making me abundantly happy (the house, the kids, soccer) and things sucking the energy from my life (my store). There was way too much to do for one woman, and I was missing out on the life I'd envisioned for myself. I got to join the family in Nashville for the game versus Paraguay, but missing the subsequent USWNT game with Doug and the kids really got to me. I was so happy in our house I wanted to spend all my time working on it without constantly thinking about how I should be spending more time at the store. I had tried to sell the store but each of the three times I'd gotten into the process, the deal had fallen through and the buyer had backed out. I woke up one morning after about two weeks in the house, and told my husband it was time to close the store. I could move the services portion of it back into the house, but the retail side had to go. Moving and changing careers … all in one month.

The decision making was gut wrenching but the plan execution was much easier. I started to sell down my inventory, and prepared to close down after the holiday season. When my landlord got into trouble with their bank and started making life difficult for us renters, I moved our close to the end of July thinking I would move home and just do private shows and office hours at the house for holiday shopping. My decision was reinforced when my sister became ill and was hospitalized for several weeks of late June and July. I was able to spend a few days with her, but as my parents aged and my sister was ill, I felt the pull to do more for my family than an entrepreneurial life allowed. The stepped up closing schedule meant I'd have more time with the kids for their summer break, but it was a tight timeline.

Although not so tight I stopped going to games. The Tennessee match was fantastic fun, seeing a city I've never seen before embrace US Soccer with passion. The pregame bar was great fun, with high backed banquettes that people were standing on as we sang and got fired up for the match. Nashville was a game of firsts, with the kids inaugural dress up as Betsy Ross and Uncle Sam. Raphael read for the first time on the morning of the game, reading "eggs and pancakes" from the hotel breakfast menu. At the game, I met one of my all time favorite stadium security guys, "Big Kenny." Kenny and another guard wanted me to stop standing on a seat to lead the section, concerned I'd fall or break the seat. I told him, "If I break the seat, I'll pay for it. I came here from Des Moines to have a good time."

"You came from Des Moines? Girl, you knock yourself out." Kenny said. Most stadium security doesn't care what your story is, and they'll refuse to have any fun with you. Not Big Kenny. Later in the game I was standing in the front section and he came down to clear the walkway. He said to the people in the front section, "People you need to make some room for this lady, she came a long way to see this game." Love it. Nashville gave us a great day of partying before a great match environment, reinforcing that our new 10 hour drive limit was well worth the trip.

In July, Doug and I went up to Detroit for the Gold Cup match against Canada, while our kids partied it up with their Grandparents. It was the first time I'd been to a soccer game in an indoor stadium, and our first game with the new "Midwest Mama" stadium flag. Doug and I have always been fans of giant American flags that cover the supporters' section at soccer games during the National anthem and after goals are scored. Stadium flags look cool, and I had developed a weird superstition that US Soccer only played well when A) there was a stadium flag at the game and B) I was within arms' reach of it. Trouble was, the two flags among supporters were the Big Ass Flag (a 30x60' flag) in New Jersey or Boston, and the Baby Ass Flag (a 20x30' flag) also living on the East Coast. We were tired of no one bringing the flags out to the Midwest, where we were most likely able to attend matches. If we took up donations I figured we could save up for a flag and never have to rely on outside forces to get my good luck juju on. I started to stalk giant flags on Ebay, and when one popped up for $200 less than any other flag I'd seen, I pounced, despite being significantly short donations to cover the entire amount. We'd decided after suffering repeated frustration of no one bothering to bring one it was worth chipping in a couple hundred bucks to cover the cost of having one at our beck and call. The flag arrived at my store, and my kids and I unrolled it in all its glory, whopping it up at the awesomeness of our newest exhibit of extreme soccer passion. Glorious: 30 feet of flag unrolled across tables in the event space of my store. The only thing left to do was name it. We didn't want to continue the "names with curse words" thread. I wasn't offended, but it seemed less appropriate to have a Midwestern flag named with "stadium language." A twitter conversation lead us to the spin on the Big/Baby direction to a Mama flag in the Midwest, and the Midwest Mama was born.

Driving into Detroit just in time to make the tifo drop off at the stadium, we embarked on our first real tifo set up of positioning the flag in the section, making sure it wouldn't block aisles when it was unfurled. Giddy, we did the test run with two of us running the corners up to see how it looked over the section. Beautiful thing, our sparkling clean, not yet anointed with beer or face paint flag spread out over a couple hundred seats. We headed back to the pre-party bar, already feeling like we were set up for a great day.

Waiting for food at the grill outside the bar, rumor spread through the crowd Alexi Lalas had arrived and was inside the bar. Doug had played at a college camp with Alexi many years prior, and when I met Lalas at Rally, Doug mentioned it would be cool to see him again. We traipsed into the bar, but were dismayed to see young fans swarming around Lalas like ants on a fresh sugar cube. There was no way we wanted to postpone food long enough to make it through the fray, but we didn't have to make that call as Lalas looked up through the crowd and saw me, and said one of the more awesome sentences I've heard in my life: "Tanya! I was hoping you'd be here!" Pretty sure I heard angels singing as the sea of 20- and young 30-something fans parted and I was able to walk right up to the table. I re-introduced my husband, who seemed half-amused and half-impressed at my feat of soccer star stalking, to Alexi Lalas. It marked the last time I cared about what "those" young upstart fans thought about me, middle-aged-mom-of-two-kids at "their party." Yeah, kids. This is my party, and you're always welcome, just try not to be snotty about how young and fabulous you think you are, m'kay? Made my whole freaking trip, that Alexi Lalas.

The game just continued my weekend getaway love affair with US Soccer. We thought there would be a good sized Canadian crowd, with the border not far from the stadium. But the crowd was pleasantly pro-American and being indoors meant it was air conditioned and very loud. The game was a beauty, from the first time I saw my flag unfurl over a crowd for the anthem to the goals by two of my favorite players, Dempsey and Altidore, to the tremendous atmosphere: happiness from start to finish.

The following week, we took the kids to see US vs. Guadeloupe at Kansas City, a far more forgiving three hour drive away. Kansas City has always been a blessing and a curse for us. So close we never want to deal with getting a hotel room, which means we typically miss their epic night before parties. Particularly right on the heels of the trip to Detroit, we did not need to be burning vacation or hotel money on a midweek game. We rolled into the stadium parking complex just as the tailgate was getting started. Sun shining perfection was wonderful for the tailgate, but had no impact on our players. Dempsey had the worst game of his career missing impossible to miss goals all day long. Luckily, Altidore had put USMNT up 1-0 in the 9th minute, but that was the end of our joy for the day, the rest of the game could easily be called "Agony of Dempsey".

By the time I closed my store in early August I'd suffered weeks of soul crushing fatigue. My work relationship turned bad didn't make it any easier to break off the once rosy love affair with the store I had started. My customers would come in and tell me how sad they were we were closing which, while sweet, only made things worse. As if I was trying to get a toxic significant other out of my life, but all my besties kept telling me how much they loved him. By the time the final auction closed, I was desperate for a change of scenery. I got in my car the next day and started driving East with my kids. The longer I drove, the better I felt. Before I ever got to a soccer game, visiting old friends members of our soccer family helped start forming a vision for what my life could look like post-store ownership. We bolted across the Midwest to Pittsburgh with very few friends available to visit before Pennsylvania. From there we jumped from friend to friend: meeting up with college buddies, eating at high school friend Jesse's restaurant, staying with my high school boss and forever mentor Marina's house, and stopping to stay at Kaela and Tai's home for wayward soccer travelers before getting to my parent's house in Boston for a break before continuing on to the cabin in New Hampshire.

It was in the sun splashed mountain ranges of western Pennsylvania as my highway snaked through ravines that my Twitter feed erupted with the news US Soccer had hired Jürgen Klinsmann to be our coach. All things were perfect in the world ... my dream coach finally hired. Still bitter he hadn't been our coach for the 2010 World Cup, his hiring only added to the sensation that everything was going to turn out OK. It made me drive with extra vigilance for fear things couldn't possibly be so right without me driving off the cliff ruining everything in a horrifying fireball. I'm optimistic until everything gets too perfect and I find myself looking around every corner for lurking impending doom. I wonder if it's part of being Jewish ... the sinking sensation things can't possibly work out well in the end (could they?)

We stayed at my parents' cabin in New Hampshire for several days, enjoying some time off the road and in the White Mountains. It was tough leaving the idyllic lake house and face the hundreds of miles we had ahead of us, but the next destination was tantalizing: the US vs. Mexico rivalry in Philadelphia. Always a "friendly" in name only, since every US Soccer supporter knows there are no friendlies with Mexico. We spent too much time visiting with family and arrived at the field a bit later than we expected and missed the chance to bring in our banner for the tifo set up by minutes, sad after carrying the banner cross country. Nevertheless, there we were. Hours before kickoff at a US vs. Mexico tailgate not really knowing anyone. The kids were sick of sitting in the car, so we set out for adventure walking the tailgate. I watched as my passionate soccer fan kids became increasingly frustrated no one was singing at the tailgate. It was very low key compared to Midwest tailgates, perhaps Easterners were too cool to start singing before the beer is really flowing. Whatever the reason my kids were not having it. Aviva marched up to a group of guys from New Jersey and shouted full of eight year old fury, "Hey, why aren't you guys singing?"

They looked bewildered, so she continued, "C'mon you guys!" and started to sing, shaming the tailgaters into singing along with her. My heart filled with joy at my mini capo (capo is soccer supporter for song/ chant leader), getting the crowd warmed up, as she collected high fives from the guys and we went further on down the row of tailgaters.

Raphael was supremely jealous his sister had stolen the show. He begged for his turn at a tailgate full of strangers. My son, barely four years old, desperate to lead a chant with me seeking a group that wouldn't let him fall flat. Scanning the tailgate I found a merciful looking group tailgating behind a giant white van. They appeared to be having fun, so I gambled they'd play along with my son's capo dreams. My bet paid huge dividends as we were about to meet the American Outlaws of Richmond, Virginia.

My son strutted up to them and with gusto started singing "Everywhere We Go." The faces of our instant friends at AO RVA lit up when they realized the chants were coming from my little boy. They followed along in happy fervor. When he finished, he collected not only high fives, but an honorary AO RVA membership, complete with t-shirt and drinks. We stayed and chatted with them, meeting Richard, Brian, Pedro, and the RVA members who would forever more be a part of our soccer family. Their chapter remains one of my favorites, with three years of meeting at games, tailgating, and experiencing their friendly outreach to soccer fans and casual bystanders alike. They have also produced one of the scarves I could not resist, "In Y'all We Trust." Just another great organization helping me go broke $20 at a time.

The tailgate was wonderful, and for me, it was a huge thrill to miraculously catch my hero Jürgen Klinsmann's first game at the helm of USMNT. His lineup was a mix of old school USMNTers like Bocanegra and Cherundolo juxtaposed with newer guys like Fiscal and Castillo's first cap. An interesting feeling out of our roster did not score him his first victory over Mexico, who scored in the 17th minute before allowing USMNT to tie on a 73rd minute equalizer by Robbie Rogers. Rogers' goal was later made famous when he came out as the first openly gay player in MLS. Many chances for the US to win but we were left to seek satisfaction in optimistic baby steps that we tied the Mexican team who had beaten us in the Gold Cup final less than two months earlier.

We didn't really have a plan for when to return to Iowa, since my free spirit loves the flexibility of road tripping, but the school year was breathing down my neck. I decided we could spend a few more days visiting my hometown friends before catching the Philadelphia Union game on our way home three days later. I love living in Iowa but it's difficult leaving behind the Jersey world that's still more familiar to me. My childhood friends, Mark (met in 7th grade Jazz Band, currently in Brooklyn) and Nicole (met in Kindergarten, currently in central Jersey) claim they see me more than they see each other but it doesn't dull the isolation I feel living in Iowa. At least my time with them feels sanctified by the effort it takes to achieve our often brief visits, and I'm grateful when soccer "forces" three unstructured New York metro days.

Nicole was kind enough to let us set up camp in her New Jersey home with her husband and daughter, giving us a jumping off point around an hour outside New York City. I booked time with Mark and his son in at the Metropolitan Museum of Art. After 45 minutes of MoMA playground, the kids were drenched in sweat, ready to go inside for a cool down. Our mini docents walked through the galleries examining sculptures and paintings, architectural pieces and stained glass. We talked about art history as I caught up with Mark and enjoyed being New Yorkers by association. Perfect day for me watching my kids on their NYC road-not-traveled walking the Met getting their city grove on. Yes, I love Iowa, but my impractical heart yearns for the ridiculously expensive but energetically alluring NYC metro life of my childhood.

The day finally arrived when we had to start driving back to Des Moines. Car packed, we headed to Philly and their not-so-nice part of town stadium. I hoped the ridiculous amount of money we paid to park would offer some protection for our fully loaded car. Our seats were in the corner near the Union supporters known as the Sons of Ben. (How am I just now realizing that the logical abbreviation for the Union is "PU" and their fans are SOBs?) We sat on their side for the first half and enjoyed their singing, but it wasn't enough to hold us in our seats once we got word our friends Tony and Misel were in attendance with their daughters. At halftime, we walked over to spend the second half catching up on Tony's latest adventures refereeing and traveling while watching the Union battle it out with FC Dallas to a 2-2 tie. Even at a tie for a team I didn't care about, we had a blast watching MLS and experiencing a new city's supporter culture. The groundwork was laid for the following summer's MLS Roadtrip.

28

Eurotrip 2011

As my 30s drew to a close I struggled to come up with some big, earth-shattering idea of how to mark the end of another decade. I thought about training for a Fall marathon but was so focused on closing my store and our new old house I didn't start training early enough. I couldn't reopen my store until we closed the house purchase and I couldn't work on the house until we closed, nor did I want to unpack everything and jinx the purchase. Frustrated and restless when US Soccer announced the European friendlies for November 2011 the same week my parents asked what I wanted for my birthday present ... a beautiful plan emerged. My parents funded the trip and I plotted how to get as much out of Europe as I could in 10 days.

Two weeks before I left our financing fell through on the house when the appraisal came back stating the roof, foundation, boiler, and exterior paint weren't in good enough condition. In a panic, we tore into everything but the roof, working almost around the clock for over a week, rebuilding the foundation with the help of neighborhood volunteers and scraping off and painting the worst of the exterior. Painting required massive four level scaffolding positioned and repositioned around three sides of our 4000+ square foot house. It was the craziest week and a half, and when I left I still didn't know if we'd done enough to finance the house. At least I'd exhausted myself to the point I slept on the international leg of the flight.

My flight from the states landed at 7:30 AM on November 10th.

Overwhelmed at arrivals, jet lagged and groggy, I realized it had been decades since I'd traveled solo. I was accustomed to Doug planning everything out, then we would divide and conquer the tasks required to exit an airport. Pausing to regain my composure from the verge of panic I slowly worked through the required steps of collecting luggage, getting through customs, and finding my way to the metro. I must have looked especially pathetic staring perplexed at my metro map. A Parisian guy found me, showed me the way through mass transit to my hotel. As we parted, he gave me a number to text if I wanted a tour guide later. After confirming his offer stood even after pointing out my wedding band, I agreed to meet. Solo travel 101 level mastered!

Checked into my hotel, got my phone working on the European system, and got showered and changed for the day around Paris. I walked out of my hotel and wandered up the alley of cafes and street art, happy to be breathing in Europe and all it's wonderful charming culture. I peeked in galleries and wandered around touristy things. My soccer friends were due to arrive the next day, so I figured this was a good day to wander through the Louvre and streets of Paris. I wandered past the spot where I'd seen Scottish fans moon Americans in 1998, and strolled through the Louvre gardens. I decided to spend the afternoon there, blitzing the galleries I had time for without worrying I only had hours for a place I could spend days. I checked off the Mona Lisa, Venus de Milo, and the Impressionist gallery, stared at Degas and Monet paintings for an appropriately long time, walked past statues of mothers with babies and lovers in embrace, and by dinner, felt fully acclimated to Parisian culture and time.

I met my subway navigation hero by Notre Dame, and we headed out to an English pub that he was convinced was wonderful, but was actually only an amusingly vague attempt at a French impression of "English pub." A dreadful attempt, and I convinced him to leave after a beer. We found a much more Parisian café with good wine and delicious food I could not translate for dinner, and felt myself fall back into the grove of visiting Paris. We finished dinner and walked through the market a bit when he asked me if there was anything in particular I wanted to see. Was it too touristy and inconvenient to see the Eiffel Tower at night? He said that it wasn't, but about 40 minutes by transit. We headed for the metro and little more than 40 minutes later arrived within sight of the tower gracefully arching into the night sky. We walked up to the base and while he left to go find a restroom I was startled by a blaze of glimmering lights in the sky. The hourly light show had started and I was alone to gaze in unabashed American wonder, dazzled by the LEDs sparkling like a thousand diamonds in a jeweler's display light. Breathtaking. Just enough fog to refract the lights into a glowy haze, without obscuring the top of the tower. It seemed everything in life had perfectly aligned and an unofficial wonder of the world had been revealed to me.

I'd been to Paris twice before and enjoyed it, but never understood how people could fall in love with the city until that night. Gazing at the Eiffel Tower and later walking back to my hotel along the Seine in the gorgeous, hazy, mist I finally understood how enchanting Paris could be. The delicious food and wine, the intoxicating scenery, even the mist … the city made light rain seem wonderful. Maybe as a teen, I wasn't ready to appreciate Paris, then during the 1998 World Cup, I didn't really get to see Paris as itself rather … for better or for worse … as a Coupe du Monde host city. But on this trip, by myself, contemplating my upcoming birthday, my newly imagined life, and all my future held, Paris had me under its spell, at least for the night.

Ready to meet my soccer buddies, I enjoyed a proper French breakfast of coffee and croissants and set out to explore the city in the gleaming sun. The perfect day for sightseeing is blurred in retrospect by my excitement for the game that night. I'm sure I saw lovely things before finding the agreed upon pre-game bar. Our rallying point was difficult to find, requiring two stops for directions but eventually, I could hear Americans singing and turned the corner to find a small pub with red, white, and blue cloaked Americans spilling out the door. There were the guys from Arizona, who I'd only know as "Pheonix" until this trip. When I discovered they were also continuing on to Slovenia, I felt obligated to remember Ed and Dale (with the memory cue Chippendale, because it usually turns into a wild night when they are involved). Jason from New York arrived, one of a little group of Jewish fans affectionately referred to as #JewCrew on social media, and Bob, a traveler from Boston, who wasn't tribe, but seemed to fit in well enough with Jason and I to earn honorary Jewish status for the trip. We drank and I face painted, and soon enough, it was time to head to the stadium.

We marched to the stadium as a group singing to baffled Parisians and telling jokes and stories, occasionally stopping along for photos of the stadium lit up at night. Predominantly travelers from the US with a few expat Americans living in Europe who'd come in for the game, once we reached our seats we entertained ourselves cracking jokes and chanting soccer songs until kickoff. I'd finally found an experience that mimicked Korea travel with everyone as hard core as the next guy.

We sang our hearts out, but in the end, the US lost, and we were left to drown our sorrows in the restaurant across the street. We ate and laughed, fortifying ourselves with food and beer for the trip back to our hotels. We joked the French weren't capitalist enough to have enough scarves left for us to purchase after the game and other American observations on our French experience. Once the crowds had died down, we headed for the metro, luckily making it in time to catch a late train back to civilization. The platform was deserted and sketchy, and I was grateful to be headed the same direction as Jason.

The next day, we were all departing Paris at different times, but Jason and I were leaving late enough to meet for lunch. When Bob overslept his flight home, he joined us. We found a cozy café and spent a few hours drinking wine and talking, eating lamb stew and bonding over our travel experience. These experiences are what makes soccer travel alluring to me now: regardless of score getting the opportunity to know a diverse group of smart, funny, people who start out fellow supporters and end up lifelong friends. It's those bonding experiences that have formed most of my adult friendships.

Once the boys left, I had a few hours to wander Paris with my bags. My train was scheduled to depart at 7 PM, so I did some last minute shopping for my Paris obsessed daughter, then headed to the station in time to collect some provisions for the overnight train to Florence. I'd never been to Italy before because I was saving it to travel with my mother, who had studied abroad as a college student in Florence. At almost 40 it was time to see the fabled city of my mother's youth even if I couldn't convince her to join me. I was looking forward to traveling by train: where you can meet people, have interesting conversations, walk around, and generally have a more relaxing travel experience than flying. Trains are good for my procrastinator's soul … leaving things like buying dinner until the last minute. My laid-back day ended with me running for the train in dramatic fashion, then eased with the simplicity of finding a single seat among the six person cabins.

My travel companions were a couple from Hong Kong, a young man from Ivory Coast, and two women from Florence returning home together. We started out with just a simple hello drinking our own drinks and eating our own food, but not long into the train ride the Italian women began getting texts and phone calls and speaking rapid fire, excited Italian. They became so agitated we all started to laugh and they smiled and laughed with us, explaining the very corrupt Italian Prime Minister, Brunlusconi, was finally resigning. Their phone calls were reports from home of leaving his residence, arriving for the announcement, and just as they finished the explanation, he resigned, inspiring another round of drinks and maliciously gleeful cheers of "Fuck Brunlusconi!" Once we had bonded over this wonderful moment in Italian history, we talked about the reasons for our various trips, exchanged cultural stories, and drank many rounds cursing the former Prime Minister. I suggested they sing their national anthem which they did, I sang mine, the guy from Ivory Coast sang his, and the gentleman from Hong Kong performed theirs. Having convened a full on meeting of the United Nations and an international cultural exchange of epic proportion we shared food and drinks, laughing at each other's stories like old friends. Although no one was able to speak German with me, I listened to others speaking French, impressing the Ivory Coast guy with "C'est la vie" when he couldn't plug in the phone for me while I was stuck precariously up on the top bunk.

Madcap adventure didn't end once we drank the liquor cart dry. The couple from Hong Kong dozed off, but the Italians and Ivory Coaster would get up periodically to cram themselves into the bathroom of our non-smoking train to smoke out the window, only to return laughing hysterically at themselves. We'd just converted the car to sleeping when the police woke up the car next to us to search their bags at 3 AM. We never did hear what criminal activity caused the prolonged commotion, but it sounded serious, and ended the illegal smoke breaks for the rest of the night. We got to sleep a few short hours before our dawn arrival in Florence, but it was worth it for all the adventures we shared. Before we left the train, I exchanged phone numbers with one of the Florentine women, Antonia, and planned to meet for dinner.

Determined to enjoy as much as I could of Florence in the 36 hours I had there, I got off the train at 7 AM and stopped about two blocks from the train station for espresso and cannoli for breakfast. I bit into the crust through the rich filling, I realized that if this was the worst Florence had to offer, it was far superior to anything I'd eaten in the states. Full of Italian food and drink, I went on to my guest room near the center square. Charming and lovely, just like you'd expected Italy to deliver, even on my low budget travel. Once I'd ditched my stuff and showered I set out to explore the city.

I was there on Sunday and made the mistake of touring the architecture the first day, not realizing that the museums would be closed on Monday. Walking Florence was wonderful and the weather was perfect for wandering through churches and courtyards and haggling with street vendors. Heavenly sweet perfection, a taste of how lovely Florence could be on the blitzing schedule soccer demands. My schedule only allowed for glimpses of the most spectacular things a city had to offer, so I asked upon arrival what must not be missed. I followed my hotel clerk's suggestions, stopping along the way for surprises like finding the same alley where Des Moines photographer John Gaps III had stood to take a photo I'd purchased a few years prior for my mom. Of course, my imitation photo wasn't as well lit, but it would do for proof of the magic of finding the same spot. I spent the day wandering before heading over to Antonia's house.

Her charming daughter and a few of her friends chatted with me as she took the simplest of ingredients and made the most magical pasta and sauce I had ever experienced. I was inspired to never have sauce from a jar again, finally enlightened in the ease of making mind-blowing fresh sauce. We ate as her daughter asked questions in Italian for her mother to translate for me. A wonderful night I didn't want to end, but understood her desire to put her daughter to bed after being away traveling. I followed her suggestion to find entertainment at the local wine bar right downstairs. A quick check of my Facebook on her wifi alerted me a friend of mine from high school had discovered my Florence fly-by and was living nearby. I messaged back if she wanted to meet I'd be at the wine bar.

I sat next to a couple men from Sweden who were on a wine tasting trip. We struck up a conversation about food, wine, and soccer. Before long they were sharing their gourmet food and expensive wine flight while making more affordable recommendations for me by the glass. They finished their tasting and left me to turn to my other bar neighbor, where a well-dressed older gentleman sipped red wine. He spoke very little English but we were able to mime out I was an American soccer fan traveling by myself in celebration of my upcoming birthday, which as it turned out, was the same day as his. He carefully explained he was a leather purse craftsman, a prototype maker for an Italian fashion designer. We were just wrapping up when Meghan, my friend from high school walked in to my complete surprise. The buzzing hum of Italian wine bar conversation was shattered, embarrassingly so, by our mutual shrieks of excitement in seeing each other for the first time in 20 years. I explained to my startled drinking partner who this woman was, said goodnight, and set off into the night to find a more appropriate place for noisy Americans.

We went out for espresso and Florentine desserts, including a local treat that can only be described as a penis shaped rum cake, which of course is exactly what you'd order, catching up with a friend from teen years. Meghan had been working in Florence for several years and was engaged to be married. We talked about Brunlusconi, life in Italy, my soccer travels, and how much things had changed since our high school graduation. Discussing the strengths and weaknesses of Italian and American society, in a courtyard with gardens and sculpture and fountains, while devouring Italian pastry seemed like the perfect way to squeeze every possible moment out of my time in Florence.

The next day, I packed and left my bags at the hotel for pickup on the way to the night train and set out for my last day exploring Florence. Talking to a street artist about a painting I wanted to purchase, I struck up a conversation with a Canadian woman who was on holiday from her studies in England. We made our purchases and decided to wander the city together since our sightseeing goals for the day were similar. While I enjoy traveling solo, it was nice to have Zara to talk to and enjoy the city with for the day. We went across the river to the gardens that overlook the city, and even managed to find the place Antonia mentioned I should try. Pumpkin ravioli for lunch was rich and creamy with flavors swirled into delicious combinations in my mouth. We drank wine and talked about our dreams and aspirations for the rest of our trips and the rest of our lives … everything I needed as I contemplated my next decade. We said goodbye in the late afternoon, and I caught the bus to the train station, sad to part ways but looking forward to seeing Slovenia for the first time.

I boarded the night train to Ljubljana, Slovenia, and settled in amidst the college age backpackers and prepared to catch up on my writing. Little did we know, the torture about to dominate our lives. For on the train was a man with the worst smelling feet I have ever smelled. Foot stink that makes your eyes water, the kind of smell you worry about getting into your clothes. The kind of smell you can taste and feel sinking into your pores. Truly horrifying. We were in the middle of a great conversation, myself, the 21 year old Croatian across from me and the two guys from San Diego in the banquette across the aisle from us, when the smell of vile, moldy, sweaty feet hit us. I tried to ignore it, fearing the stench was from the shoes the backpackers had tied to the outside of their bags, but the smell was so strong and had just started, it had to be someone who just removed their shoes. Then I saw him … the guy one row behind me, sleeping with his shoes off. I tried to be polite, I swear. But I could barely concentrate on what I was saying, as the smell intensified, I became more and more distracted and unable to think in any language.

Unable to take it anymore, I commented to my travel mates I could barely breathe from that horrible smell. A fast exchange of "Ugh, I smelled it, but didn't want to say anything" "Talking about it is just making it worse" and various smelly situation stories being exchanged. We spoke English, which I knew the smelly guy didn't speak. The stinky feet monopolized (without exaggeration) the next hour of conversation. We'd stop and I would open the doors and try to air out our car. I had to keep pushing the automatic door buttons for the two doors to outside and the door to our compartment over and over, trying to move some air through the train. My attempts pushed the odor further into the car, striking the next rows of seats spawning more stench jokes and conversation, only this time in Croatian. I could have left, seeking out a new seat in another car, but there was a sense of camaraderie among the people in that train car. We were in it together, no one wanting to move luggage or leave travel acquaintances behind.

When the train was moving, the air flow made the situation less horrible, but when the train stopped as the San Diego guy said tortured, "That's when it's the worst." We would start talking about something else, and then someone would walk past and drag the smell up with them and returning us to agony. I began to be grateful for the smell of cigarettes from smokers walking back from between the cars. Anything to distract from the stench. As the woman entered our car to check passports at the Slovenian border you could see the look on her face become instantly disgusted. She stepped back and covered her nose, as the train erupted in laughter at her expression.

We tried various forms of dealing with the smell. We tried covering our noses with our shirts and scarves. The San Diego guys had hand sanitizer, which brought blissful relief when rubbed under the nose, but only lasted as long as it took to evaporate, then the smell returned. The Croatian girls had wipes, which they waved back and forth, temporarily spreading the scent of the wipes around. For a while, the man put his shoes back on during the passport check, which was a blissful relief. But soon enough, he'd kicked them off and we were back where we started.

At this point, it was almost midnight and new sleep-friendly methods of smell fighting were employed. One of the Croatians had a sleep mask, with wet wipes tucked under each eye. One of the San Diego boys wrapped his sweatshirt around his head, complaining they had just done laundry and now he'd have to re-wash everything. In one instance, the Croatian gentleman across the aisle from the girls blessed the air which seemed to work until we realized the shoes were put on for one more time. How could the smell perpetrator possibly not get we were all talking about him? Sir Stinks Alot would put his shoes on, and we would all stop talking and try to sleep, but then he would take them off, waking us up. The funny thing was, the torture of it all was so bonding our whole section started talking to each other. Mostly about feet, but also about where we were all traveling and what one should see along the way. I got some good travel tips out of it but didn't keep in touch with those people from the train. As if we'd been best prison buddies, never to be spoken of again, once we were on the outside.

Mercifully, we arrived in Ljubljana. Let me preface that I did not want to come to Slovenia. There had been a rumor that the US would play Germany on this date. I was all about going to Germany to visit friends, speak the language, and have a chance to see my favorite team play my second favorite team. When Slovenia was announced, I was upset and almost decided against making the trip entirely. I don't speak Slovenian and had only heard of the country because they were in our group in the 2010 World Cup. After grumbling for a few days, I realized I could still see my German family and friends after Slovenia, and decided to continue with my dream trip planning.

I arrived at 2 AM on game day, to a deserted train station with no plan of how to get to my hotel, which was beyond reasonable walking distance. My assumption that train stations would have cab stands proved false, but there was a pizza stand open. He called a cab for me while I devoured my late night snack. I checked in and slept until 15 minutes before breakfast closed, establishing myself as the lost in time American girl with the hotel staff. I spent the mid day checking out the city of Ljubljana with two other American fans, and headed to the stadium bar around 3:30.

Our first stop in the stadium neighborhood was to pick up tickets. I had no idea how small our contingent was until we got to the stadium and were directed to the visiting fans ticket booth. I walked up and as I was fishing my passport out of my back pocket to show ID to pick up will call, I said "Hi, my name's Tanya." Before I could get my passport out, the woman smiled, welcomed me, and handed me an envelope with my name on it. I stood there bewildered for a moment, trying to figure out how she could know my tickets by first name, as it slowly dawned on me our group must be very, very small. I asked how many envelopes she had and she replied there was about a dozen. When tickets can be claimed with a first name and no ID, it's going to be a VERY small crowd, perhaps the smallest away fan base I'd ever been a part of. We laughed about our tiny supporter section, and headed over to the All Star Bar, stumbling upon the Slovenia Supporters selling scarves at the roadside. I fell in love when I saw the top "Majhna in ponosna - little and proud," perfect for our trip on a few levels, it required immediate purchase. How could I not fall in love with Slovenia? I talked with the guy selling them, who turned out to be a leader of the supporters for Slovenia. We had a good time chatting, and as I was leaving, he gave me a really nice Slovenian flag. All I can say is, you had me at "majhna in ponosna."

There were five Americans at the All Star Bar and several Slovenians confused to find us there. The stadiums in Europe are all alcohol free, a far cry from the standard American Outlaws game day libations and a problem considering how unbelievably cold and damp it was. I had stopped upon arrival and purchased a thick knitted hat, but even when combined with several layers of clothing, there seemed to be no defense from the icy cold mist enveloping the city as the sun set. One of the locals tipped us off to Kuhalo Vino, a hot spiced wine that went down real easy. We compared notes on travel and dealing with foreigners and the language gap, bringing us to the phrase of the night, "What you say is very interesting." Perfect for when foreigners try to communicate with you but are unable to make themselves understood. It was a well used phrase for the night, and makes me crack up every time I've thought about it since.

Full of food and warm wine, we headed to the stadium. No longer looking for a "supporter section" we set out to find "our section, the row" I wondered if they'd have riot gear cops around a single row. We got to our seats about two thirds the way up the lower deck, almost in the corner. I hung the AO Des Moines banner in front of our corner and went down to the front row where the US boys were warming up. The seats were so close to the pitch we were practically on the field, imitating the intimacy of a women's game (often played on smaller fields). You could almost touch the players as they went through warm up drills. We interacted with the players a bit, showing off the sign one of the guys had made celebrating Carlos Bocanegra's 100th cap. It was more like relaxing watching a practice than gearing up for a game so we were startled when we realized it was minutes before the walk out, and no one had kicked us out yet. I ran up to the old seats and grabbed our stuff, updating the only other Americans (a couple of expats from Austria) that we were permanently relocating and they were welcome to join us.

I've never been prouder to belt out our national anthem. So patriotic to be there with my four new friends cheering on our boys. And when we scored it took a moment to realize that although the stadium was pin-drop silent … we'd scored! We went nuts, creating the not-so-deafening roar of five people cheering … completely unreal and fantastic all at once. The field was veiled in fog so thick we couldn't see the far side benches from our front row vantage point. I imagine from the upper deck you could not have seen much of the field at all. The Slovenians got some chants going and they had a well coordinated fan group in the end zone. Their supporters got call and response chants going with the rest of the fans in the stadium, creating an impressive atmosphere. They were great sports even when they were down goals or tied and shook hands with us post game once we'd emerged victorious. We stopped outside the stadium to take a photo with all the Americans we could collect, which was maybe a couple dozen people. We looked more like explorers on a North Pole expedition than soccer fans. Memories recorded, we were all too happy to return to the All Star Bar for more Kuhalo Vino.

Finally warm, I reflected on the day pleased in the post game afterglow at the bar happy the US was finally playing better and satisfied my dream coach Klinsmann's plan seemed to be coming together. I was glad to catch Boca's 100th cap, since I remember him as a new young guy on the team. There was something special about going to an away game with low US support. I loved being a part of a tiny little group of supporters cheering against all odds, little and proud. We walked back towards our hotels, taking a substantial detour to buy street food "burek," hot meat filled pastries … the perfect end to a night of drinking and soccer. I love all US Soccer matches, but I will always have a warm (finally) place in my heart for Slovenia.

The following day was devoted to Ljubljana tourism. I had planned on doing the City Tour, but after another late night giving in to my jet lag with heaps of free soccer on Slovenian TV, I barely made it to the 11 AM departure of the tour. Our guide was funny and charming, telling stories of Slovenian folklore, ancient Slovenian history, and pointing out interesting characteristics of local landmarks. One local sculptor would arrange the fingers of his statues with the two middle fingers together which made it very easy to identify his work. Our guide entertained us with the story of how the huge relief carved on the bronze door of the St. Nicholas Cathedral appeared very old but contained the image of Pope John Paul. It had been commissioned to commemorate the Pope's visit to Ljubljana. It contained references to the oldest printed Slovenian bible, which had been printed and shipped in barrels. The door showed the barrels, but not the printer, because he was Protestant. He then told us every city has a sculpture like this that people touch a certain part of for luck, and he had decided that the sculptor's self portrait's nose, at the bottom of the door, should be this touchstone for Ljubljana. I imagined this one tour guide, on day becoming single handedly responsible for rubbing the artist's nose off.

After touring the Ljubljana Grad, a castle on top of the hill overlooking the city, we walked across the modern bridge one down from the Dragon Bridge, the famous bridge with two huge dragons guarding it. Dragons were the mascot or icon of the city, but on the modern bridge, there were padlocks hanging from the support cables. I asked why there were so many locks hung there and our guide explained that local legend said couples who wrote their names on a lock and hung it there would be locked together in love which seemed very sweet and romantic. Then our guide said he'd heard of people coming back to cut the lock off after things went badly (lest we get too romantic). He told us about the local specialties of Ljubljana. He said Slovenians make a lot of wine but hardly export any of it and for the bonus fun fact: their national anthem is a drinking song. He also showed us the pumpkin seed oil that is a local specialty, and encouraged us to try it on salad … any authentic Slovenian restaurant would have it. A great mix of history, storytelling, and travel guide, the tour gave me plenty of choices for what to do with the rest of my time in Ljubljana. After the tour, I asked two of my fellow tour mates if they'd like to join me for lunch at a local place. The guide was right about pumpkin seed oil … it delivered a light, nutty flavor that tasted great on the salad and with our lunches as well.

My last night in Slovenia was spent drinking with friends in a few bars of strange and varied themes. The first place was sports oriented but then we went to a place with weird vignettes of scenes involving animals set in strange anthropomorphized poses ranging from fashion shoots to vague references to fetishes. Strange, but seeming appropriate for Ljubljana. We left there to wander the city streets and as we passed the castle I saw an unguarded poster for the art show I had really enjoyed on the city tour. I'd asked to buy the poster, but they weren't selling them, they'd only printed four for promotional purposes. I wanted to steal one so desperately but couldn't bring myself (even several drinks into the night) to vandalize the sweet city monument. I went back the next day and asked if I could take the poster from the reverse side of the advertising board. The castle clerk said she couldn't give it to me until after the show, which was several days after my departure. "Could you mail it to me in the States after the show? I'd really like to have it as a souvenir of the trip." I asked her.

"Absolutely. That I can do." She replied.

Yeah right, I thought. There's no way this stranger is going to remember me once the show is over, but I gave her the $10 worth of Euros, my address, and my thanks, and hoped for the best. Several weeks after I returned home, a poster tube arrived at my house, containing the poster! It was nice to have my good deed of not stealing repaid by her keeping her word to send it. It hangs in our middle parlor where I can look at it daily and completely guilt free.

From Slovenia, I flew to Frankfurt then took the train to Kaiserslautern to visit the Trommers and finally see an FC Kaiserslautern match live and in person. FCK is a second division team in the Bundesliga who've been in the top division before but have slipped to persistently flirting with promotion. Returning to Kaiserslautern felt like a homecoming for me, with so many familiar memories at their house. It's funny, the things that become special to you, like the little line drawing that hangs in their powder room, to the table where we ate breakfast on the red table cloth I remember from my childhood (or a convincingly similar one, at least). I got to see photos of Tanya's daughter, and catch up with Wolfgang and Jutta, hanging out at the house and shopping around Kaiserslautern's town center. We have often joked over the years, that if you are really good in a past life, you come back as a treasured Trommer cat, so it seemed funny but appropriate to

Skype our cats with the Trommer cats. My kids got on to say hello as well, with Raphael stealing the show.

He said "I'm Raphael, R A P H A E L." So adorable to hear him spell out his name for clarity. Aviva was very excited to chat with her Germany Grandma and Grandpa, and was entirely jealous she could not be part of this visit. It's a blessing and a curse, how well traveled our children are. They will often have to defend themselves to childhood friends who cannot fathom how much they travel following US Soccer. Someday, I'm sure, we'll get back to Germany to visit with them.

FCK vs. Bayer Leverkusen had me very excited as well. Fritz Walter Stadion is legendary in and of itself, perched on top of the hill, making the approach a climb of anticipation. We took the bus most of the way up then climbed the rest of the way to the stadium night. When the US played Italy here in 2006 it was a day game and didn't give the full effect of the stadium lit up like a beacon on the hill, drawing us in like moths to a porch light. This was my first opportunity to meet FCK supporters, and I was intoxicated by their merch table before I even entered the stadium. I bought stickers, patches, and pins … anything I thought I could fit in my overstuffed luggage, then walked through the front of their supporter section, greeting a few of the leaders and feeling mesmerized by the energy of their section, the WestCurve.

I rejoined the Trommers for curry wurst and beer, we went up to our seats where I could barely contain my excitement listening to German language soccer discussions around me while watching the team and the WestCurve warm up. The FCK Ultras lived up to their reputation as one of the best supporter groups in the Bundesliga. At least by my expectation as I don't have much to compare in German soccer, but they sounded amazing even from the opposite end of the stadium. Ultimately the team lost but the atmosphere was full of win. Every person in the stadium understood the finer points of the game. Unlike American stadiums, every sweet touch, beautiful pass, great look was followed by a gasp or a shout of appreciation, resulting in a wonderful sense of belonging for me.

My trip to Germany wrapped with a really special dinner out with my Deutsche family taking me out to a traditional German meal. Heavily invoking of my loose interpretation of travel kashrut, I accepted that the main course was a roasted pig. Here's the thing: I don't typically eat pork, since it was the first law of kashrut I learned when my childhood MuShu Pork ordering seemed to be the one thing that really offended my grandfather. But I also love to travel and discovering local delicacies. In Germany delicacy often involves pork. Really delicious: potatoes, vegetables, bread, and yes, the pork. We ate, drank, and told stories about when we were all younger. My real parents aren't the kind of people you can get drunk and let loose with so the experience of getting wasted with your parents and talking late into the night was new and quite fantastic. I didn't want the night or the trip to end.

The next day, I boarded my plane back to the States, reveling in my nearly perfect trip of meeting new friends, seeing old friends, and watching great soccer matches. More and more, it was becoming clear to me the secret to happiness was a life lived passionately, in my case seeking out love of soccer expressed around the world. I'd grown up thinking I wanted to do something that allowed me to travel to exotic places and meet fascinating people and here I was, living my dream and loving every second of the adventures soccer set before me. I arrived back in the US, ready to face my big birthday, my new life, and embrace the next phase of life … marked by the next phase of World Cup qualifying.

29

The Road to Brazil is Wet, Hot, and Snowy

2012 kicked off 2014 Brazil World Cup qualifying in June with the first match against Antigua and Barbuda in Tampa, Florida. My Korea '02 friends Andy Gustafson and Greg Ellis were living in Tampa and had launched a full court offensive to get me to come down for the game. I resisted, because who goes to Florida right after it starts warming up in Iowa? I do, apparently, because friends who won't let friends miss World Cup qualifiers. Andy offered me a place to stay, Greg was entirely convincing that I must make it happen, and fortunately flights weren't too expensive off season. I packed the banner and the stadium flag and flew down for a few days of soccer, drinking, and hanging out with my soccer family.

I got into Tampa the day before the game and headed down to the American Outlaws night before party with Greg. Beer flowed and the place was packed with familiar faces from my Slovenia travel buddies to the girls from Texas. Sunil Gulati, the head of US Soccer walked in. I'm fairly confident my exchange with him was far from inappropriate but did not pass for remotely in the neighborhood of sober. Something about Florida tapped into Spring Breaks I never spent getting wasted at some trashy nearby resort. I dialed it back a bit, reminding myself that I might want to remain functional enough to find my way back home of my own devices. I had settled into a nice happy buzz when Justin Brunken, one of the American Outlaws founders walked in, looking exhausted at 10 PM from his day of travel. I said hello and asked how he was. "I'm getting to old for this shit." He replied.

"You recognize the irony of you saying that to me, don't you?" I smirked.

Looking confident, he replied, "Oh, I am definitely older than you."

"Ha! I promise you, you are not." I said, now thoroughly amused, confident in my position, but not sure exactly how old he was, particularly with the look of bravado on his face.

"I'm THIRTY." He said, with utmost confidence he had beaten me soundly.

"I'm FORTY." I grinned with the all the happiness of "but you think I look like I'm in my twenties!" I'm pretty sure I left soon after, convinced I'd seen the high point of the night.

We got up the next morning and had coffee and went to get Cuban sandwiches for lunch. My pork travel clause now even more loosely interpreted but whatever … they were delicious. You can't pass up authentic local cuisine, it's in the rules. We watched soccer on Andy's gigantic TV, eating sandwiches and catching up. Jon and Jen Strauss showed up from Boston and it was an official soccer family reunion. We spent the afternoon hanging out, drinking, and talking, and in no time the afternoon had flown by and it was time to head to the stadium.

We arrived in time to do early entry to set up the flag then came back out to enjoy the tailgate. Andy brought great beer and the crowd was amped up and entertaining. I met new friends like a guy nicknamed Big Fudge, a name that struck me as hilarious for a white Southern kid. The Southern chapters were well represented with people I'd not gotten to meet yet. Lager Haus had a "beer patrol" police car with a pretty authentic looking paint job, and people were in high spirits, with or without gratuitous free beer.

This atmosphere lasted until about the time we walked into the stadium, when the skies opened up and torrential rain poured down on us. We were already in our seats when stadium security came out and asked us to take shelter, we protested with various chants about not leaving and singing in the rain. Eventually, we left to take cover in the walkways that ran the long end of the stadium but there were too many people crammed into too small a space. I was not convinced we were any safer and became increasingly frustrated as game time came and went and we were still not allowed back to our seats. The rain finally let up enough to send up back in and the game started a bit late. Completely soaked, as were the flags and banners, but you couldn't help but enjoy the show put on by the US. Donovan's corner kick allowed Carlos Bocanegra to tie Balboa's career 13 goals as a defender in the 8th minute, allowing us to relax and enjoy the match early on. Dempsey converted a late in the first half penalty kick, setting up 2-0 at halftime. 2-0 is the most dangerous of leads, because it feels confident, but isn't really safe. Antigua and Barbuda gave me a bit of nerves with a shocker of a goal in the 65th minute cutting our lead in half and inspiring a late rally by the US. Shot after nail biting shot until A&B's keeper succumbed to the attack in the 72nd minute leaving us soaked but victorious at 3-1.

Andy was kind enough to shoulder the giant water logged flag out of the stadium allowing me to ponder how I was going to get a soaking wet flag now two to three times heavier back to Des Moines without it breaking me physically, financially, or suffering death by mold. Back at Andy's we unfurled the flag in his garage taking up the entire two car space draped over as many stored items as possible increasing our available square footage by elevation change. Not the perfect flag protocol, but given our desperate times and lack of a military detail we were getting the job done. We sat in the kitchen, veterans of Korea 2002, myself, Greg, Andy, joined by Rishi, who came to visit and retell stories of the trip with Jon and Jen, reliving the soccer of our younger days ... the perfect start to 2014 World Cup qualifying.

I returned to Des Moines refreshed with renewed excitement about following USMNT to Jamaica for the Fall qualifier. Doug and I had honeymooned in Jamaica in 1995 and we'd always talked about doing a 10th or 15th anniversary trip back there. Supporter schedule made more send to travel in September 2012 and toss the anniversary trip idea. We needed a regroup. Doug had been unhappy at work and I was settled into working on the house enough to need a break. With the kids back in school it seemed like the perfect time to spend a few days in Jamaica followed by a few days in Columbus. In Soccer World, Columbus Ohio be construed as a romantic getaway.

We drove to Chicago and slept overnight at a hotel that would let us park free while we were gone. We flew out first thing and arrived at the AO hotel a day before almost everyone else. We got checked in, hung the AO Des Moines banner on the balcony, and headed out to explore the property. Lying in the sun on a beach in Jamaica is about as far as I could get from my world of demolition, remodeling, paint stripper, and kid pick up … and it was lovely. We had extended talks about life in general for the first time in forever. We talked at length about Doug's career dissatisfaction earned through years working for a company that seemed to have no understanding for how to retain employees. They treated people horribly, forced salaried employees to clock in and out, limited lunch to 30 minutes, and micromanaged capable people. It had been a nightmare job for a few years and didn't shown signs of improving. We came to the conclusion he would start looking for freelance work with the end goal of replacing his income and quitting within a year. Our conversation paid huge dividends three weeks later when his miserable employer was kind enough to downsize his position and offer six month severance. Doug said it was hard not to shout with joy as they told him he no longer had a job having fully prepared while on our soccer break. When has the soccer universe not provided everything we need?

Other soccer fans arrived the next day ratcheting up the party around the pool bar to a nice respectable level. We met Casey from Sacramento and were having a nice afternoon of rum and soccer talk when another AO joined us so drunk he struggled to put sentences together. Not at all hiding his total inability to maintain eye contact (eyes up here, friend) it was one of those awkward conversations where one person is several drinks ahead of everyone else, and doesn't seem to realize it's time to let the crowd catch up. Mercifully, we were heading up to the AO cocktail hour reception and in a failed attempt to exit the pool, the drunk guy ended up flat on his back on the pool deck. We figured that would slow him down for a while and went upstairs to change for the party.

But no! He soon resurfaced at the cocktail hour, although seemed to have no recollection of meeting us, amusing me to no end. We "chatted" for a few minutes, a euphemism for me mocking him as he openly stared at my breasts slurring his words asking me questions he'd asked just 90 minutes earlier at the pool. I finally had to come clean.

"Do you really have no recollection of meeting me at the pool?" He stared blankly at my face for a few moments before returning his gaze to my cleavage.

"We met?" is what I think he slurred out.

"Yes, at the pool, maybe an hour or so ago." More blank stares.

"Well, you don't have to be a bitch about it." Oh, drunk guy charm. Because I'm a bitch for pointing out you're too wasted to recognize a woman you've now hit on twice without realizing it's the same woman, with bonus points for doing it in front of her husband … both times. Yes, I'm clearly the one failing here, friend. More from my drunken friend later.

The cocktail hour was otherwise great. People we hadn't seen in a while, including the guys we'd met as they were filming in South Africa, Jon and Ashwin from One Goal, who were making videos about traveling American Outlaws. They interviewed us and we got to catch up on what they'd been doing since completing their South Africa project, "Laduma." We enjoyed our interview, and they seemed pleasantly surprised to hear stories from our soccer long term USMNT support. The best part of our talk with them came a few weeks later when their Travel Channel show trailer came out. Their trailer introduced a reality show with various characters giving video quotes, then freeze framing on that person with graphics of the "character's" name scrawled across the screen. They featured great quotes from guys I really like such as Fera and Hexsel, but as it went on I was rolling my eyes at another video featuring the 20-something boys of American Outlaws. Then my own face popped on the screen talking about the game vs. Jamaica with typical Tanya bravado. My face frozen on the screen with my name (spelled correctly!) in the lights of YouTube. My opinion got whiplash it turned so fast. I'm happy for all the AO press, but I do particularly enjoy the pieces looking beyond the 20-somethings to a few of us old enough to traveled to the France World Cup in 1998.

Joining us at the bar was a destination wedding party from Manchester, England. As luck would have it, there were several soccer fans in their party, including the groundskeeper for Manchester United making a great night of exchanged soccer stories. Mostly ManU supporters but one very funny drunk guy who supported Bolton

Wanderers, and loved to sing about them every chance he got. At random he'd launch into singing about the wacky wacky wacky wacky Wanderers then roll up his sleeve to show off his Bolton tattoo. There's something hilarious and wonderful about England fans interacting with US soccer fans. They're so pleasantly surprised real supporters exist in the States they become giddy and charming and will chat for as long as you allow about American thoughts on world soccer.

American Outlaws had arranged a scrimmage of Outlaws vs. Montego Bay United practice team. I played in the lowest division of my rec league, but no way I was missing this. We took a mini bus to their practice grounds and played their coaches and second team players. One of their players was from the World Cup team from 1998. Exciting enough to play on the same pitch as a former World Cup player but he fouled me, knocking my head hard enough into the ground I was pretty sure I was going to 1) black-out 2) puke 3) cry. All of which were totally unacceptable options as the one coed on the field. I managed to hold it together and savored my forever bragging rights: fouled by a World Cup player.

My one regret of the trip was not following Ashwin, Jon and the guys to the school boys game immediately following our match. We wanted to go to the Montego Bay game the following day and the idea of also going to see their team of high school aged boys seemed silly. We should have known when we drove by the stadium packed with a raucous crowd it was time to let go of our plans to shower and have a nice dinner. I broke my own rules to follow adventure whenever it presents itself. Next time, I won't be so quick to judge a school boys game and will trust my host. If the host thinks it's cool, I should probably go. Lesson learned.

The trip to the USMNT game was quite a trek. We were staying in resort central Montego Bay but the game was played at "the Office", Jamaica's national stadium in Kingston. Google will tell you it should have been a three hour drive but I call bullshit. It has to be at least four or five hours on a good day and driving in Jamaica isn't really designed for consistently good days. On our drive, in addition to the usual stops for a 50 person bus to use the restroom and refuel on drinks and snacks, there was an accident which ended up a defining adventure of the road trip.

About an hour outside of Kingstown traffic on our beautiful two lane road came to a standstill. River on our right and gorgeous wooded areas on both banks creating a canopy over us while we waited. And waited. And waited. We had plenty to eat and drink and fun people to talk to but the discussion slowly turned from concerns we wouldn't have any time to pre-game at the bar to near panic we would miss kick off. With no traffic from the other direction, cars began to pull forward into the oncoming traffic lane to try to see what the holdup was. Word finally reached us there had been a car accident which included a fatality.

I wish I could tell you we handled this news with the somber reverence appropriate for the loss of human life, but we were barely holding it together at this point. We managed to stop short of complete irreverence but there were guys trying to pick up women from surrounding cars (who later called these prospects, introducing themselves as "I'm so and so, we met at the fatality.") Never have the words "the fatality" been uttered with such amusement as this trip.

An ambulance arrived but all lanes of traffic were still completely blocked. One shoulder offered a wall of stone and trees, the other side dropped off to the river. Thus began the game of Car Jenga, where one car would gingerly back up into an impossibly small space to allow the ambulance to slip by and the another vehicle would have to shift positions and so on until 30 minutes later the ambulance had traveled a half mile. Probably best this was already a fatality because I can't imagine this going well for someone waiting for this ambulance.

Finally through after several hours camped out, we continued to the stadium. I'd done my elaborate game day makeup and one of the guys who'd watched me do it asked me to paint a Captain America shield on his head. Happy to do it, only we didn't get started until the fatality had almost been cleared so I had to finish it while the bus was moving. It felt like I was molesting him trying to hang on for balance while painting his head without breaking his neck but I got it done. Don't think he'll need too much therapy … he hasn't sent me a bill at least.

We finally arrived in Kingston with just enough time to stop at the restroom, grab a quick beer, and head to the stadium. The walk from the bar was short through streets full of Jamaicans headed to the game. We marched as a group singing and chanting our way through the chaos of Jamaican supporters, jerk chicken grills, guys hawking noise makers, and police officers looking vaguely amused with us. We got to our seats and had just enough time to get the banner set and make a beer run before kickoff. Luckily the fatality hadn't cost us any more time because the only US goal of the match came just moments after kickoff. Dempsey scored on our end, whipping our little section into an early frenzy, only to have our hopes dashed in the 24th and 62nd minutes, as Jamaica was finally able to defeat the US after a 10-0-8 run by the USMNT.

Heartbroken post game having seen our reign over Jamaica end and mourning the loss, we watched the Jamaicans storm the pitch. I thought about what it was like for the US when we finally started beating our long term foes. We wanted to travel to Jamaica to watch the US beat them, but watching them celebrate a new achievement in soccer quickly grew on us. As thousands of Jamaicans filled into the field, we decided to join them in their celebration. If not three points I would at least score my first pitch invasion. Sharing the joy of the Jamaicans celebrating their victory was almost as sweet as savoring our own win. The grass was so dense and firm, it was a pleasant sensation just to walk on, and I was standing where Dempsey had just scored from not 2 hours prior. Not a win, but it very special.

We headed back to the bar where the bus was parked and drowned our sorrows in food and beer. Once everyone returned from the stadium we loaded the buses and headed back towards Montego Bay. Most of us were exhausted from the long day travel, the fatality, and soccer. The Drunk Guy we met at the welcome reception and a few of his drunken friends were on our bus and not at all interested in sleeping. Apparently, none of them got the memo you can use quiet voices to speak when everyone around you is trying to sleep. They "entertained" the bus of weary travelers with their private, idiotic drunken stories of mayhem and immaturity. The group of us at the back of the bus silently exchanged looks and earplugs, but even with earplugs in and in a state of complete exhaustion, no one could sleep over the racket created by Drunk Guy and his merry band of frat-party-gone-wrong. I had resigned myself to not sleeping and plotting their shaming in my writing when I heard one of the guys speaking about the two single women on the trip who were riding in the other bus.

"Hey, did you see those tattooed girls on the other bus?"

"Yeah, man, she was ..."

Honestly, I don't really know what he said after that, because at that point the blood was rushing through my ears in a fierce burst of anger. The women in question were Amy, my roommate from AO Rally, and her friend and the tone Drunk Posse was speaking about them in filled me with rage. I was on my feet and to their row in seconds listening to them chat raunchily about women who should be considered their sisters, and I launched into a soliloquy in defense of all women everywhere, to say nothing of their fellow bus riding hostages.

"Are you aware there is a bus full of people riding with you, who have no interest in your loud drunken exploits, nor are we interested in listening to you trash talk our fellow AOs. Those women are my friends, and I will not sit here and listen to you demean them one second longer. Why don't you try growing up, shutting up, and letting the rest of us get some sleep?"

I turned back to my seat, leaving them to whine to Hexsel about how they weren't doing anything wrong, poor persecuted boys they were, while I returned to the back of the bus to several understated high fives, satisfied at least tonight, they'd have to think twice before talking about women as if they were objects and not people. I tried to rest, thankful these boys would be middle aged by the time my daughter is old enough to date.

The best part of this whole exchange? Drunk Guy wasn't done yet! He want around our tiny group of friends talking about what an awful person I'd been to him ruining his little mobile frat party. He complained I had no place on the trip, because who was I? Where had I been in 2002, when he had gotten up in the middle of the night to watch the games in what I imagine to be his adorable living room. Perhaps with a juice box of apple juice and some Cheerios? Yes, Drunk Guy Super Genius said all this to people who were good enough friends of mine to relay the message of his bravado back to me in short order. Oh sure, I was steaming mad for a while, but you know ... don't get mad, get even.

I couldn't believe my luck while dining with my husband that evening, when Drunk Guy showed up in a party of ten or so guys. This was going to be great. We finished dinner, and as we were walking out, we stopped by their table for me to deliver my speech.

"Hey" I said, looking directly at him. "I just wanted to apologize." He smiled what I like to think was his last smile for a while. "You're right" I said "I don't know what you would have said had I let you keep talking about my girlfriends. I made a judgment based on listening to you bragging all weekend and made the preemptive move to shut you up before I heard any more. I'm so sorry for pre-judging you." By now my voice was so thick with sarcasm, his smile had faded to a grim frown. "Oh, by the way, I heard you were wondering where I was during those 2002 games in Korea. I was in the stadium in Korea. I hope that clears up your confusion on who I am as a supporter." I turned on my heel and walked out, feeling entirely satisfied in leaving him speechless. They say living well is the best revenge, but it's possible proving you've lived well for over a decade might be sweeter.

Despite a few bad apples, traveling for US Soccer will show you far more about how awesome supporters are. On the morning of our last day in Jamaica, our checking account went on fraud alert and was locked down, leaving us with no access to travel cash and wondering if we'd be able to make it through the airport, let alone to the next game in Columbus. We figured we probably had enough to make it, but I was a little freaked out to be traveling with almost no cash. A couple we'd just met from Georgia loaned us a hundred bucks without hesitation, just to make sure we'd make it OK. It blew my mind someone we just met would so readily have our back in an emergency, but that's what our soccer family is like. People who are absolutely amazing, like family once out on the road together.

We made it back to the States, deciding to chance it going to Columbus, trusting that everything would work out with our checking account (but surviving on peanut butter and jelly for the rest of the trip, just in case we only had $100 to get home). I didn't want to miss out on the revenge match against Jamaica, and I love going to Columbus for games. The city has old school heart for soccer makes me smile. Some of my earliest caps were in Columbus, and the nostalgia factor was pretty high. We picked up our car at O'Hare in Chicago and headed East towards Ohio.

Columbus had a fantastic tailgate party set up with a beer truck and sandwiches from a company called "Dead Pig," which was written in pink script on their food truck. The crowd around the American Outlaws tent was funny and entertaining, and we got to meet the extended soccer families of our travel buddies from Jamaica, as catch up with several of our old friends. Detroit had brought in a huge bus, headed up by James Cates, one of our friends from the Korea trip. James and his son Jimmie always crack me up with their stories, and they're great guys. While I was catching up with James, he mentioned since the tailgate was packed, I should come on the bus if I wanted a break from the potty lines. I walked over to check out their road trip bus … a pretty sweet ride … and a welcome break from the crowds outside. I was talking with James when a 20-something guy got on the bus and looked at me with distain.

"Who are you?" he said, with a tone that clearly stated "And what the fuck do you think you're doing here?"

I didn't even have a chance to stammer something out about manners or anything before James leader of this guys road trip said "Who is she?! You don't know who she is? Huh, you should know who she is."

I wanted to high five James right then and there and throw my arms around his neck in gratitude. He took a moment of pure frustration with the state of young men in supporter world and turned it into a huge compliment. This Rude Guy and Drunk Guy from the Jamaica trip are what's wrong with some of the younger of American Outlaws. They're prone to assume I follow soccer to travel with my husband, cannot fathom I travel by myself, or worse … that he "let's" me travel by myself. Then there's the male fan that considers my soccer life "abandoning" my kids, a concept I can't believe still exists today. Haven't we reached the day when women can stay with their kids or not with the same lack of judgment men do? Working from home, I would have to go to more soccer games than humanly possible to equal the time away from my kids that my husband spends away from them working 9-5. Why are we even having this conversation about my well adjusted kids? Taking time to do something you love away from your kids only makes you a more awesome mom when you're with them the other 350 days a year. Do we seriously look at women of any age and question what they have to offer the world of sports? C'mon people, we can do better.

After basking for a moment in James' compliment, I said good bye and headed back out to the tailgate, drank some more beer before marching into the stadium. The supporters section was split into two with a stage covered in late-addition bleacher seats lodged in between. Everyone seemed really amped up for the match that promised to deliver not only revenge for our loss to Jamaica a few days prior but all the Americana heart of a match played on the 11th anniversary of 9/11. There were police and firemen from New York on hand for an honorary celebration during the anthem and the entire crowd seemed to buzz with excitement even before kickoff. Once the game got underway things got completely crazy. The firemen came around and high fived us after the anthem then Frankie Hejduk ran through the crowd, doing his insane antics that all soccer fans know and love. In no time the supporters section was completely nuts and crazy loud.

Looking around the stadium, I realized it wasn't just the supporters section. I nudged my husband and he nodded. It was the first time we had seen an entire soccer stadium cheering in unison for the USMNT. I felt time slow down as I absorbed this milestone of how far the US has come in the soccer world. I was watching this huge crowd all standing and singing not against arch rival Mexico, but against Jamaica barely out of the CONCACAF minnow pool by beating us a few days prior. It was so beautiful being a part of that crowd in a blip on the soccer history timeline. Maybe no one else noticed but thrilled it me to tears. America had finally arrived as a soccer loving nation.

Thankfully, we can count that historic game as a win. After a first half fraught with goal post striking heartbreak and chance after failed chance, Herculez Gomez finally buried a free kick in the back of the net and lifted the USMNT 1-0 over Jamaica. Powerful as the energy had been all game, it now exploded in joyful. The roar from the crowd was a deafening sound wave that crackled into the night. It was happy and intense and further underscored everyone in stadium understood this game and how important it was. For me, that was a thing of beauty.

The next stop on the road to Brazil 2014 was in Kansas City for the qualifier against Guatemala. This game was supposed to be a great family bonding moment. It fell right after our firstborn's 10th birthday and marked our 100th cap family cap. But the actual road to get there was a little rocky. My sister had been ill on-and-off for over a year, putting an enormous strain on my parents already emotionally taxed to the hilt with the stress of my 1990s eye drama. We had celebrated the double digits birthday with my family and the trip had ended very badly in an argument that ended with my parents saying they never wanted to see us again. Maybe I should have realized this was something said in the heat of the moment, but really, when my parents dropped that bomb, not even my usually unbeatable optimism held up. I left in shock, assuming I would never see my family again, flew back to Des Moines, and immediately hopped in a car and drove down to KC for the night before party.

You could argue perhaps I should have headed right to my therapist's office, but my whole soccer family was waiting for me in KC and the thought to cancel the trip never crossed my mind. I couldn't get there fast enough. I spent the flight to Des Moines journaling and trying to sort out where our visit had gone so far off track and the car ride to Kansas writing, crying, and in stunned silence. Once we arrived and I was in the company of my soccer friends I tried to forget the trip to my parents ever happened.

I was still shell-shocked enough I didn't want to talk about what had happened, but told the whole story to a few of my closest friends just to make sure someone knew what was up if I ended up drunk and sobbing on the ladies room floor. The unanimous response was some version of "that's horrible, we're going to get you drunk." These are all people I've been drinking with for a very long time … what could go wrong? Professional caliber drinkers trying to get me, another pro-level imbiber, drunk when I have zero desire to hold them back. Yeah, nothing could go wrong there.

Shots, too many to count, and beers were plentiful. Surrounded by the love of my soccer family, I was a very happy girl with not one single thought toward crying in the corner. I was also extraordinarily drunk and just well known enough to make life interesting. Someone introduced me to Ives of the Soccer by Ives blog fame, an introduction I was in no shape to handle with even a scrap of professional decorum. He was amused, but still speaking to me at the next game, so I'm going to count it as a win albeit on the technicality he's probably accustomed to drunken soccer fans fawning all over him while mispronouncing his name. Yep, I'm awesome, really awesome, when wasted.

Then there was the walk back to the hotel with my friends. I was just sober enough to smoothly walk out of the bar with a cup of beer I believed to contain a couple ounces of beer. There was a soft voice in the back of my head saying something about not needing any more alcohol but I rarely listen to that girl. I walked with Kaela and Jon back to our hotel, only partially aware of the cup in my hand, listening to them banter back and forth. If you follow Kaela (@local_kitchen) or Jon (@WeberKing) on Twitter, you know they can be hilariously funny. You may have noticed Jon loves to mock me about living in Iowa, being from New Jersey, or both. I do not remember what he said that night to finally flip my switch, but whatever it was, my brain thought, "Hey, I know a good thing to do with this extra beer" and with a flip of my wrist, the beer was on its way to Jon.

There are two things you must understand: 1) There was a lot more beer in that cup than I thought there was and 2) considering how drunk I was I had laser sharp aim. The beer hit Jon so squarely in his back hardly a drop hit the ground as it soaked his entire shirt and the top of his jeans. I was so impressed with my accuracy it never occurred to me to run for it. Plus, I was the only one who left the bar with any ammo. It was remarkably (mercifully) warm for October … in Jon's favor as he stripped out of his beer soaked shirt and walked the rest of the way topless through downtown Kansas City before demanding I relinquish my jacket to get him through the hotel lobby. He eventually forgave me, but it was a few months before he stopped glaring at me. He has not stopped mocking me although it seems to be a little less frequent (at least when there's beer within reach).

The rest of the evening has become a event of epic family folklore. I remember most of the night, but the time at the hotel is fuzzy. Doug instructed me to be quiet and whisper, and I stage whispered back, loud enough to wake my daughter.

"I am whispering."

I'm told the rest of the night ended like this: I flop in the middle of the bed, still dressed. My husband does not appreciate this.

"You need to move over."

"No. I'm tired."

"No, seriously, you're taking up the whole bed."

"Shhhhh … you're keeping me awake." I said. My daughter chuckled, now awake.

"You have to move."

"Be quiet, I want to sleep. If you keep talking, I'm going to punch you in the face." I'm not really a violent drunk but I've been known to make threats.

My husband, seeing an opportunity says, "Stand up and punch me in the face."

That's the line that has lived on in infamy. I don't remember any of this so I think it's all myth, but it makes for a good story. And it makes me chuckle every time the PSA comes on about "What will your children remember about their childhood?" ads for substance abuse. Yep, my children will remember my drinking, but fortunately in very isolated circumstances. My son, at age 6, said that he thought the drinking age should be 40, because by then, people would know how much they could drink without getting out of control. By the time my kids are in high school, they should have had plenty of teachable moments about why you shouldn't drink … the rest of them coming from people outside the family I hope.

The next day, I recovered quickly enough to join our group for brunch downtown before going out to the stadium to set up the tifo for the game. For this game we had banners to hang from the upper deck, the stadium flag, and a tifo with colored pieces of paper over two sides of the stadium. We brought the kids with us to set up the tifo for the first time and had the proud parent moment of seeing my son rack up several firsts: first time he carried the backpack with the stadium flag by himself and the first time he learned to zip-tie banners. This extended our age achievement markers for supporter kids: follow songs by age two, lead a group by three and a half, zip tie banners by age five.

USMNT served up a rocking party atmosphere for the 3-1 win over Guatemala with Dempsey scoring twice and assisting Bocanegra on the third goal, we had a blast until it came time to leave. I folded the Midwest Mama flag with the help of half a dozen supporters while Doug went up to retrieve our banners from the upper level. We'd carried our banner plus two sweet hand painted banners for Prairie Clayton (@ Hoover_Dam), who we'd just seen in Boston. As I worked to roll our 20 x 30' flag tight enough to squeeze into our backpack, my phone rang.

"Prairie's banners are gone." Doug said, dropping my heart to the floor.

"What do you mean? Did someone else get them for us?" I hoped.

"No one saw them. They're gone."

I felt awful. We spent the next hour tracking down stadium security and looking through the local pile of banners but couldn't find her work. I called Prairie and tweeted a photo of the missing banners but we had kids to put to bed. We left gutted, praying for a miracle.

Several days later, my phone rang. A serious voice said he was Chris Wyche, VP of Stadiums Operations. His tone was so gruff, I thought I was in trouble.

"I want you to know that we take this sort of incident very seriously. We were able to go back through security footage and trace what happened with your banners."

OK ... I'm not in trouble. Phew.

"Ms. Keith, I want you to know that we've identified the people who took your banners and they will return them to us so we can return them to you."

Thank goodness ... I could finally relax about having banners disappear on my watch! We talked about supporters, the Sporting stadium, and the Sporting KC program. By the end of the phone call he had invited the family down for a match and stadium tour, which we took and were blown away with how cool the organization was. I could go on about the design of the stadium and quality of the staff or how cool it was shadowing an MLS VP Stadium Ops as he interacted with his staff on game day, but the most impressive thing was the US Open Cup trophy sitting on his mini fridge. Like no big deal, just the Lamar Hunt trophy, sitting here. It was very cool.

The story doesn't end there. One of the guys who stole the banner tweeted a photo of it hanging in his dorm room the following July, telling soccer reporter Grant Wahl it looked better in his dorm room. By the time I woke up on central time, the Twitter war on this guy was going strong. I woke up to the beeps of Twitter notifications as @

WeberKing tweeted "Does @TanyaKeith know about this?" Not the best way to greet the day. The entire thing is documented on my blog at www.soccerfamilystyle.com on a July 18, 2013 post, but the short story is this: soccer fans are very cool people until you steal from one of their friends. So if you're going to steal, I suggest you don't go on Twitter and brag about it to reporters.

30

Battle of the Hoth

Spring Break 2013 kicked off the Hexagonal of 2014 World Cup qualifying in Denver, Colorado for USMNT vs. Costa Rica. It was my goal to get to all the home games of the Hex and in Denver we had several local friends join us. AO Des Moines had grown since our 2010 founding and over a dozen people from our chapter traveled to Denver. It made me so happy that so many of our AO DSM friends were joining our soccer travel family. Kim and Barry were with us thankfully, since Kim sets up the best tailgates, and they brought along Ryan. Vicky and Matt were there without their kids to drink and laugh and entertain us. Corey rode with Trevor who had his new warm knitted Bird Hat. Trevor is one of my favorite local fans. He's hilarious at games and online, and he's a huge Iowa State University Cyclone fan, in addition to his soccer obsessions. He gets so emotional at games I'm completely endeared to him. He wears a plastic cardinal bird hat to Cyclone games so when I saw a knitted eagle hat on Etsy, I had to point it out to him. Not with us because he was still overseas in the military was the there in spirit Steve, who moonlights as an excellent brewmaster although he drinks no alcohol. I love seeing friends old and new at USMNT games, but having a core of people traveling from Des Moines was especially cool.

The game would live in infamy. Temperatures dropped all day. As the snow started to fall, my son stood on the hill by our tailgate in his Captain America costume with a flag that was twice his size pointing to the stadium as if he were a general planning to take the field at dawn.

243

By kickoff, the snow had piled on the field and US Soccer officials in dress shoes ran behind shovels in a desperate attempt to clear off the lines so the game could be played. The game started but it was snowing so hard officials had to shovel off the lines when play was at the other end of the field throughout the match. Players' hair caked with snow as inches accumulated on the pitch. Aviva made a snowman that was bent over, symbolizing Tim Howard's back injury. Raphael did his best to keep his tiny fingers from freezing, his resolve restored by a halftime break in the heated restrooms. We were still tied at zero a few minutes into the second half when play suspended and it looked like the referee might call it off. Fans chanted "Let them play!" The supporters section buzzed with speculation.

"What happens if they call it?"

"Will they replay it?"

" I can't believe this game."

Several tense moments passed as both teams and the referee conferenced at midfield with both teams. It seemed like forever, but eventually play resumed, and soon after, the US scored and the fans went crazy in the surreal soccer winter wonderland. The score stood at 1-0, with a post game protest by Costa Rica failing because they didn't file it within the time allowed. Fans came up with several nicknames for this game that was played in a Snow Globe, but my favorite was "Battle of the Hoth," named after the famous snow battle scene in Star Wars. One of the craziest games I've ever seen, and by far the heaviest our flag has ever been … frozen flag is much heavier than wet flag.

31

USMNT vs. Germany, 20th Anniversary Edition

I have a rule about not traveling to friendlies during World Cup Qualifying. Priorities. I would much rather go to qualifiers than burn the budget on fun but meaningless games. But when US Soccer announced the Centennial Match would be US vs. Germany at RFK Stadium in Washington, D.C., I knew I had to go. I had promised myself whenever the US next played Germany after Jürgen Klinsmann was hired, I would go ... but did it have to be right in the middle of qualifying? June was already busy and adding another flight to my budget seemed impossible. Still, no way I was going to miss this match. I called my D.C. friends in search of a place to stay.

You may remember my first cap for any international team was USMNT vs. Germany in the US Cup, on June 13, 1993. I was already excited that I would pass my 20th anniversary of supporting US Soccer during qualifying, but to have my 20th anniversary celebrated with a first cap redux was too good to be true. It was a way to honor both my teams simultaneously. I'd been so happy to watch my hero Klinsmann scoring in the 14th minute but when Tom Dooley answered with a goal 10 minutes later for the Americans ... The AMERICANS? My USMNT fandom was born.

Flash forward 20 years, and I made it to D.C.. My one goal for coming to D.C. was to finally meet Klinsmann. My Facebook wall had been littered with friends who met him at the airport, at practices I didn't get to attend, and/or at the Centennial Celebration in New

York City. I was more than a little jealous. After all, I'd been a fan for DECADES, and here were people who had lukewarm trust in Klinsy with photos with him plastered all over Facebook, mocking me. I was one more Facebook photo away from a full on toddler-force tantrum … something had to be done.

First stop was the Nike Store event in Georgetown, a mob scene of kids who were too big to shove out of the way unnoticed. I tried not to think about the multiplier of the average age to my age, and I got positioned near the front … on the side that ended up the far side of Klinsmann and Tim Howard (my son's current obsession) and near side to Clint Dempsey and Michael Bradley. Not a losing position. Every single person on stage was amazing but given my goals as a mama and fan girl, I should have been on the opposite side. Taylor Twellman emceed a Q&A I half heard over the blood rushing past my eardrums, then the autograph frenzy began. Nothing organized, with guys signing civilized behind a table, but a mosh pit of youth soccer players and I jockeying for position. I ended up getting Bradley's and Howard's autograph for both my kids (go Mom!) but I'm pretty sure Klinsmann vaporized soon after the autographs started. I asked one of my US Soccer contacts if Klinsmann was still in the building. After checking, he said no but if I found him at the Public Practice he would try to help me get my photo.

The next day, I went down to RFK to watch the German practice at 11 AM. I didn't get super involved, since I can only recognize a few of their players, but had a nice morning chatting with the German ex-pats who were there. I managed to score Louis Podolski's autograph but the highlight came as the practice was breaking up. I noticed Alexi Lalas walking around with a hard-to-miss purple umbrella to guard against the noon-time sun. I was wearing my 20 year old t-shirt from US vs. Germany thinking to myself about my life following US Soccer for the past 20 years. There's Lalas, one of the players that played for the US in the 1993 game. I called hello to him and he nodded in greeting in return.

"That's a shirt from way back." He called up to me.

"Yeah, I had to dig way back in the closet for it. This was my first cap." I said, thrilled he'd recognized it (it does show the '93 USMNT kit). Then Lalas blew my mind.

"Tom Dooley had a heck of a game that day, right?" Are you kidding me? How many games has he played for the US (it's 96, I looked it up) and how many has he announced, let alone watched, and he had the details from a particular game from 20 years ago. The man knows his soccer, and he signed the US side of my shirt. Take that, Lalas haters.

The day continued to get more and more awesome. Between practices, we were hanging out at the Supporters Club sign in, which was next to the press area. I got faux stalked by Tom Fraehmke, a Facebook friend of mine who sent me creepy messages about where I was standing until I found him and got to meet him in real life. I liked him on Facebook for talking about soccer and German language, but in person made the pleasant discovery he's tall enough to make me feel petite at 5'8" … something I always appreciate.

While we waited for gates to open, we were greeted by former Nats goalkeeper Kasey Keller, and ESPN broadcaster Ian Darke. Keller was quiet, but stopped for photos and autographs, and Mr. Darke stayed and chatted with us for a while, talking about just hanging out like a regular guy chatting up soccer. He's very thoughtful and insightful, and a pleasure to talk soccer with, so I was almost sad when they said it was time to head into the stadium. Once inside, and positioned on the track with the rest of the Supporter's Club members, I had a chance to hang out and tell stories with a few of my travel buddies, JMazz, American Bootsy, Amy and Robert Huschka. I'm convinced some of the best storytellers in America follow US Soccer. We mock each other like siblings in the best dysfunctional family ever, telling stories about the adventures in soccer travel:

"Hey, Garrett, you suck!" "You've been demoted to other Garrett!" (this was directed to Garrett from Massachusetts, because Garrett from US Soccer was looking particularly fly in his fancy shoes that day). Max (aka "Alaska") was cracking jokes and telling stories of his adventures around the US, soccer related and otherwise. A few friends who shall remain nameless told the "remember that time at the strip club when we ran up a $3000 tab?" story. There's no story involving a $3000 bar tab anywhere that isn't funny, but particularly ones that involve pantomimes of trying to communicate in a foreign language "No, we just want a strip club, not a brothel." That's a classic.

Back to soccer! Practice broke up, and the players were extraordinary, taking lots of time to sign autographs and pose for photos. I met more players than I can fathom, but no Klinsmann. After the session, security started to clear us out, and I began to panic. I had had such a perfect day, only to fail in my ultimate mission. Intolerable. Desperately, I searched the crowd for my US Soccer contact, and shouted to him across the security area. He mouthed "Did you meet him?" I shook my head no. He held up one finger to wait, and took off. I drug my feet as much as possible, and when we were cleared to the stadium seats and asked to leave, I said "I was told to wait here …" and was just about to justify my staying in a last ditch attempt to avoid getting bodily thrown from the stadium, when Michael popped up from the player tunnel and asked security if he could take me with him. They agreed, and I went through, vindicated and beyond excited. I half ran, chasing down into the locker room level of RFK. We turned into a hallway, where I recognized several members of the soccer media on one side of a fence. I was told to stand on the other side, just past them. I stood and waited, watching a guy from MLS.com wrapping up an interview. More players began to funnel down the hallway, some stopping to answer questions, a few pausing to give me a nod. I asked Beasley for a photo, since he is my husband's favorite, but otherwise, I tried to be cool and just wait. Dempsey walked by and I must have had a particularly obvious "she's not press" look on my face, in awe he was right there in front of me. He got a look of recognition on his face and then (in slow motion with epic movie music playing somewhere) silently walked up and shook my hand. I stood frozen, heart in my throat as he kept walking. I somehow squeaked out "Wow, thanks."

By the time I regained my senses, Klinsmann was right in from of me, startling me back to reality. I called out in German, asking "Can I have your …" Shit. What's the word for autograph? I came up with "writing" but he was already walking over, thank goodness, able to translate through the IQ lowering effects of fangirl overload. I told him how I'd been a German soccer fan, and came to see him play 20 years ago, how I remembered the goal, and when the US came back to almost equalize, I became a US Soccer fan, culminating with "I'm a US Soccer fan because of you, and I just wanted to say thanks, and can I get a photo with you?" That's how I ended up with my coveted Klinsmann photo, complete with him smiling almost as wide as I am.

USMNT vs. Germany was bound to be uber-emotional just based on it being my 20th anniversary as a supporter, but my plans kept improving. My college roommate from Carnegie Mellon offered me a place to stay and said she'd come to the game with me. I posted to Facebook I'd be in town, and did any of my D.C. area friends want to join me at the game? Matt Erickson, owner of 76 Words, and the guy that took me to his prom, asked me to grab him three tickets. So now I'm going to the most meaningful game of my life, with my former college roommate and prom date. I could picture myself at the field, with Alexi Lalas narrating, "Tanya Keith, this is your life!!"

Even better, Matt was moving out of his office, taking his company out into its own space for the first time. There's something very sweet about knowing someone through 4th and 5th grade Academically Speaking, attend prom, then watch their company grow into independent space. That would have been crazy enough, but then I had all this soccer goodness poured all over it. It turned out that Courtney, my ex-roommate, couldn't host me, so I crashed on Matt's couch for the weekend, and thus subjected him to a front row of my soccer obsession. He tolerated the Nike event well enough, and got to meet my South Africa husband, Scott, as well as Kaela and Andy at the night before party. It turns out in the very small world of D.C. business, my South Africa husband and '89 prom date not only know each other but live less than 2 blocks from each other.

Matt and I headed to the stadium just after 8 AM to hang banners and set up the stadium flag which took longer than usual but still got us out to the tailgate shortly before the rest of the crew. Our group set up by the river, which was so pretty, and seemed about 10 degrees cooler than the rest of the parking lot. Somehow, magically, we did not lose any soccer balls in our kick around dangerously close to the river bank. As people started showing up, it became clear there were more than a dozen one degree of separation relationships between Matt and I. In the Venn diagram of soccer fans and D.C. insiders, there's heavy, if not total, overlap. In fact, Matt had offered one of his two extra tickets to a guy from our hometown who graduated a few years ahead of us. His friend had declined the tickets but invited Matt to his tailgate … which turned out to be the same tailgate I'd invited him to attend.

We ate, drank, face-painted, and talked, occasionally kicking a ball around. We did one pass through the lot to go visit our friends from New York, and to visit my AO RVA friends. Too soon it was time to go into the stadium. With assigned seats we rolled in barely in time for anthems. It was fun, having the Midwest Mama flag farther back in the section than usual, since people were excited to be a part of the flag management. I was excited to find one guy wearing an Ampel Man shirt. Ampel Man is a graphic design icon from East Berlin, a red walking man that adorned traffic lights, telling you when to walk or stop, don't cross. It was a subtle reference to German culture adding another layer of happiness to my day.

The game kicked off, and the joy of the day was just getting started. In the 13th minute Jozy Altidore scored on a fantastic shot and breaking his 19 month scoreless streak. Gleeful giddiness poured out of me. I couldn't remember ever leading Germany in a match, but before I could collect myself and take a photo of the score board, right in front of me, I witnessed the impossible. A German central defender had the ball at the edge of the penalty area and under pressure, passed the ball to his wing, who was also well marked and made a quick back pass to the German keeper, Marc-Andre ter Stegen. Every soccer coach simultaneously made a Top Gun "never leave your wing man" reference, thinking "Never, never back pass on frame!" Ter Stegen was immediately under intense pressure from three US attackers and in a startled moment of indecision he hesitates, and the ball rolls impossibly slowly into the German net. Now we were up 2-0, dos a cero!! It's not just for Mexico anymore!

After a German goal was called back for being offside, we headed into halftime, up by the most dangerous lead in soccer. When Germany came out after half and scored once, I thought we were in trouble, but a pair of clinical, beautiful rifle shots from Clint Dempsey put the score at 4-1. What strange new world is this?

But we weren't done yet. Germany made a late game sub and with brutal quickness, the score was 4-3 and I was praying we could hold it the last seven minutes. It had already occurred to me this game was an almost perfect flip of the scoring summary from US vs. Germany twenty years prior. I wanted my day to come complete full circle. As the players moved from one end of the field and back, I prayed alternately that neither would score, and leave my 4-3 in perfection. I'd found myself begging the US *not* to score for the first time in my life. Then the Germans would find their attacking end and I'd be begging forgiveness hoping by thought alone I hadn't cost the win by not wanting to run up the score. It was such a long seven minutes until the final whistle and referee signaling the end of the game. They'd done it. US Soccer had made the perfect ending to the perfect weekend, perfect game.

32

Summer of '13

So much better than Summer of '42 or '69, I spent the rest of Summer 2013 chasing my team around the US, meeting many new friends, and strengthening old friendships. Qualifiers with my husband for Panama at Seattle and Honduras at Salt Lake City were our soccer equivalent of date night and showed the best and worst of supporters in 2013. My enjoyment of the Seattle atmosphere could have only been heightened by a little less "we invented supporter culture" attitude from our hosts. We loved the city of Salt Lake and staying with AO Des Moines friends Tiffany and Greg Welch, who are originally from Provo. Greg gave us a great city tour including Temple Square which further bonded us as AO DSM's alt religion group. On the other hand, Salt Lake rival supporter groups made for an unpleasant experience in the stands for many of us and left me feeling the city lacked the heart to let their differences go in support of the team.

I let my homesickness for the East Coast get the best of me and road tripped to Baltimore for a last minute Gold Cup experience with Amy and Robert, JMazz and American Bootsy ... two of the super-couples of US Soccer fandom. My ticket, along with anyone else who ordered through Barra Brava, got stuck in traffic. I was relatively calm about this until about 45 minutes prior to kickoff. At about 20 minutes prior to kick, almost everyone I knew had already gone in and I was really freaking out at the thought that I had just driven 1000 miles to miss the game. I was about to break down in a full-blown, stress-induced sobbing fit when Justin Coughlan (who'd already won ambassador-of-the-trip hands down by bringing Maryland crab cakes to the tailgate for me) handed me his ticket so I could get in before kickoff. It was one of the coolest things anyone has ever done for me, especially since it meant he didn't get in until part way through the first half.

"Uncle" Jimmy LaRoue heard I was driving in for the game and decided to road trip from North Carolina. He'd gotten caught in the same traffic as the ticket guy and didn't get in until halftime. We hung out for the second game of the double header with my high school friend, Larry Boodin, and caught up on old times while unwinding after the craziness of the pre-game. Larry and I had been acquaintances in high school but have grown closer lately thanks to Facebook and our mutual interest in soccer and our mutual desire to one-up each other with photos of famous soccer players we've met. We've managed to maintain our friendship through his jealousy of my travels and my jealousy that he's met my all time favorite, Brad Friedel, and I have not. It was fun to go to a game that became such an awesome mashup of old school friends from Korea as well as literally old school classmates and the East Coast soccer family I had not seen in a while. On my return trip, I did a tour through New York and New Jersey to visit my Montclair buddies, Mark, Nicole, and Christopher Rulewich, the boy who grew up across the street from me. I made an overnight stop in Pittsburgh on the kindness of another MHS connection, Joshua Siebert, and his wife, Annie. I'd originally planned to stop further west, but I couldn't pass up staying with friends when Josh responded to my offer to meet for dinner with the additional offer of their spare room. The longer drive the next day was worth the night spent catching up with Josh, meeting his wife, and sharing stories of restoring old houses and other details of our lives in our respective cities.

The road trip also allowed me to crash the party of the provisional chapter in Iowa City for the watch party of the next round of the Gold Cup. As a marker for how far soccer had come in America, Iowa (the state I once imagined would never have a full chapter anywhere) now had provisional chapters in Cedar Rapids and Iowa City, both of which made it to full chapter by the end of 2013. Along the way, my friend Jon Strauss tweeted that his friend who was studying in Iowa City should come out to meet me ... which he did and joined the chapter that night ... such as the soccer family is. It was fun meeting up with another chapter and those I had met at previous matches even if it was at the tail end of a 2500 mile road trip.

We made the Gold Cup Final a family trip to Chicago, Illinois. US Soccer HQ "Soccer House" hosted a lunch for Supporter Club members which included a tour of the trophy room and photo ops in front of the collection of Gold Cup trophies. The lunch was great, and I enjoyed taking the kids around the various trophies telling them stories of our travels from before they were born. The game was more stressful as we wanted to stand with friends but security didn't want to allow general admission seating to take over. For most of the game, the kids and I were standing near Trevor and the rest of AO Des Moines with Doug on the other side of the section drumming. Security tried to force us into our assigned seating making me too anxious to realize I had been forced into a row right next to former National Team member, Jimmy Conrad. He was charmingly amused when I said that I recognized him and asked where we'd met. In my defense, he was wearing star-shaped shades. Realistically, if he'd been wearing a jersey with his name on it, I might still have missed it given my stress level of trying to stay in the section with the kids. Let's pretend my cluelessness was part of my charm and leave it at that.

We were also there as a family when the US qualified for Brazil 2014 against Mexico at Columbus. I was supposed to road trip out a day ahead of my family and most of AO DSM with AO Iowa City people, but as the day approached, that group wanted to leave late enough that we would miss the US Soccer pep rally. My friend, Ryan Youtz, of AO Omaha/Iowa City decided to leave the night before and drive most of the night in order to make the party. This was so upsetting to another AO IC guy that he bailed last minute on the whole trip and left Ryan holding an extra ticket. From our road trip, Ryan tweeted about it at midnight, and a woman from Seattle answered saying she wanted it if she could make last-minute travel plans. She did, and I mercilessly teased Ryan that she was to be his future wife, and that one I'd day write about their love affair that was brought together through US Soccer. As of early 2014, they were seriously dating, so my fingers are crossed that in the sequel to this book there will be a chapter about their wedding that I can title "I Was There When This Started, And I Called It."

Columbus started out an amazing weekend. My super-couple buddies Amy and Robert were there, as well as several members of the #JewCrew family who had been brought together by Matt Dziomba's Jew Crew tee shirt that had blown up the internet and my blog promoting it for a few days with American Outlaws that saw it as divisive. It may have ruffled the feathers of a few people, but certainly helped to unite our subgroup of Jewish supporters in a round of drinks at the US Soccer night before party. I got to meet Columbus Crew and USMNT legend Frankie Hejduk and talk to him for as long as I could keep up with his endless energy. I was talking one of my New England friends, Evan Cipriano when he pointed out USMNT and New England Revolution star Brian Dunseth. I was mostly a spectator in their conversation, since Evan's MLS knowledge far exceeds mine, but I enjoyed listening to them talk Revs history. They were like musicians riffing off each other, with increasingly awesome crazy soccer stories as their music. The night before was full of promise of a great weekend.

Doug and the kids met me at the tailgate as we gathered an impressive showing for AO Des Moines. Following my viral blog post at my blog, SoccerFamilyStyle.com, I was an official capo for the first time in Columbus. I lead the secondary stands for the first half then ran over to the main stands to try to work out difficulties with the sound system. When the US finally scored just as I got into the section, I decided it would be bad luck to return to my original section, and since my capo shift was over, I spent the second half freelance leading in front of my friends from AO Des Moines. My departure from my kids blew up the blogosphere after the game. A few guys from Kansas made an impressive case for sexism when they couldn't fathom that my children were be perfectly safe with their Dad, who knew where I was the whole time thanks to magical cell phone technology. In one of those "I was the greatest parent before I had kids" moments, those young men decided my children needed to be monitored by their mother 100% of the time. They tore apart my mothering and capoing skills and made online threats about how I would be treated at the next game in KC. It made me sad Sporting KC had several bad apples in their supporter groups that I found unworthy of the classiness of Chris Wyche and the Ladies of SKC had shown me. But I suppose it's better that I have a husband with less Neanderthal-like views of parenthood and children who can laugh off behavior that's ridiculous to them.

I would have been smug the whole game in KC the following month, had it not been so painful to listen to the guy they made capo on mic the entire game. It might have ruined the day except it was also Aviva's 11th birthday which was celebrated at a huge AO DSM tailgate. Kim put together a great celebration including cake, and we celebrated alongside friends from one of the chapters I helped establish, AO COMO (Columbia, Missouri). We spent the game sitting with Chris Gleason, another one of my new favorite people. He beams positive energy, loves the kids, and has a great sense of humor. I had texted him our location while I was running kids to the bathroom, and he came down and sat next to Doug while I was away. Doug defended my territory, saying "My wife's sitting there."

"I know your wife." Gleason said, flashing my text message. Only in laid-back soccer culture world does this conversation not end in a fist fight. My soccer family wouldn't let a few bullies from SKC ruin my firstborn's golden birthday celebration for me. We laughed it off, took our victory lap win, and watched the post-game laser show which made for the most awesome 11th birthday a mini fan could wish for.

33

The Next Twenty Years

The past two decades following US Soccer have given me everything I needed to make a happy life. Through wins and losses, my love of this sport has carried me through so many challenges and multiplied my joy over and over. Finding my passion and living my life in pursuit of it has given me a direction I have not found elsewhere. Following soccer has given me the focus to achieve so much more than I would have by just moving aimlessly from one job or project to the next. My soccer friends have become a soccer family strong enough to last a lifetime. I couldn't be more grateful for the experiences I have had standing and cheering with so many great people as we've watched US Soccer grow.

I know this isn't the end of my story. The US Soccer team will be joining me in Brazil in summer 2014, and I have begun my third decade of supporting US Soccer. This journey has taken me to over a dozen states (not including the drive through on our own family's various soccer road trips) and to eight countries. I have seen players go from promising kids to superstars, to retirement and to superstardom again. I have watched the rise of MLS soccer, and my favorite journey of all has been American soccer culture flourishing into its own. I've watched as European and Latino supporter culture began infecting the American public, defended by Lalas in 1994 asking us to just go with it, as we watched the strange traditions of international soccer take over our stadiums. Those of us who caught the bug early started to spread the love for soccer like a fantastic, colorful plague across the US. Slowly at first as MLS struggled into being and then into relevance, the journey traveled with Sam's Army as they figured out the dos and don'ts of organizing Americans into a supporter nation.

Today, soccer culture seems to spread like wildfire with a new American Outlaws chapter popping up everywhere you look as fledgling competitor supporter groups try their wings. What will the next twenty years look like? How will AO, MLS, and US Soccer face the demands of a growing soccer fan base? How will the rise of soccer as a true major league level sport impact greater American culture? What will America look like when the majority of adults have grown up playing youth soccer and following the professional game in leagues and countries around the world.

Sometimes I catch glimpses of the new world order when I'm eating or drinking somewhere and a soccer game is turned on without me having to request it. It happened at kids' night at our local Gateway Market on the night of Jamaica vs. Mexico World Cup Qualifier. It was a slow night at the market when we arrived since select soccer practice for my daughter had kept us at the fields until almost 8 PM. I had been daydreaming that the man across from me at the counter was wearing a Minnesota United shirt instead of the Minnesota Vikings shirt that he was actually wearing when I was startled back to reality by a kitchen worker asking me if I had been watching the news they had on. I said no, you can change the channel particularly if you want to turn it to the Jamaica vs. Mexico game, intending to joke with her because why would she turn the game on. But she WAS turning the game on for the kitchen staff who wanted to cheer on Mexico's El Tri as they cleaned up for the night. I couldn't believe it. When my attempts at friendly banter failed due to my lack of Spanish language skills, I held up my US Soccer track jacket logo and immediately they knew that I knew, and we had this lovely moment of smiles and implied winks. Yeah, we knew it was going down tonight, and by the end of the week, it could be all but over for Jamaica. The friendliest worker shouted "Mexico! $100 they win!" I laughed and said I wouldn't bet on Jamaica, but if he wanted that bet in September, I'd be happy to eat free for months. Although we don't share a language, Mario and I now wave to each other every week in solidarity of soccer in America, even if not for the same team.

It happened again at our AO bar for the US vs. Jamaica qualifier. We were displaced from our regular back room at the Keg Stand by an arena football party. Initially frustrated, I was filled with pride as our numbers swelled prior to kickoff. One of our members pulled me aside and said conspiratorially, "I looked into their room and we have way more people than they do." Then another commented "I like it out here, people are coming in to check us out including the people at the arena football party." Then the US scored, and instead of being annoyed, waitresses and bouncers alike were coming to me all smiles and saying they loved the atmosphere we were creating with our shouts and cheers. It was a far cry from our early attempts to find a bar favorable to a soccer crowd.

Someday this is what it is going to be like. We Americans will not gather around the water cooler to talk Monday Night Football. We'll gather, as we do now in the virtual world, to talk soccer. American soccer fans will not be relegated to the bottom of the social totem pole but revered for the passion with which we support our teams. We'll play in home-field advantage stadiums across the US as more and more children grow up with dreams of playing for the United States. The American Soccer fanbase can only grow as it becomes easier and easier to get our high level soccer thrills at home.

I do not know exactly what it will look like with variables like MLS expansion and NASL teams becoming more prominent, but the landscape of American teams are shifting. The US is ripe for another mind-blowing performance at the World Cup, based on my highly unscientific method of recognizing that '94 and '02 were hot years while '98, '06 were not. Not to mention, 2010 had so much unrealized potential that I am still smoldering over it. Will 2014 be the year we shock the world again? And will it be the '02 type of shock and awe or G-d forbid, the '98 shock and horror? Will Sam's Army ever regain their market share? Where is the next big supporter group lurking … planning the next leap forward in supporter culture? Will it come from within or splinter off? Only time will tell, but I hope you'll be watching along with me as it unfurls across the United States like a glorious billowing stadium flag, a lovely riot of color and joy that is following soccer as a 21st Century American.

About the Author

For the past 20 years, Tanya Keith has traveled around the world following US Soccer. First as a referee, then as a coach, player, supporter, and parent, she has experienced American soccer from all angles, and shared her experiences on her blog, www.SoccerFamilyStyle.com. Across the United States and through eight different countries, Ms. Keith has watched Americans grow from a small group of fans in the early 90s to stadiums full of supporters today. Passionate Soccer Love is her memoir of stories collected following the rise of US Soccer.

Ms. Keith lives in Des Moines, Iowa, where she tries not to terrify Midwesterners with her brash Jersey Girl attitude. She lives with her husband, Doug and their two kids, Aviva and Raphael, or Wonder Woman and Captain America, as they are known among soccer fans. When she's not watching soccer or writing about soccer, she works on restoring the 125 year old Hatton House in the River Bend neighborhood.